Nonproliferation and the National Interest

Nonproliferation and the National Interest

America's Response to the Spread of Nuclear Weapons

Peter A. Clausen

Late, Union of Concerned Scientists

HarperCollins*CollegePublishers*

Executive Editor: Lauren Silverman
Project Editor: Diane Rowell
Design Supervisor: Lucy Krikorian
Cover Design: Kay Petronio
Production Manager/Assistant: Willie Lane/Sunaina Sehwani
Compositor: Circle Graphics Typographers
Printer and Binder: R. R. Donnelley & Sons Company
Cover Printer: The Lehigh Press, Inc.

Nonproliferation and the National Interest: America's Response to the Spread of Nuclear Weapons

Library of Congress Cataloging-in-Publication Data

Clausen, Peter A.
    Nonproliferation and the national interest : America's response to
the spread of nuclear weapons / Peter A. Clausen.
        p.   cm.
    Includes index.
    ISBN 0–06–501395–6
    1. Nuclear nonproliferation.   2. United States—Foreign
relations—1945–   I. Title.
JX1974.73.C53   1992
327.1′74′0973—dc20
                                                    92-17191
                                                    CIP

92 93 94 95 9 8 7 6 5 4 3 2 1

To Pat and Bill, with all my love

Contents

Preface

The proliferation of nuclear weapons looms as a fundamental threat to global security in the final years of the twentieth century. Few questions will have a greater impact on the success or failure of efforts to construct a peaceful world order in the aftermath of the Cold War. Indeed, if "the bomb" continues to spread to additional nations, the mellowing of the East-West conflict may prove to have brought only a Pyrrhic victory over the menace of nuclear war.

As the 1990s began, the gathering influence of proliferation on world politics was apparent. The Persian Gulf war drew belated attention to Iraq's determined pursuit of nuclear weapons, which Bush administration officials portrayed as a leading justification for military action against that country. Destruction of the Iraqi nuclear program became an urgent U.S. priority in the ensuing conflict. The later discovery of the impressive scale of Iraq's nuclear weapons program, most of it based on imported technology and facilities, raised fundamental questions about the adequacy of the existing nonproliferation regime. The Gulf war also stimulated broader awareness of Israel's unavowed but substantial nuclear capability, and the potential for conflagration inherent in the intertwined proliferation of atomic, chemical, and ballistic-missile weapons in the Middle East. In another region of chronic conflict and instability, India and Pakistan—both de facto nuclear powers—moved to the brink of war over the disputed territory of Kashmir in early 1990. The implicit nuclear dimension of the crisis prompted a high-level U.S. diplomatic effort to defuse tensions. In addition, the breakup of the Soviet Union posed novel proliferation threats. Overhanging these developments, a fateful deadline approached—the 1995 renewal date for the Non-Proliferation Treaty (NPT), the centerpiece of global efforts to stem the spread of nuclear weapons.

Proliferation is not a new issue. The inexorable diffusion of nuclear technology was foreseen even before the United States tested the first atomic bomb at Alamogordo, New Mexico, in July 1945. Three months earlier, Secretary of War Henry Stimson had warned President Truman that America could not hope to enjoy an enduring nuclear monopoly. Moreover, Stimson wrote, the problem of controlling the bomb's spread, and the U.S. attitude toward sharing the weapon with other nations, would become "a primary question of our foreign relations."

The decades since World War II have borne out this forecast. The Soviet Union tested an atomic bomb in 1949, ending the U.S. monopoly. In the next fifteen years, Britain, France, and China joined the circle of acknowledged nuclear weapon states. Thereafter, proliferation continued apace, but in a more veiled and ambiguous manner. Israel, India, Pakistan, and South Africa advanced toward the bomb along various clandestine and deceptive paths, without openly admitting it. A number of other nations—including Argentina, Brazil, South Korea, Taiwan, Libya, Iran, and Iraq—actively sought nuclear weapons at one time or another.

Stimson's prediction that the diffusion of nuclear weapons would present severe foreign policy challenges has been amply confirmed as well. From the start of the atomic age, the United States recognized a powerful interest in preventing proliferation. At first this meant attempting to thwart Soviet acquisition of the bomb—a self-evident goal in the emerging Cold War of the late 1940s. But U.S. policymakers also came to believe that the spread of nuclear weapons even to friendly countries should be discouraged. Largely at American initiative, an elaborate international framework—the "nonproliferation regime"—was established to support this objective. Gradually strengthened over the decades, the regime includes the International Atomic Energy Agency (IAEA) and its inspection system, the NPT, and cooperation among the industrial countries to control and restrict exports of nuclear technology. Despite weaknesses, this framework has unquestionably helped delegitimize the ambitions—and retard the progress—of would-be nuclear powers. It is equally evident that this success would not have been possible had the United States not discerned a vital national interest in nonproliferation.

But the close historical link between nonproliferation and U.S. self-interest has another side. Efforts to prevent the spread of nuclear weapons are not cost-free; they cut across a whole range of issues and policies that engage other important American interests. Nonproliferation impinges, directly or indirectly, on questions of American-Soviet relations, U.S. ties with European and Asian allies, regional conflicts in the Middle East and elsewhere, energy and trade policies, and U.S. economic and military aid to Third World countries. Inevitably, these intersections create policy dilemmas and trade-offs, because vigorous nonproliferation efforts often do not fit easily with the pursuit of other objectives.

Amid the clash of competing interests, the actual priority of nonproliferation in U.S. policy has fluctuated widely over time and from one country to another. Notwithstanding America's historic leadership role in nonproliferation policy, American efforts to stop the spread of nuclear weapons have in practice been ambivalent, equivocal, and selective—and, as a result, too often ineffective. In the 1950s, Dwight Eisenhower found a strict approach to nonproliferation difficult to reconcile with a strong Western alliance, or with the economic and political lure of sponsoring nuclear power overseas. Lyndon Johnson's determination to secure the NPT in the 1960s drove a wedge between the United States and its Cold War allies, as did Jimmy Carter's campaign against the nuclear "breeder reactor" ten years later. Ronald Reagan faced an irreducible tension between U.S. laws designed to punish Pakistan's quest for the bomb and his desire to arm that country against the Soviet threat in neighboring Afghanistan. George Bush went to war against Iraq when geopolitical interests and nonproliferation objectives coincided, but he found himself in a dilemma when he tried to maintain good relations with China while seeking to curb proliferation-prone Chinese nuclear exports. And for more than two decades, the President and Congress have favored Israel with a tacit exemption from U.S. nonproliferation efforts.

This book is a history of American policy on the spread of nuclear weapons. Following Henry Stimson, it treats the subject as "a primary question of our foreign relations," centering on the nexus between nonproliferation and U.S. foreign policy. This vantage point has the merit of being realistic. It anchors the study of nonproliferation in its political and historical context, and underlines the fact that America has opposed the spread of nuclear weapons, not as a moral or humanitarian imperative but out of hard-headed calculations of interest. Policymakers have defined the problem not in abstract terms but through the prism of their broader foreign policy goals, principles, and prejudices. This prism has shaped their sense of the nature and urgency of the problem, and their assessment of the costs and benefits of alternative responses to it.

The goal of this study is thus to probe the underlying logic of American choices and actions on nuclear proliferation. It explores the chronic dilemmas and conflicts that have beset U.S. policy in this field, and attempts to illuminate the sources of ambivalence and mixed motives that have inhibited that policy. A better understanding of the past, in turn, is crucial to making nonproliferation policy more coherent and effective in the future. Accordingly, the book attempts to extract from the historical record lessons and guidelines for avoiding past pitfalls in addressing the proliferation challenges ahead.

The study is organized chronologically, tracing the evolution of American nonproliferation policy from its origins during World War II. In each period, the book explores the interplay between nonproliferation and the major themes of U.S. foreign and national-security policy. Three recurring patterns mark this history: a conflict between heavy U.S. reliance on nuclear weapons to deter the Soviet Union and the attempt to deny these weapons to other countries; a tension between limiting the burden of U.S. overseas commitments and addressing the security needs of would-be nuclear powers; and a reluctance to exert strong U.S. pressure against the nuclear programs of close allies and client states. Running through the course of U.S. policy, these dilemmas largely define America's reluctance, at critical junctures, to pay the true costs of nonproliferation. As the final chapter argues, however, the ending of the Cold War may create opportunities to soften, if not escape altogether, these historical constraints and inhibitions. To do so, the United States will need to articulate, and act upon, a clear sense of its national interest in stemming proliferation.

Chapter 1 examines the attempt of U.S. policymakers to come to terms with two revolutionary challenges simultaneously after World War II—the Soviet Union and nuclear weapons. Focusing on the debates over the Baruch Plan, cooperation with Britain, and the growing U.S. dependency on nuclear weapons, the chapter shows how the emerging Cold War shaped the evolution of U.S. policy on control of the bomb.

Chapter 2 traces the origins of Eisenhower's plan for peaceful nuclear cooperation, the creation of the IAEA and its safeguards system, and the early development of the civil nuclear market. The chapter emphasizes the multiple motivations behind the shift from denial to cooperation, which served important U.S. foreign policy and commercial interests in addition to nonproliferation.

Chapter 3 reviews the development of NATO nuclear relations in the 1950s and early 1960s, focusing on the deployment of tactical nuclear weapons in Europe, the decision to aid the British nuclear weapons program but not the French, and the alliance crises over nuclear sharing and the Multilateral Force (MLF). This chapter shows how changing U.S. assessments of the risks and requirements of extended deterrence influenced nonproliferation policy under the Eisenhower and Kennedy administrations.

Chapter 4 reviews U.S. policy in the Non-Proliferation Treaty (NPT) negotiations, with emphasis on the treaty's stressful impact on U.S.-European relations. The chapter shows how U.S. pursuit of the NPT meshed with two broader themes of U.S. foreign policy in the mid-1960s—superpower détente and an expansive, interventionist concept of U.S. global security interests (epitomized by the intervention in Vietnam).

Chapter 5 explores further the relationship between U.S. foreign commitments and nonproliferation in the 1960s and early 1970s. The cases of Israel and India are examined to show the dilemmas and cross-pressures affecting U.S. nonproliferation policy and the changing premises of U.S. policy from the Kennedy-Johnson era globalism to the Nixon administration's emphasis on multipolarity and greater self-help by U.S. allies and clients.

Chapter 6 analyzes the Ford and Carter nonproliferation initiatives and the controversies they inspired in the foreign policy context of the mid- and late 1970s. The chapter focuses especially on the debate over plutonium use between the United States and its allies and the attempt to prevent a nuclear arms race between India and Pakistan. Its main theme is the gap between the more ambitious nonproliferation policy adopted at this time and the decline of U.S. influence due to the diffusion of global power, the energy crisis, and post-Vietnam U.S. retrenchment.

Chapter 7 reviews U.S. policy in the 1980s, showing how the renewal of Cold War tensions after the Soviet invasion of Afghanistan—and the Reagan commitment to a reassertion of U.S. power overseas—led to a reduced priority for nonproliferation policy. The chapter analyzes the links between anti-Soviet and nonproliferation policies toward South Asia, the Middle East, and China, as well as changes in U.S. policy on civil nuclear cooperation and plutonium use under Reagan.

Chapter 8 reviews the major historical patterns revealed by the study, and addresses the problems of integrating nonproliferation and other national interests in the post–Cold War world. With particular reference to the Persian Gulf war, it considers the implications of the Cold War's end for the dynamics of the proliferation threat, its impact on U.S. interests, and the possibilities for U.S. and multilateral nonproliferation policies.

ACKNOWLEDGMENTS

I am indebted to the many people who provided me with valuable help as I worked on this book. I gratefully acknowledge the assistance of the following individuals, who granted an interview and/or provided advice: Emanual Adler, Helena Cobban, Warren Donnelly, Lewis Dunn, Robert Gallucci, Tom Graham, Morton Halperin, Ben Huberman, Neil Joeck, Spurgeon Keeny, Robert Komer, Paul Leventhal, Gary Millhollin, Joe Nye, Joe Pilat, George Quester, George Rathjens, Randy Rydell, Larry Scheinman, Gerard Smith, Roger Smith, Leonard Spector, Raju Thomas, and Paul Warnke. In addition, Al Carnesale, Robert Gallucci, George Quester, and Leonard Weiss each reviewed parts of the manuscript and gave me important comments. Finally, I am grateful to the following for providing me with documents and other materials and feedback: the Center for Science and International Affairs; Tom Blanton, Virginia Foran, and Ann Herpel of the National Security Archives; Randy Rydell; and Roger Smith.

I would like to thank Howard Ris, executive director of the Union of Concerned Scientists, for his help and support, and my editor at UCS, Jan Wager. Last but by no means least, I am indebted to my wife, Pat McMurray, and my son, Bill Clausen, for their constant love and encouragement.

PETER A. CLAUSEN

Postscript: Early in the summer of 1991, Dr. Peter Clausen passed away. In his final weeks, Peter asked a long-time friend and colleague, Dr. Steven Baker, of the Monterey Institute of International Studies, to help in updating and revising portions of this book. The Union of Concerned Scientists gratefully acknowledges Dr. Baker's very generous help. UCS would also like to thank the following reviewers, who provided helpful comments about the manuscript: Timothy Luke, Virginia Polytechnic Institute and State University; Timothy Lomperis, Duke University; and Curtis Reithel, University of Wisconsin-La Crosse.

About the Author

On June 24, 1991, Dr. Peter Clausen passed away at the age of 46 after a long struggle with cancer. From 1983 until his death, he was director of research for the Union of Concerned Scientists, overseeing most of the organization's policy analyses on nuclear arms control, the Strategic Defense Initiative (SDI), and nuclear proliferation issues.

A nationally known expert on nuclear proliferation, Dr. Clausen became involved in the field as a political analyst with the Central Intelligence Agency in the mid-1970s and later as a nuclear specialist with the U.S. Department of Energy. Dr. Clausen was coauthor of two major UCS assessments of SDI, *The Fallacy of Star Wars* and *Empty Promise: The Growing Case Against Star Wars*. He also directed two major UCS arms control reports, *In Search of Stability* and *Presidential Priorities: A National Security Agenda for the 1990s*. He received a Ph.D. in political science from the University of California at Los Angeles.

Chapter
1

The Monopoly Era: The Bomb and Russia in American Policy 1945–1950

*A*s World War II ended, American diplomacy came face to face with two enormous challenges. One was the Soviet Union, which had emerged from the war as the dominant power in Europe. The other was the atomic bomb, whose awesome destructiveness had been demonstrated at Hiroshima and Nagasaki. Both had been keys to victory over the Axis, but both now cast ominous shadows over the postwar landscape. Either challenge alone would have been daunting. But the task was not only to manage them both at once, but to deal with each in relation to the other. For it was clear that the fate of U.S.-Soviet relations and the future of the bomb were intimately connected.

Little else was clear, however, including the nature of the two problems themselves. A basic question was whether either could be managed within the framework of traditional statecraft. Was the Soviet Union an ideological power committed to world revolution, or a conventional great power with which the West could do business? Did the atomic bomb transform world politics, making nationalism and war obsolete, or was it simply a new and more powerful military weapon?

The situation seemed to require a choice as to which posed the greater danger: To define one as the problem implied that the other was part of the solution. The belief that the Soviet Union was the overriding threat to American security led inexorably to the view that the bomb was a national resource, not to be shared. The belief that the bomb was the greater threat called for partnership with the Soviet Union to control atomic energy.

The logic of the Cold War finally prevailed. The failure of the Baruch Plan (which would have subjected atomic energy to international control) and the passage of the 1946 Atomic Energy Act (which sought to preserve the American monopoly through secrecy and denial) marked the first watershed of U.S. nonproliferation policy. For the first but hardly the last time, a grand design for controlling the bomb fell victim to Cold War realities. Meanwhile, nuclear weapons were assuming a central role in U.S. security policy—tentatively at first, but decisively by the end of the decade. By then, the American atomic monopoly had been broken; the Soviet Union had joined the nuclear club and Great Britain was waiting in the wings.

The brief monopoly era was in a sense the prehistory of U.S. nonproliferation policy. Behind the heated debates on international control, there had been little systematic thinking about how the bomb's spread would actually affect international relations and U.S. national interests. Theorizing about such questions was made difficult by the bomb's novelty and by the special nature of the first two cases of proliferation—America's bitterest adversary, and its closest ally. Nevertheless, these formative years foreshadowed many of the problems the United States would later face in attempting to reconcile nonproliferation with its broader foreign policy agenda.

DEBATING NUCLEAR POLICY, 1945

The debate on postwar control of the bomb, begun even before the weapon had been tested and used, emerged in the fall of 1945 as a contest between two sharply differing approaches. On one side were the proponents of international control, who regarded nuclear weapons as the dominant security threat of the postwar world and argued that, unless they were removed from national hands, proliferation and nuclear wars were inevitable. On the other were advocates of a nationalist policy, who saw the bomb as America's "winning weapon" and urged a policy aimed at exploiting and protecting the U.S. monopoly.[1]

The technical and political assumptions of the two groups were in large part mirror images of each other. Advocates of internationalism dismissed the possibility that the United States could monopolize the bomb, and placed their hopes on U.S.-Soviet collaboration. Nuclear nationalists disparaged cooperation with Russia and envisioned a long and fruitful era of U.S. monopoly. It was as if hard-headed realism on one issue induced naive credulity on the other.

Support for international control had been building during the final stages of the war. Within the inner circle of U.S. defense research

---

[1] See Gregg Herken, *The Winning Weapon* (New York: Vintage Books, 1982). The phrase is from Bernard Baruch's speech to the UN Atomic Energy Commission, June 14, 1946: "Before a country is ready to relinquish any winning weapons, it must have more than words to reassure it."

advisors, the idea was championed by Vannevar Bush and James Conant—the White House science advisor, and the president of Harvard, respectively—who in September 1944 urged Secretary of War Henry Stimson to begin planning for the postwar management of atomic energy.[2] Manhattan Project scientists were also a center of advocacy for an international approach. The June 1945 Franck Report, which had argued in vain against use of the bomb on Japan, was a key manifesto. "Unless an effective international control of nuclear explosives is instituted," the scientists argued, "a race for nuclear armaments is certain to ensue following the first revelation of our possession of nuclear weapons to the world."[3] As the war ended, Stimson embraced this view and recommended it to President Harry Truman.

At a special cabinet meeting on September 21, 1945, the day of his retirement, Stimson offered a proposal for direct negotiations with the Soviet Union on atomic control.[4] In his memorandum to President Truman describing the plan, Stimson squarely identified the bomb as the central issue of U.S.-Soviet relations: "To put the matter concisely, I consider the problem of our satisfactory relations with Russia as not merely connected with but as virtually dominated by the problem of the atomic bomb. . . . Those relations may be perhaps irretrievably embittered by the way in which we approach the solution of the bomb with Russia."[5]

Stimson described a basic choice between treating the bomb as a traditional (though devastating) military weapon, "to be assimilated into our pattern of international relations," and treating it as something "too revolutionary and dangerous to fit into old concepts." Rejecting the first, he argued against the allures of atomic monopoly—the temptation to use America's "momentary superiority," either for diplomatic leverage in the ongoing peace talks ("having this weapon rather ostentatiously on our hip," in Stimson's often-quoted phrase) or for military advantage to offset Soviet power in Europe. The attempt to exploit the monopoly would not only fail, Stimson claimed, but would simply hasten its end, stimulating "feverish activity on the part of the Soviet [sic] toward the development of

---

[2] Richard G. Hewlett and Oscar E. Anderson, Jr., *A History of the United States Atomic Energy Commission. Volume I: The New World, 1939–46* (University Park, PA: The Pennsylvania State Univ. Press), pp. 325–31.

[3] On the atomic scientists' movement, see Alice Kimball Smith, *A Peril and A Hope* (Chicago: Univ. of Chicago Press, 1965). The Franck report is printed in Appendix B, p. 560. During the war, these concerns had been vigorously pressed by Niels Bohr, who argued in vain with Churchill and Roosevelt for a sharing of work on the bomb with the Soviet Union. See Richard Rhodes, *The Making of the Atomic Bomb* (New York: Simon & Schuster, 1986) pp. 522–38.

[4] See Herken, *The Winning Weapon*, pp. 27ff., and Hewlett and Anderson, *The New World*, pp. 418–21.

[5] Reprinted in Henry L. Stimson and McGeorge Bundy, *On Active Service in Peace and War* (New York: Harper & Row, 1948), pp. 643–46.

this bomb in what will in effect be a secret armament race of a rather desperate character." Nor was there promise in using atomic cooperation as a "carrot" to open up the Soviet political system, a strategy Stimson himself had earlier advocated.

Instead, Stimson called for an immediate approach to the Soviets, without preconditions, aimed at establishing a cooperative partnership for the control of atomic energy. Specifically, the United States would offer to cease its atomic weapons program if the Soviets (and British) would do the same, and to impound its existing bombs. The three countries might then enter into an agreement to cooperate in the development of atomic energy for peaceful purposes. Stimson stressed the importance of approaching the Russians directly rather than at the United Nations, where the offer would be mired in "loose debates" among "nations who have not demonstrated their potential power or responsibility," and would not be taken seriously by the Soviets.

Stimson granted that there were risks in cooperation: "We may be gambling on their good faith and risk their getting into production of bombs a little sooner than they would otherwise." But this, he argued, was not a compelling objection to his plan. The Soviets would acquire the bomb in any case, and the timing of that event was less significant than the character of the Soviet Union and its relationship with the West when it did occur. A sincere offer of cooperation could open the way for a far-reaching improvement in U.S.-Soviet relations; a monopoly policy would only reinforce Soviet hostility and suspicion. "The only way you can make a man trustworthy is to trust him," Stimson claimed, "and the surest way to make him untrustworthy is to distrust him and show your distrust."

Stimson's proposal, despite the endorsement of Under Secretary of State Dean Acheson, generally met with a skeptical, if not hostile, reception.[6] To many in the administration and the military, as in Congress and the public at large, giving up the bomb was unthinkable and the virtues of monopoly self-evident. Influential advocates of this view were Manhattan Project director General Leslie Groves and Secretary of the Navy James Forrestal.

Politically, the opponents of cooperation shared a distrust of Russia and an assumption that the postwar U.S.-Soviet relationship would be adversarial. An offer to cooperate on atomic energy, they argued, would be interpreted by Stalin as a sign of weakness; instead of allaying his insecurities, it would encourage him to challenge the West all the harder. Thus Forrestal dismissed Stimson's plan as a dubious attempt "to buy [the Soviets'] understanding and sympathy. We tried that once with Hitler," he wrote. "There are no returns on appeasement."[7]

George Kennan, then serving at the U.S. embassy in Moscow and already deeply pessimistic about postwar U.S.-Soviet relations, shared

---

[6] For Acheson's support, see "Memorandum by the Acting Secretary of State to President Truman," *Foreign Relations of the United States (FRUS), 1945, Vol. 2*, pp. 48–50.

[7] Walter Millis, ed., *The Forrestal Diaries* (New York: Viking Press, 1951), p. 96.

Forrestal's misgivings. Four years later, Kennan would become a convert to international control, but in 1945 he regarded the Stimson plan as dangerously naive and "a frivolous neglect of the vital interests of our people."[8] He was scornful of Stimson's belief that a "friendly" American overture would significantly affect Stalin's calculations and help steer Soviet nuclear policy along cooperative lines. "There is nothing—I repeat nothing—in the history of the Soviet regime," he cabled Washington,

> which could justify us in assuming that the men who are now in power in Russia, or even those who have chances of assuming power within the foreseeable future, would hesitate for a moment to apply this power against us if by doing so they thought that they would materially improve their own power position in the world. This holds true regardless of the process by which the Soviet government might obtain the knowledge of the use of such forces, i.e., whether by its own scientific and inventive efforts, by espionage, or by such knowledge being imparted to them as a gesture of good will and confidence.[9]

In Kennan's view, the nature of the Soviet state made cooperation unthinkable on a matter as sensitive as atomic energy. Others' reasons for opposing sharing went beyond distrust of the Soviets; in their view, the atomic bomb was a key to the advancement of U.S. interests in the postwar world. This was a theme with many variations, having in common a reversal of Stimson's priorities: Instead of trying to enlist the Soviets in managing the nuclear threat, the object was to use the bomb to counter the Soviet threat. To this group, international control was undesirable whether or not it was feasible.

In military terms, the bomb was already being regarded by some as the lynchpin of future U.S. security, essential to countering Soviet power in Europe and Asia. Although they would not prevail for another two years, advocates of an "air-atomic" strategy were already pressing for a nuclear-based defense policy. They saw the bomb as an ideal opportunity to exploit America's technological advantages and compensate for its weaknesses, particularly in the area of manpower. Postwar demobilization was in full swing (reducing U.S. armed forces from 12 million at the time of the German surrender to 3 million a year later), and Congress was firmly opposed to reinstituting the draft. Nuclear weapons seemed to offer a way of offsetting the Soviets' huge land armies without the economic and political costs of remobilization.

The bomb also held temptations as a negotiating lever, particularly for Secretary of State James Byrnes. As Stimson was warning against bargaining with the bomb "on our hip," Byrnes was at the London Foreign Ministers Conference intending to do just that—hoping to use "nuclear diplomacy" to force Soviet concessions on peace settlement issues. His hopes were quickly disappointed, however. The Soviets, he learned at

---

[8] George F. Kennan, *Memoirs, 1925–50* (New York: Bantam Books, 1969), p. 312.

[9] Keenan, *Memoirs, 1925–50*.

London, "are stubborn, obstinate, and they don't scare."[10] Soviet Foreign Minister V. M. Molotov failed to be intimidated by the bomb and tauntingly hinted that the Soviets had it as well. From this episode, Byrnes concluded that the bomb was too blunt an instrument to be useful diplomatically; the threat to use it to enforce demands at the bargaining table was simply not credible. "There is no powder in the gun," observed Vannevar Bush, "for it could not be drawn."[11] By the end of 1945, Byrnes was carrying a version of Stimson's approach to the December Foreign Ministers Council in Moscow. But the image of the bomb as a diplomatic lever, whether as a carrot or a stick, died hard. It remained a recurring theme in U.S. thinking about the bomb and an effective argument against surrendering it to international control.

An equally stubborn illusion was the belief the United States would enjoy a long-lived nuclear monopoly. The atomic scientists had anticipated the power of this myth and its high potential for distorting policy judgment, and tried early to discredit it. The Franck report had cautioned that "the experience of Russian scientists in nuclear research is entirely sufficient to enable them to retrace our steps within a few years, even if we should make every attempt to conceal them." But few top officials absorbed this message. Most were convinced that other nations, and in particular, the Soviet Union, would require a decade or more to duplicate America's success. General Groves was an influential disseminator of this myth, which became an article of faith for President Truman.

This faith did not rest on a belief that the basic science of nuclear explosions could be monopolized; policymakers generally understood that this body of knowledge was widely known in the international scientific community. Indeed, within days of the bombings of Japan, on August 12, 1945, the United States had released a detailed history of the Manhattan Project, entitled "A General Account of the Development of Methods of Using Atomic Energy for Military Purposes Under the Auspices of the United States Government, 1940–45." Known as the Smyth Report, it was a primer on the science and technology of nuclear weapons, describing at length the principles of the bomb and the production of fissile materials.[12]

---

[10] Cited in Herken, *The Winning Weapon*, p. 43.

[11] Herken, *The Winning Weapon*, p. 37.

[12] Hewlett and Anderson, *The New World*, pp. 406–7; Vincent C. Jones, *Manhattan: The Army and the Atomic Bomb* (Washington, DC: U.S. Army Center of Military History, 1985), pp. 556–62. The report was ordered by Groves primarily to publicize the achievements of the Manhattan Project and deflect possible postwar criticism of the way it was managed. But another motive was to protect the inner core of sensitive information about the bomb and deter leaks by revealing at one stroke everything deemed suitable for public release. A statement accompanying the report captured the spirit of this effort. It called for "the utmost cooperation by all concerned in keeping secret now and for all time in the future, all scientific and technical information not given in this report or other official releases of information by the War Department." The report's scope surprised both those who approved of it (particularly the scientists, who hoped it signaled a return to the free exchange of information in the atomic field) and those who didn't (including the British).

The Smyth Report belied a serious hope that the essential information about the bomb could be kept secret. At the same time, it accented the confidence of Groves and others who believed that, even armed with such information, the Russians could not match America's achievement. This conceit was rooted in the belief that the Soviets lacked the engineering skills, industrial capacity, and raw materials to operate a nuclear weapons program. "So far as the scientific knowledge is concerned," Truman told a press conference in October 1945, "all the scientists know the answer, but how to put it to work—that is our secret."[13] For Groves, the key to preventing proliferation was the control of uranium, the basic raw material of the bomb. Wrongly believing that uranium was scarce, he thought the Soviet bomb effort could be thwarted by cornering the world's supply of the ore. As Richard Rhodes notes, "He might as well have tried to hoard the sea."[14]

During the war, the United States and Britain, working through the Combined Development Trust, had bought up uranium in areas not under their control, and gained a ten-year option on the future production of the Belgian Congo mines—the largest source of the ore at the time. Groves's goal was to meet the needs of the Manhattan Project and to deny uranium to others "not only for the period of the war, but for all time to come."[15] At the war's end, Groves claimed that the Trust controlled 97 percent of the world's high-grade uranium deposits and that Soviet uranium, if indeed there was any, was in low-grade deposits that would require "a revolution in extraction techniques" to exploit.[16]

In reality, uranium is abundant in the earth's crust, and is easily obtained from low-grade ores. That fact, and the overriding national security incentive that the Soviets now had to find uranium, made it very unlikely that the United States could control the raw materials necessary for nuclear weapons. Again, the Franck report had described the situation accurately: "Even if we do not know the size of the deposits discovered so far in the USSR, the probability that no large reserves of uranium will be found in a country which covers 1/5 of the land area of the earth (and whose sphere of influence takes in additional territory) is too small to serve as a basis of security. *Thus we cannot hope to avoid a nuclear armament race either by keeping secret from the competing nations the basic scientific facts of nuclear power or by cornering the raw materials required for such a race.*"[17]

---

[13] Harry S. Truman, *Year of Decisions* (New York: Signet Books, 1965), p. 585.

[14] Rhodes, *The Making of the Atomic Bomb*, p. 500.

[15] Jones, *Manhattan*, p. 296.

[16] Herken, *The Winning Weapon*, pp. 109–10.

[17] In Smith, *A Peril and A Hope*, p. 563. Emphasis in the original. Groves's error was to extrapolate from the operating pattern of the prewar industry, which served a small market centered on the genuinely rare element radium—a wholly inappropriate basis for projections into the era of atomic weapons. See Rhodes, *The Making of the Atomic Bomb*, p. 638.

Behind the sharp divisions among senior U.S. officials, there were clear signs during the closing months of 1945 that the President himself was inclined toward the hard line of Groves and Forrestal. As Truman began to regard confrontation with the Soviet Union as inevitable, the idea of cooperation on atomic energy became increasingly unreal to him. When he spoke about nuclear policy, he did so in strongly nationalistic terms. At his October 8 press conference, he attributed the bomb to America's unique combination of industrial capacity and raw materials, and announced that if other nations were to "catch up," they would have to "do it on their own hook, just as we did."[18] A month later, in his first major foreign policy speech, he referred to the bomb as a "sacred trust" to be used to advance American aims.

Truman rejected Stimson's proposal for a direct approach to the Soviets on nuclear cooperation. The issue would be taken up instead at the UN Atomic Energy Commission—just the public, multilateral forum Stimson had advised against. Meanwhile, the closely linked question of domestic arrangements for atomic energy was being taken up in Congress, where the issue was controlled by staunch atomic nationalists led by Senators Arthur Vandenberg, Brien McMahon, and Bourke Hickenlooper. When Secretary of State Byrnes, acting on his own, raised the atomic control issue with Stalin in December, Truman was furious. Facing a revolt by congressional leaders and his own administration hard-liners, the President cabled new instructions to Byrnes in Moscow, and on his return to Washington rebuked him for insubordination. Expressing his growing impatience both with Russia and with the accommodationist diplomacy of the secretary of state, Truman announced that he was "tired of babying the Soviets."[19]

In early 1946, the Cold War gained momentum. Hopes for agreement on an overall peace settlement faded amid continuing U.S.-Soviet disputes over the fate of Germany, the consolidation of Soviet power in Poland, and other issues. The reality of a postwar world organized around rival spheres of influence gradually replaced the universalist vision of great power cooperation as the guiding premise of American foreign policy. In February 1946 the emerging common wisdom was captured in George Kennan's celebrated "long telegram" from Moscow. Kennan's message, as he later put it, was one that Washington "was ready to

---

[18] Truman, *Year of Decisions*, p. 534.

[19] The following month, Byrnes announced his resignation, though he remained as Secretary of State for another year. On the Moscow meeting and its aftermath, see Herken, *The Winning Weapon*, pp. 69–94, and Truman, *Year of Decisions*, p. 552. Byrnes was carrying a version of the Stimson plan, which provided for staged cooperation on atomic energy, beginning with the exchange of general scientific information and moving toward progressively more sensitive areas. A major complaint of the proposal's critics was that the sharing of information would begin before agreement had been reached on controls or safeguards. They demanded a tight linkage at every stage between cooperation and Soviet acceptance of controls. See also Dean Acheson, *Present at the Creation* (New York: Norton, 1969), p. 135; and Hewlett and Anderson, *The New World*, pp. 473–77.

receive." [20] His analysis of the political and ideological sources of Soviet hostility, his categorical dismissal of the possibility of U.S.-Soviet cooperation, and his call for a Western policy of firm resistance to Soviet expansion were eagerly embraced by policymakers trying to make sense of events, and had enormous influence. As if to confirm Kennan's analysis, the following month's Iran crisis produced the first real confrontation of the Cold War.

THE ACHESON-LILIENTHAL REPORT AND THE BARUCH PLAN

Against this inauspicious background, the U.S. government first studied in depth the problem of preventing the bomb's spread. The result of this effort, the Acheson-Lilienthal report, probably came at least a year too late to shape the course of events. Yet, decades later, it remains a keen analysis of the proliferation problem and a prescient indictment of the later course of policy in this field.

The study, commissioned to prepare the United States for the opening of the UN Atomic Energy Commission in June 1946, was directed by a committee under the new Secretary of State Dean Acheson. Acheson in turn appointed an expert board of consultants chaired by David Lilienthal, the head of the Tennessee Valley Authority and a prominent New Deal liberal. [21] The board had access to all pertinent information, and a broad mandate to explore the requirements of an effective nuclear control system.

Acheson and Lilienthal hoped to use the project to challenge the prevailing assumptions of U.S. nuclear policy. Both were skeptical of nuclear secrecy and concerned that policy was being made in ignorance of key technical and political facts (including the secret wartime arrangements for U.S.-British collaboration). In particular, they saw the study as an opportunity to break General Groves's virtual monopoly on atomic information and hence loosen his grip on nuclear policy. As Lilienthal wrote,

> The assignment would force an examination of the crucial question: *What* is there that is secret? Are those facts really "secret" in the sense that is assumed by our international policy. . . . If my hunch . . . that in the real sense there are no secrets (that is, nothing that is not known or knowable)

---

[20] Kennan, *Memoirs, 1925–50*, p. 310.

[21] The members of the Acheson committee were Gen. Groves, Vannevar Bush, former Asst. Sec. of War John McCloy, and Harvard President James Conant. The board of consultants consisted of four individuals who were closely involved in the scientific and industrial aspects of the U.S. weapons program—J. Robert Oppenheimer, Chester Bernard, Charles Thomas, and Harry Winne. For a detailed account of their meetings, see Hewlett and Anderson, *The New World*, pp. 534–40.

would be supportable by the facts, then real progress would be made. For then it would be clear that the basis of present policy-making is without foundation. For present policy and commitments are made on the Army-sponsored thesis that there are secrets. And since it is in the Army's hands (or, literally, Gen. Groves') to deny access to the facts that would prove or disprove this vital thesis, there has been no way to examine the very foundation of our policies in the international field.[22]

Ironically, Lilienthal would assume control of the U.S. nuclear program a year later, only to become responsible for implementing an Atomic Energy Act that embodied the essentials of the Groves approach.

In March, the board of consultants presented Acheson's committee with a plan for international ownership and control of atomic energy. The scheme was radical but not utopian. It did not call for world government or an end to war. As Acheson cautioned, "We should not . . . expect an agreement to do away with Soviet-American tensions or the possibility of war."[23] Nor was Lilienthal oblivious to the threatening world situation. Acheson had shown him Kennan's long telegram and had briefed the committee on the Iranian crisis, bringing "a note of grim reality to the whole business."[24] Nevertheless, the committee tried as much as possible not to tailor its approach to political realities, but rather to follow the logic of the nuclear problem itself; this method led inexorably to a policy of international control.

The report began with the premise that the United States could not hope to maintain a monopoly on nuclear weapons. Echoing the earlier warnings of the atomic scientists, it stated that the scientific knowledge of nuclear explosives was "well known to competent scientists throughout the world."[25] The study predicted that economic development, national rivalry, and security concerns would all spur the spread of national nuclear capabilities: "Atomic energy plays so vital a part in contributing to the military power, to the possible economic welfare, and no doubt to the security of a nation, that the incentive to other nations to press their own developments is overwhelming."[26]

A second key assumption, which shaped the Acheson-Lilienthal analysis and all subsequent attempts to deal with proliferation, was the

[22] David E. Lilienthal, *The Journals of David E. Lilienthal: Volume II: The Atomic Energy Years 1945–50* (New York: Harper & Row, 1964), pp. 11–12.

[23] Acheson, *Present at the Creation*, p. 152.

[24] Lilienthal, *Journals, Vol. II*, p. 30. Lilienthal found Kennan's analysis convincing but not discouraging; to him, it underscored the urgency, rather than the futility, of an international solution for the bomb (p. 26).

[25] *A Report on the International Control of Atomic Energy* (the "Acheson-Lilienthal Report"), Washington, DC, March 16, 1946, p. 2. Reprinted in *Peaceful Nuclear Exports and Weapons Proliferation: A Compendium*, Committee on Government Operations, U.S. Senate, April 1975, pp. 127–98.

[26] *Acheson-Lilienthal Report*, p. 2.

intrinsic overlap—in knowledge, materials, and technology—between peaceful and military applications of atomic energy. A weapons program and one devoted to exploiting atomic energy for medical research or electric power generation would be "in much of their course interchangeable and interdependent."[27] This overlap poses a core dilemma of nonproliferation policy: How can the development of atomic energy for peaceful purposes be reconciled with the prevention of weapons proliferation? The blunt answer of the Acheson-Lilienthal report was that it could not be, if atomic energy remained under national control.

Rejecting the approach that subsequently became the basis of the global nonproliferation regime, the authors concluded that "a system of inspection superimposed on an otherwise uncontrolled exploitation of atomic energy by national governments" could not provide confidence against diversion to military uses: "The facts preclude any reasonable reliance upon inspection as the primary safeguard against violations of conventions prohibiting atomic weapons, yet leaving the exploitation of atomic energy in national hands."[28] The policing of national programs would be an impossibly large task, requiring a huge, intrusive, and essentially adversarial agency; as many as 300 inspectors might be necessary to guard a single uranium enrichment plant, and even then there would be no guarantee against diversion. In these circumstances, the system would be unlikely to gain international confidence and might even aggravate international tensions.

The only hope for an effective inspection system, then, was "to reduce its scope to manageable proportions, to limit the things that need to be inspected."[29] To achieve that objective, the plan limited national atomic programs to a very restricted sphere of "safe" activities, while reserving "dangerous" activities to an international Atomic Development Authority (ADA).

As its name implied, the ADA was seen not primarily as a policing agency (since there would be little to police), but an operational one with exclusive authority to conduct research and development in weapons-related areas. The sphere of "dangerous" activities was sweepingly defined, encompassing virtually the entire nuclear fuel cycle beginning with raw materials.[30] (Though it had little else in common with General Groves's views on the issue, the report shared his conviction that control of uranium was the key to nonproliferation.) The ADA would assume ownership and control of uranium mining; own and operate nuclear reactors and separation facilities for the production of fissile

---

[27] *Acheson-Lilienthal Report*, p. 4.

[28] *Acheson-Lilienthal Report*, p. 9.

[29] *Acheson-Lilienthal Report*, p. 8.

[30] The distinction between "safe" and "dangerous" activities was Oppenheimer's. See Hewlett and Anderson, *The New World*, pp. 536ff.

plutonium and uranium-235; and undertake all explosives research and development. It would also license and inspect the "safe" activities (involving no access to militarily significant quantities of fissile materials or the facilities for producing them) that states and private concerns would be permitted to engage in, and would provide the materials for them. These activities would include medical and other scientific research involving small amounts of fissile material, and—in the future—the operation of power-generating reactors using "denatured fuels" (diluted with nonfissionable isotopes) unsuitable for use in explosives.

This sharply unequal division of labor would effectively remove the element of national rivalry from the development of atomic energy and greatly reduce the inspection burden. Because the ADA would have a legal monopoly on such activities as uranium mining and the production of fissile materials, the detection of any national activity in these areas would be a prima facie violation: "It is not the motive but the operation that is illegal."[31] It would also give what later came to be known as "timely warning" of violations, imposing a long lead time on any state attempting to circumvent the system to produce atomic weapons. "Danger signals" would "flash early enough to leave time adequate to permit other nations—alone or in concert—to take appropriate action."[32]

The strategy for implementing the plan was recognized as critical to its political fate. The challenge was to map a route to international control that would satisfy other nations (and especially the Soviet Union) of U.S. good faith, while protecting America's position during the transition. To assure the latter, the Acheson committee insisted on a step-by-step linkage of controls and cooperation in lieu of the "integral" approach preferred by the board of consultants.[33] The United States would disclose progressively more sensitive atomic information at each stage in the implementation of the plan—first the general scientific information needed for discussion of the proposal; then more practical technical know-how as the ADA began to assume its functions; and finally complete information on nuclear explosives when the system was fully in place and operational.

While acknowledging that the plan would probably accelerate the loss of U.S. dominance in atomic energy, the report stressed that the United States would control the process at each stage. "Should the worst happen and, during the transition period, the entire effort collapse, the United States will at all times be in a favorable position with regard to atomic

---

[31] *Acheson-Lilienthal Report*, p. 40.

[32] *Acheson-Lilienthal Report*, p. 9.

[33] See Lilienthal, *Journals, Vol II*, p. 27. This distinction had sparked the controversy over Secretary of State Byrnes's nuclear proposals at the Moscow Foreign Ministers Conference the previous December.

weapons."[34] Most important, the United States would reserve the right to continue manufacturing nuclear weapons, and to control its own nuclear production facilities, until the end of the process.

> The plan does not require that the United States shall discontinue such manufacture either upon the proposal of the plan or upon the inauguration of the international agency. . . . That decision, whenever made, will involve considerations of the highest policy affecting our security, and must be made by our government under its constitutional processes and in the light of all the facts of the world situation.[35]

The report was forwarded to Byrnes, who recommended it to Truman as the basis for American policy at the United Nations. To the dismay of Acheson and his colleagues, Byrnes also advised Truman to appoint Bernard Baruch, the Wall Street financier and self-styled "advisor to presidents," to present the plan at the UN. Baruch, disdaining the role of "errand boy," insisted on putting his own stamp on the proposal. In doing so, he remained largely faithful to the substance of the Acheson-Lilienthal plan, but subverted its underlying spirit.

Baruch transformed the tone of the plan from conciliation to belligerence. While the original report had stressed cooperative development and downplayed enforcement, Baruch emphasized the need for "immediate, swift, and sure punishment" for violators. "It would be a deception, to which I am unwilling to lend myself," he told the UN, "were I not to say to you and to our peoples that the matter of punishment lies at the very heart of our present security system."[36] Further, the veto power held by the five permanent members of the UN Security Council was not to apply in cases of enforcement under the plan. Baruch's approach thus highlighted precisely those issues that the Acheson committee had hoped to finesse in early discussions so that the substance of the plan could be considered on its merits. His changes, Acheson believed, "were almost certain to wreck any possibility of Russian acceptance" of the plan:

> The Soviet Union was undoubtedly doing all in its power to develop nuclear weapons at the moment. . . . If so, the "swift and sure punishment" provision could be interpreted by Moscow only as an attempt to turn the United Nations into an alliance to support the United States threat of war against the USSR unless it ceased its efforts, for only the United States could conceivably administer "swift and sure" punishment to the Soviet Union. This meant the certain defeat of the treaty by Soviet veto.[37]

---

[34] *Acheson-Lilienthal Report*, p. 61.

[35] *Acheson-Lilienthal Report*, pp. ix–x.

[36] Speech to the United Nations, June 14, 1946.

[37] Acheson, *Present at the Creation*, p. 155.

But Baruch was complacent about this risk. "America can get what she wants if she insists on it," he told Lilienthal. "After all, we've got it and they haven't and won't have it for a long time to come."[38]

As Acheson predicted, the Soviets quickly rejected the Baruch plan, offering an alternative that reversed the U.S. sequence. The Soviet plan proposed outlawing the bomb at the outset, requiring the United States to surrender its nuclear capability. Only then would other nations have to submit to international controls. In addition, the Security Council veto would be retained. An impasse quickly developed, and the ensuing debates became a sterile exercise in political posturing and blame-placing. The United States finally pushed the Baruch plan to vote on the last day of the year, winning a meaningless "victory" when it was approved 10–0–2, with the Soviet Union and Poland abstaining.

International control of atomic energy had become an early casualty of the Cold War. Although Baruch's tactics made it more certain, the outcome would probably not have been greatly different even if the Acheson-Lilienthal plan had been presented in its original spirit.[39] The difference was more in the sincerity of the effort than the likelihood of success. Nuclear control had become a zero-sum game: Any plan requiring the Soviet Union to open its nuclear program to outside inspection and control while the United States retained its atomic monopoly would have been unacceptable to the Russians. The Baruch Plan, as Henry Wallace pointed out, effectively asked the Soviets to give up their only cards before the game had begun.[40] But it was no more likely that the United States would deny itself an escape clause and surrender its monopoly without guarantees against the Soviet nuclear program. As Truman wrote Baruch in July 1946, "We should not under any circumstances throw away our gun until we are sure the rest of the world can't arm against us."[41] As if to underline the point, the United States was at that moment conducting a series of nuclear tests in the Bikini islands—the first atomic explosions since Nagasaki.

While the UN debated, the U.S. Atomic Energy Act of 1946 (the McMahon Act) became law. Though its main purpose was to establish civilian control over the atomic energy program, the act's international implications were far-reaching. It reflected a firmly nationalist approach,

---

[38] Lilienthal, *Journals, Vol. II*, p. 123.

[39] Serious prospects for cooperation on atomic energy may well have been foreclosed even before the war's end. Given Stalin's suspicions of the West, his knowledge through spies of the Manhattan Project (and of Anglo-American nuclear cooperation that not only excluded but was in part aimed against Russia), and—perhaps most important—the U.S. use of the bomb against Japan, it is likely that the Soviet Union was determined at the end of the war to acquire its own nuclear weapons. See McGeorge Bundy, *Danger and Survival: Choices About the Bomb in the First Fifty Years* (New York: Random House, 1988), pp. 176ff.

[40] See Herken, *The Winning Weapon*, pp. 181–82.

[41] Harry S. Truman, *Years of Trial and Hope* (New York: Signet, 1965), p. 25.

enshrining the policy of secrecy and denial, and defining as "restricted data" all information pertaining to the production or use of fissile materials. The law's strictures applied to peaceful as well as well as military uses: " . . . Until Congress declares . . . that effective and enforceable international safeguards against the use of atomic energy for destructive purposes have been established, there shall be no exchange of information with other nations with respect to the use of atomic energy for industrial purposes."[42]

THE COLD WAR AND THE BOMB, 1947–1949

Desultory debates on international control continued until May 1948, when the UN Atomic Energy Commission adjourned, but they were essentially a sideshow. The Commission's final report confirmed this failure, conceding that "agreement on effective measures for the control of atomic energy is itself dependent on cooperation in broader fields of policy."[43] By this time, the bomb was moving toward the center of U.S. defense policy.

In retrospect, America's nuclear dependency was surprisingly slow to develop. For nearly two years after the war, the U.S. nuclear threat was virtually a bluff, consisting of only a token stockpile of unassembled bombs and a minimal capability to deliver them.[44] Early plans for the use of atomic bombs were basically paper exercises, lacking both the hardware to implement them and a coherent view of the new weapons' military and strategic implications. The bomb was still too novel and too scarce to claim its eventual role at the heart of American strategy.

But as the Cold War intensified, the bomb assumed a growing importance.[45] In early 1947, as the Truman Doctrine and Marshall Plan were being formulated, the President was briefed for the first time on the low

---

[42] U.S. Atomic Energy Act of 1946, sec. 10(1).

[43] *Documents on Disarmament, 1945–59*, United States Arms Control and Disarmament Agency (Washington, DC: GPO), pp. 171–72.

[44] See David Alan Rosenberg, "U.S. Nuclear Stockpile, 1945 to 1950," *Bulletin of the Atomic Scientists*, May 1982, pp. 25–30. Rosenberg estimates that in mid-1947 the United States possessed nuclear cores for only 13 bombs, and was producing bombs at a rate of less than one every two months. The low stockpile figures were due to several factors including raw material constraints, the technical problems of scaling up to a mass production basis, and bureaucratic rivalry and secrecy. The early scarcity of nuclear weapons strongly influenced thinking about their military usefulness, fostering the view that the weapons would make sense only against very high value targets. See Fred Kaplan, *The Wizards of Armageddon* (New York: Simon & Schuster, 1983).

[45] See Herken, *The Winning Weapon*, chaps. 10–13, and David Alan Rosenberg, "The Origins of Overkill: Nuclear Weapons and American Strategy, 1945–60," *International Security*, Spring 1983.

stockpile figures and told that an alarming gap existed between the nation's military requirements and its actual nuclear capabilities. A year later, the Soviet-sponsored coup in Czechoslovakia and the Berlin blockade created a brief war scare and, more enduringly, a perception that the Soviet threat was essentially a military one.

As containment came to be defined increasingly in military rather than economic and political terms, and budget constraints and public aversion to the draft blocked a remobilization of conventional military forces, a central role for nuclear weapons followed naturally. The result was the triumph, almost by default, of the advocates of an atomic military strategy. During the Berlin crisis, nuclear-capable (though unequipped) U.S. bombers were stationed in Great Britain. In the same period, the United States conducted a new series of weapons tests, increased the stockpile to around 100 bombs, and adopted plans for an all-out "atomic blitz" against Soviet cities at the outset of a war.

With the formation of the NATO alliance in April 1949, American nuclear weapons became the guarantors of Atlantic security. But only months later, the Soviet Union conducted its first nuclear test, abruptly ending the U.S. monopoly several years ahead of government expectations. Nuclear proliferation had begun.

ANGLO-AMERICAN NUCLEAR COOPERATION

Great Britain was not far behind. While the Soviet Union was clearly the central focus of early U.S. nonproliferation policy, nuclear relations with Britain were an important second strand. At issue was the fate of the close wartime nuclear collaboration between the two allies. Britain tried to revive this link after the war, but the United States resisted, seeing little to gain—with the important exception of access to British-controlled uranium—and considerable risk in encouraging the U.K. nuclear effort. In the prevailing U.S. view, Britain's program was redundant and worse—an unwanted competitor for scarce raw materials, a likely source of security leaks, a dangerously exposed target in the event of Soviet attack, and a commercial rival in the postwar world. The resulting friction previewed later Atlantic nuclear debates and cast Britain in an "ally-as-victim" role that would become a familiar motif of U.S. nonproliferation policy.

Britain had begun research on nuclear weapons even before the United States. Its conclusion that fission weapons were feasible, in the 1941 "Maud Report," had been instrumental in persuading Washington to embark on the Manhattan Project. Once under way, however, the U.S. effort soon surpassed and dwarfed Britain's, and cooperation between the two countries was strained by this inequality. The United States, which previously had eagerly sought British help, now saw it as superfluous and began to limit the access of British scientists working on the project to what was strictly germane to prosecuting the war effort.[46]

In response to British complaints, President Roosevelt agreed to new guidelines for cooperation in two secret agreements that were later much regretted by the United States. The first was the August 1943 Quebec Agreement, which called for "full and effective collaboration" and a pooling of "all available British and American brains and resources" in the interest of the speediest possible development of a bomb. The agreement also provided that neither country would use the bomb without the other's consent or communicate any information about it to third parties.[47] Finally, in a concession meant to allay U.S. suspicions about British commercial motives, Prime Minister Winston Churchill placed the future of Britain's civil nuclear program in American hands:

> The British Government recognizes that any post-war advantages of an industrial or commercial character shall be dealt with as between the United States and Great Britain on terms to be specified by the President of the United States to the Prime Minister of Great Britain. The Prime Minister expressly disclaims any interest in these industrial and commercial aspects beyond what may be considered by the President of the United States to be fair and just and in harmony with the economic welfare of the world.[48]

Thus, in a strange twist, America's first agreement for nuclear cooperation hinged on assurances that the fruits of cooperation would not be diverted from military to peaceful purposes.

Postwar arrangements were addressed again in the Hyde Park aide-memoire of September 1944, in which Roosevelt and Churchill agreed that full collaboration in both military and civilian aspects of atomic energy would continue after Japan's defeat "unless and until terminated by joint agreement." This agreement was held so closely that Truman's foreign policy advisors were largely ignorant of it until months after the war; the congressional drafters of the 1946 Atomic Energy Act did not learn of it until almost a year after the law was passed.

As the war ended, the two countries had widely diverging outlooks on the future of their nuclear relationship. Britain looked forward to close cooperation, both to assist its own national nuclear program and as a key link in a broader postwar Anglo-American partnership through which the

---

[46] See Andrew J. Pierre, *Nuclear Politics: The British Experience with an Independent Strategic Force 1939–1970* (London: Oxford Univ. Press, 1972), pp. 34–38.

[47] The latter provision may be seen as the world's first formal nonproliferation agreement. Citing it, the United States terminated the participation of French scientists (considered politically unreliable) at the Chalk River project in Montreal. The episode was a defining movement in the development of France's nuclear resentments against the English-speaking countries. On Franco-American nuclear relations, see Bertrand Goldschmidt, *The Atomic Complex: A Worldwide Political History of Nuclear Energy* (LaGrange Park, IL: American Nuclear Society, 1982).

[48] Text in Pierre, *Nuclear Politics*, p. 345.

United Kingdom hoped to maintain a leading world role. The United States was on a totally different wavelength. Preoccupied with the Soviet Union, the American nuclear debate was forming around the opposite poles of international control and national monopoly. For all their differences, both poles shared an aversion to a special bilateral U.S.-U.K. nuclear link, which risked compromising U.S. independence while undercutting any approach to the Soviets.

A painful reckoning was unavoidable, and was made worse by the Truman administration's maladroit handling of the issue.[49] At a Washington summit meeting of the United States, Britain, and Canada in November 1945, British Prime Minister Clement Atlee appeared to have gained his objective. Following a public declaration on international control, the governments endorsed a secret memorandum providing for "full and effective" nuclear collaboration, and formed a subcommittee to draft a new charter for cooperation to replace the Quebec Agreement. Under the new accord, the United States would assist Britain in constructing its own nuclear production facilities and relinquish its exclusive claim on Belgian uranium in favor of an even split with London.

But Atlee's victory was short-lived. The United States immediately backtracked, largely at the urging of Groves, who—after helping the new agreement—was stricken with second thoughts. As recounted by Lilienthal, an agitated Groves came to Acheson (until then unaware of the secret nuclear arrangements) and, describing "the mess we are in," pleaded with him to "get us out of it."[50] Groves claimed that the draft agreement was tantamount to a military alliance with Great Britain, and that the proposed split of uranium would bring U.S. weapons production to a halt. Acheson saw other dangers in the plan, fearing that it would undermine U.S. proposals for international control and, if disclosed, "would blow the administration out of the water."[51] At the same time, he had serious misgivings about reneging on the Hyde Park and Washington understandings. "Our Government," he wrote later, "having made an agreement from which it had gained immeasurably, was not keeping its word and performing its obligations. . . . Grave consequences might follow upon keeping our word, but the idea of not keeping it was repulsive to me."[52]

Under the pretext that it constituted a secret treaty in violation of the newly adopted UN Charter, the U.S. disavowed the plan. The British,

---

[49] The following discussion draws on Pierre, *Nuclear Politics*, pp. 112–20, and on the official history of the U.K. atomic program, Margaret Gowing, *Independence and Deterrence: Britain and Atomic Energy 1945–52, Vol. 1: Policy Making* (London: Macmillan, 1974), chaps. 3–4.

[50] Lilienthal, *Journals, Vol. II*, p. 25. See also Hewlett and Anderson, *The New World*, pp. 477–80.

[51] Lilienthal, *Journals, Vol. II*, p. 26.

[52] Acheson, *Present at the Creation*, p. 164.

Lilienthal recorded, were informed that "they must just resign themselves to the fact that, although we made the agreement, we simply could not carry it out; that things like that happen in the Government of the U.S."[53] In notifying Atlee, Truman added insult to injury by claiming, disingenuously in the British view, that the Washington plan had envisioned only the exchange of basic scientific information, and never meant to embrace cooperation in plant design and operational matters. "I would not want to have it said," he wrote, "that the morning following the issuance of our declaration to bring about international control we entered into a new agreement the purpose of which was to have the United States furnish the information as to construction and operation of plants which would enable the United Kingdom to construct another atomic energy plant."[54]

The Truman administration having closed the door to meaningful nuclear cooperation, Congress then locked it with the passage of the Atomic Energy Act in the summer of 1946. The British greeted this double verdict bitterly, as a betrayal of U.S. commitments and a blow to Britain's postwar designs. Significantly, however, the British now began to regard an independent nuclear program as an alternate means of pursuing those designs. In January 1947, less than six months after Truman signed the McMahon Act, Britain decided to build its own atomic weapons. While Britain's foremost interest in the bomb was national security, another important motive was to gain a measure of equality with the United States in order to revive the Anglo-American partnership. As one British scholar observed,

> Almost all officials and most politicians outside the pacifist wing of the labour party sincerely believed that Britain would never be able to look the United States in the eye, would never be treated as more than a useful or elderly relation until it became a member of the nuclear club.[55]

If the collapse of bilateral nuclear cooperation was traumatic for Britain, it also created problems for the United States. It left hanging two loose ends that the United States was particularly anxious to tie up. One was a provision in the Quebec Agreement that gave each country a veto over the other's use of the atomic bomb. Washington had forfeited a chance to terminate this mutual veto when it backed out of the November

---

[53] Lilienthal, *Journals, Vol. II*, p. 26.

[54] Truman, *Years of Trial and Hope*, p. 28. The relevant part of the draft agreement was as follows: "There shall be full and effective co-operation in the field of basic scientific research among the three countries. In the field of development, design, construction, and operation of plants such co-operation, recognized as desirable in principle, shall be regulated by such ad hoc arrangements as may be approved from time to time by the Combined Policy Committee as mutually advantageous."

[55] Alastair Buchan, "Britain and the Bomb," *The Reporter*, March 19, 1959, p. 23, cited in Pierre, *Nuclear Politics*, p. 77.

1945 agreement for continued U.S.-U.K. collaboration. Eliminating it now became something of an obsession. The veto was viewed as an encroachment on U.S. military autonomy and a serious domestic political liability. Indeed, congressional outrage at this affront to American sovereignty was such that Senators Vandenberg and Hickenlooper warned the administration that it could endanger approval of the Marshall Plan.[56]

The other matter of keen U.S. interest was uranium. Though the United States would emerge in the 1950s as the world's largest uranium producer, in the early postwar years it was heavily dependent on shipments from the Belgian Congo, whose output through 1956 had been bought up by the allied Combined Development Trust. With the severing of U.S.-British cooperation, the allocation of this output between the United States and Britain became the main focus of nuclear relations between the two countries.[57] The issue was a continuing source of friction, especially as the Cold War intensified and the United States started planning for significant growth in its then-meager stockpile of atomic weapons. The start-up of the British program created a competitor for supplies, and was all the more unwelcome for this reason. The United States was chronically worried about raw material shortages at this time (an ironic predicament in view of later battles over America's shortcomings as a "reliable supplier"), and protested that Britain's plans could force cutbacks in American weapons production.[58]

Using its leverage on the uranium and veto issues, the United Kingdom was able to reopen the door to technical cooperation—but only a crack. In January 1948 the two countries adopted a modus vivendi under which the United States agreed to share information in nine relatively nonsensitive areas (such as health and safety) of nuclear science and engineering. In return, America's share of uranium was increased; the United States gained the entire output of the Congo through 1949, and an option on additional supplies from the British stockpile if necessary to support its production requirements. The Quebec veto over use of the bomb was lifted, as was the provision giving the United States control over the postwar British commercial nuclear industry. In practice, the modus vivendi proved a one-sided boon to the United States, provoking another round of British recriminations. The United States had "consumed the bait while avoiding the hook."[59]

---

[56] Pierre, *Nuclear Politics*, p. 129.

[57] See Gowing, *Independence and Deterrence*, chap. 11.

[58] Gowing, *Independence and Deterrence*, pp. 247–49. In July 1946, the two countries had temporarily agreed to a fifty-fifty split of Congo production, a formula that the United States found increasingly unsatisfactory. Truman complained that "the British were now getting more than they could put to any practical use, while we were left short." Truman, *Years of Trial and Hope*, p. 360.

[59] Gowing, *Independence and Deterrence*, p. 349.

In 1949, however, the Truman administration changed course and made a concerted effort to restore full nuclear cooperation. Though the attempt failed in the face of congressional opposition, it signaled an important evolution in U.S. thinking about nuclear proliferation. There were two main reasons for the change.

First, with the signing of the North Atlantic Treaty in April 1949, the United States and Britain were now formal allies, and close military coordination was being established across a broad spectrum. It seemed increasingly artificial, and potentially costly in military and political terms, to exclude nuclear weapons from cooperation. Acheson and Lilienthal, now secretary of state and chairman of the U.S. Atomic Energy Commission respectively, were strongly of this view. Both wanted to bring nuclear relations into line with the larger pattern of Anglo-American solidarity and end the debilitating friction ("a haggling match about swapping uranium for 'secrets,'" in Lilienthal's words) that had marked the recent period.[60] And, with international control no longer a serious prospect, their earlier apprehension that collaboration with Britain would undermine U.S. policy at the United Nations had disappeared. Another strong advocate of restoring full nuclear cooperation was General Dwight D. Eisenhower, who had left his position as army chief of staff to become president of Columbia University in early 1949 but remained an important advisor on nuclear policy.

The second reason to look more favorably on bilateral cooperation was the progress of the British nuclear program, which by 1949 was well under way and within a year of bringing its first production reactors into operation. In both countries, it was now widely expected that Britain would be the second nuclear weapon state. On its own, the United States estimated, Britain would have a bomb in about four years; American assistance might shorten that time by 18 months or so.[61] Denying assistance was now irrelevant if the goal was to prevent British proliferation. Cooperation, on the other hand, could increase U.S. influence over Britain's program. In the framework of a joint program, Britain might even agree to concentrate its production facilities and weapon stockpiles on U.S. soil, reducing their vulnerability to Soviet attack.

Acheson, Lilienthal, and Secretary of Defense Louis Johnson, acting as a subcommittee of the National Security Council, summarized the case in a March 1949 report to Truman:

> The United Kingdom will have plutonium and atomic weapons with or without our help. Moreover, without our help the United Kingdom will retain complete freedom of action and may indeed become a serious competitor with us for scarce raw materials. . . . Full and effective cooperation with the United Kingdom in all fields of atomic energy, including weapons, would

---

[60] Lilienthal, *Journals*, Vol. II, p. 555.

[61] Acheson, *Present at the Creation*, p. 316.

provide the opportunity for the United States to secure certain safeguards and an economical distribution of effort in the common security. This alternative would be consistent with the main lines of our foreign policy both as it relates to our posture toward the Soviet Union and toward our allies.[62]

Truman approved the NSC recommendation to restore full atomic collaboration between the two countries, but encountered vehement opposition at a meeting with congressional atomic energy leaders at Blair House on July 14, 1949. A subsequent session with the full membership of the Joint Committee on Atomic Energy proved "a failure just short of a disaster," in Acheson's description, with Senator Vandenberg and others attacking the plan as "a sellout to the British and a giveaway of invaluable secrets."[63] It was the prototype of a recurring debate. The administration, anxious to strengthen bilateral relations with a valued security partner, sought an exemption from strict nonproliferation rules. Congress, acting as the guardian of a universalistic policy, resisted.

Acknowledging congressional realities, Truman authorized exploratory talks with the British with the proviso that the sharing of actual weapons data be excluded.[64] Negotiators then searched in vain for a new cooperative arrangement that would satisfy both Congress and the British. But the former in effect demanded a U.S. takeover of the British program, while the latter—remembering the betrayal of 1946—were determined to preserve at least the core of an independent capability.[65]

As the talks began, their context was suddenly altered by the October 1949 Soviet nuclear test. This development might have brightened the chances for Anglo-American cooperation—humbling the believers in America's unique nuclear abilities and raising doubts about the logic and fairness of denying its ally what the common enemy now possessed. But in fact the Soviet test only reinforced the mood of atomic nationalism, and preoccupation with security leaks, in Congress and the public. In this atmosphere, the final blow to British hopes was the arrest in February 1950 of Klaus Fuchs—a member of the wartime U.K. team at Los Alamos—on charges of spying for the Soviet Union. The ensuing political backlash, soon magnified by the onset of McCarthyism, doomed any remaining chance of restoring cooperation. Britain went forward alone and tested its first nuclear weapon in 1952.

---

[62] "A Report to the President by the Special Committee of the National Security Council on Atomic Energy Policy with Respect to the United Kingdom and Canada," Washington, March 2, 1949, *Foreign Relations of the United States (FRUS), 1949, Vol I*, p. 456. See also Acheson, *Present at the Creation*, p. 315.

[63] Acheson, *Present at the Creation*, p. 319. The exchanges are recorded by an appalled David Lilienthal in *Journals, Vol. II*, pp. 543–52.

[64] Truman, *Years of Trial and Hope*, p. 348.

[65] Pierre, *Nuclear Politics*, p. 133. For a detailed account of the negotiations, see Gowing, *Independence and Deterrence*, chap. 9.

THE RACE BEGINS

The Soviet test was a watershed in two senses. It marked the beginning of the "horizontal" proliferation of nuclear weapons to additional countries, and it prompted the first great "vertical" escalation of the Cold War arms race. The possibility that the United States might reassess its growing dependence on nuclear weapons vanished along with the American nuclear monopoly. Within months, Truman initiated a large increase in U.S. nuclear weapons production and approved the development of the hydrogen bomb.[66] Two more increases were authorized before Truman left office, resulting in the construction of eight new plutonium production reactors, ten new uranium enrichment plants, and a massive concurrent growth of U.S. nuclear weapons and "required" targets in the Soviet Union.[67] By the end of Truman's term, the H-bomb had been tested and the U.S. stockpile had grown tenfold to around 1000 bombs. The age of atomic scarcity was over and the age of overkill had begun.

Though inexorable, the trend was not uncontroversial. The H-bomb decision was opposed by the General Advisory Committee of the AEC, including Oppenheimer, and by Lilienthal, who resigned as AEC chairman in early 1950. Another critic was George Kennan, who had become increasingly estranged from the military and nuclear emphasis of U.S. policy. In late 1949 he drafted a long memorandum advocating the international control of atomic energy that he had scorned at the time of Stimson's proposal.[68] In poignant contrast to the long telegram of 1946, the message was completely out of phase with the emerging policy consensus. This time it was Acheson—Stimson's former advocate and now the leading architect of U.S. Cold War policies—who was scornful. "If that is your view," he told Kennan, "you ought to resign from the Foreign Service and go out and preach your Quaker gospel."[69]

CONCLUSION

In its formative years, American nonproliferation policy was dominated by two overarching, and related, questions—the fate of U.S.-Soviet relations, and the place of the bomb in U.S. security. As policies in these two areas took shape, they established a context that framed, and severely narrowed, the realistic options for controlling the spread of nuclear weapons.

---

[66] The impetus it gave to U.S. H-bomb research was "one of the positive effects" of the Soviet test, in Truman's view. *Years of Trial and Hope*, p. 352.

[67] Rosenberg, "The Origins of Overkill," pp. 22–23.

[68] *FRUS 1950, Vol. I*, p. 40; Kennan, *Memoirs, 1925–50*, pp. 497–502.

[69] Walter Isaacson and Evan Thomas, *The Wise Men* (New York: Simon & Schuster, 1986), p. 489.

The emergence of the Cold War ensured the failure of international control of atomic energy. It sealed the victory of American advocates of a nationalist nuclear policy and made Soviet proliferation inevitable. Contrary to the hopes of Stimson and the atomic scientists, who sought to fit postwar international politics to the requirements of nuclear control, the bomb was instead fitted to the traditional logic of national interest and the balance of power. If there were to be, in Charles Bohlen's words, "two worlds instead of one," then there would also be two bombs.[70]

But while the Cold War doomed international control, it did not necessarily dictate that nuclear weapons would become the centerpiece of American national security policy. This development owed more to domestic economic and political considerations than to the emergence of U.S.-Soviet rivalry per se. Yet it was equally fateful in its implications for nonproliferation policy. It planted a double standard at the heart of that policy, making it a case of "Do as I say, not as I do." "We cannot . . . carry conviction," Acheson conceded during the H-bomb debate, ". . . in advocating and directing the effort for international control and abolition of nuclear weapons if at the same time our military reliance upon them is growing."[71]

Kennan, in his dissenting memo, drew the implicit conclusion: The decision to rely militarily on the bomb meant that at bottom the United States now regarded international control as undesirable in principle—"a direction in which we did not really wish to move."[72] Given a hypothetical choice between a world of nuclear weapons and one in which the Soviets were kept from having the bomb only through U.S. self-denial, the United States would choose the former. Surrender of U.S. nuclear weapons, in other words, was too high a price to pay for nonproliferation. The underlying truth was one that the United States would face repeatedly in the future: Nonproliferation was not a cheap goal; to pursue it seriously would have significant—and sometimes unacceptable—implications for other U.S. interests.

The myth of U.S. nuclear uniqueness obscured this truth, however. It created the illusion that the bomb was, as Forrestal put it, "the property of the American people," to share or withhold as the United States saw fit.[73] As a result, debates often proceeded as if proliferation were a matter of U.S. discretion, and the policy options American monopoly and international control. This self-deception led policymakers to understate the true costs of preventing the bomb's spread and encouraged two tendencies that were to become typical of U.S. nonproliferation pol-

---

[70] Cited in John Lewis Gaddis, *Strategies of Containment: A Critical Appraisal of Postwar American National Security Policy* (New York: Oxford Univ. Press, 1982), p. 57.

[71] *FRUS 1949, Vol. I*, p. 613; Gaddis, *Strategies of Containment*, p. 81.

[72] Kennan, *Memoirs, 1925–50*, p. 499.

[73] Millis, ed., *The Forrestal Diaries*, p. 95.

icy—a failure to take seriously others' motives and capabilities for acquiring nuclear weapons, and an overreliance on secrecy and denial as a means of preventing proliferation. Might the United States have pursued international control more vigorously if it had assessed Soviet nuclear capabilities more realistically? Possibly; but given the underlying premises of U.S. nuclear policy, it seems doubtful. The belief that the United States required nuclear weapons to contain Soviet power did not depend on a continued monopoly, as the U.S. reaction to Soviet proliferation made clear. Far from causing a U.S. reassessment of the trend toward greater reliance on nuclear weapons, the Soviet bomb only reinforced and accelerated that trend. This suggests that if Truman had known at the war's end how fleeting the U.S. monopoly would be, he might have quickened the pace of the U.S. bomb program even sooner in order to exploit America's head start and maximize its lead during the short time available.

A U.S. policy of nuclear exclusion and monopoly followed almost automatically from Cold War premises with respect to the Soviet Union. But toward Great Britain, the U.S. interest in nonproliferation was less clearcut. The British case raised for the first time the question of whether that interest was universal or selective: Should the United States always resist the spread of nuclear weapons? Or, given the primacy of Cold War considerations in U.S. policy, should a distinction be made between friend and foe?

The Baruch Plan and the McMahon Act both assumed an undifferentiated, universalistic opposition to proliferation. In contrast, the Truman administration's effort to revive collaboration with Britain in 1949 reflected a more selective, case-by-case approach—suggesting that cooperation potentially might serve American interests in alliance cohesion, influence over allied nuclear programs, and Western military strength. Yet even this effort was equivocal—inspired more by the desire to control the British nuclear program than to support it. As such, it indicated (as had the earlier U.S. unease over the veto clause of the Quebec Agreement) a basic American hostility to independent centers of nuclear power, whether friendly or not. What could not yet be glimpsed was that this distinctly "superpower" stake in nonproliferation would become a powerful shared interest of the United States and the Soviet Union.

It is possible that a more adroit and sensitive U.S. policy would have stopped the British bomb. But although a continuation of wartime Anglo-American cooperation might conceivably have produced a different outcome, in hindsight the British bomb, like Russia's, appears inevitable. The abrupt cutoff of U.S. cooperation was a triggering factor but not the primary cause.[74] The key determinant of Britain's decision, as Clement

---

[74] Gowing, *Independence and Deterrence*, p. 241. The U.S. cutoff "ensured that Britain's deterrent would be independent," Gowing argues, "but it was not the reason why Britain was determined to possess it."

Atlee later emphasized, was uncertainty about the postwar security role of the United States: "At that time we had to bear in mind that there was always the possibility of their withdrawing and becoming isolationist once again. The manufacture of a British atomic bomb was therefore at that stage essential to our defense. You must remember this was all prior to NATO."[75] Given these anxieties, probably nothing less than a physical allocation of nuclear weapons to the United Kingdom, under full British control, could have dissuaded Britain from its own bomb effort.

The denial emphasis of U.S. nonproliferation policy during the monopoly period was comprehensive; it extended to allies as well as adversaries, and to peaceful as well as military uses of atomic energy. Despite the conventional wisdom that this policy was a failure, alternative policies would not necessarily have been more effective. The Soviet Union and Britain were not good test cases, given the wartime roots of their weapons programs and the outbreak of the Cold War. With the failure of international control, a denial policy flowed logically from the Acheson-Lilienthal premise that national programs could not be adequately safeguarded. Even Lilienthal came to believe that "so long as we are in an atomic weapons race it is only sensible to do everything we can to slow up other countries in their efforts in this same direction."[76]

But denial was simply an instrument—and a blunt one at that—and not a fully developed nonproliferation policy. It was a tactic to buy time, but it said nothing about how that time should be used to make proliferation less likely. Nor did it offer guidance on the management of proliferation once it had occurred or become unstoppable. In the Soviet and British cases, the United States had in effect chosen to delay the inevitable rather than to accommodate it; but the Stimson proposal of 1945 and the NSC report of March 1949 indicated an alternative strategy of trying to co-opt emerging nuclear powers.

Most important, denial dealt only with capabilities for proliferation. It failed to come to grips with the underlying incentives that motivated countries to seek the bomb. With the formation of NATO at the end of the monopoly period, the United States had begun to address this problem. Already, however, there were indications that alliance dynamics would create their own proliferation pressures and dilemmas.

Here, the British case anticipated later debates over the French bomb and NATO nuclear sharing. It underscored the importance of doubts about American reliability as a motive for proliferation by friendly states,

---

[75] Francis Williams, *A Prime Minister Remembers*, cited in Pierre, *Nuclear Politics*, p. 77. See also R. N. Rosecrance, "British Incentives to Become a Nuclear Power," in R. N. Rosecrance, ed., *The Dispersion of Nuclear Weapons* (New York and London: Columbia Univ. Press, 1964).

[76] Lilienthal, *Journals, Vol. II*, p. 190. However, Lilienthal recognized the ultimate futility of a serious attempt to deny Russia a nuclear weapons capability, and changed his mind about the wisdom of applying denial to Britain.

and suggested that a U.S. policy of monopoly and denial could be self-defeating, prompting allies to undertake their own nuclear programs in order to gain influence with the United States. On the other hand, to extend nuclear cooperation in order to appease these motives could also be self-defeating, in effect sponsoring proliferation in another guise. This dilemma became more acute as atomic weapons assumed the dominant role in NATO defense, bearing out Kennan's prediction that a nuclear-centered defense policy "would raise questions as between ourselves and our allies that would be disruptive in their effect on the workings of existing alliances."[77]

---

[77] Kennan, *Memoirs, 1925–50*, p. 500. Kennan had experience in this area, having led the U.S. negotiating team in the nuclear talks with Britain in the fall of 1949.

Chapter
2
Atoms for Peace and the "Nuclear Bargain"

*I*n the 1950s the United States eased atomic secrecy in both the military and civilian spheres. In each, the shift from a policy of denial to one of cooperation was defended in nonproliferation terms. The sharing of some nuclear weapons information with NATO partners would, the Eisenhower administration believed, help preempt allied incentives for independent deterrent forces. Cooperation in civilian areas, on the other hand, could help channel foreign interest toward the peaceful applications of atomic energy and away from the pursuit of weapons. Furthermore, such cooperation could be a tool to elicit controls and commitments against military uses. This was the essence of the "nuclear bargain," which originated in Eisenhower's 1953 Atoms for Peace initiative and became the core principle of the international nonproliferation regime.

Nonproliferation was not, however, the primary U.S. objective in promoting either NATO nuclear sharing or the "peaceful atom." In the case of NATO, Eisenhower's first priority was to strengthen the Western alliance politically and militarily. Atoms for Peace, initially a ploy in the U.S.-Soviet disarmament debate, emerged in the mid-1950s as a vehicle for advancing a broad range of American political, economic, and Cold War interests. Controls against proliferation, grafted on late in the process, were porous and incomplete. The centerpiece of the regime, the International Atomic Energy Agency (IAEA) and its safeguards system, represented a control apparatus far weaker than the Acheson-Lilienthal report had deemed necessary to contain the risks of nationally based nuclear energy development.

This outcome reflected both the changing technological environment (the spread of atomic information and declining effectiveness of denial) and changing calculations of U.S. interests in the nuclear field (the desire to promote peaceful uses for foreign policy and commercial advantages). In this context, the United States overestimated the potential for a rapid and economical expansion of civilian nuclear power, while downplaying the proliferation risks of Atoms for Peace. At the time, however, these risks were judged manageable, particularly in light of America's leadership position in nuclear energy and its continuing hold on the technology of uranium enrichment. Using the European Atomic Energy Community (EURATOM) as a beachhead, the U.S. reactor technology quickly established a dominant position in the emerging world nuclear market. The strong correlation between this preeminence and the cause of nonproliferation became an enduring (and self-serving) axiom of U.S. policy.

THE ORIGINS OF ATOMS FOR PEACE

Eisenhower introduced the Atoms for Peace concept, to great world acclaim, in a December 1953 UN address. In its original form, the policy marked the convergence of two distinct trends, each exerting pressure for a relaxation of the strict nuclear secrecy enshrined in the 1946 Atomic Energy Act. One was "Operation Candor," an administration initiative to better acquaint the American public with the realities of the nuclear age and the burgeoning U.S.-Soviet arms race. Such candor, Eisenhower believed, was essential to sustaining public support for the mounting U.S. dependence on nuclear weapons. At the same time, a better understanding of the implications of nuclear warfare, in both the United States and the Soviet Union, could be a step toward peace. As the administration developed the idea during 1953, Eisenhower began to view it as the basis for a major initiative to break the stalemate in the disarmament talks between the two nations.[1]

The second trend was growing pressure from private industry and the scientific community for exploiting the peaceful applications of atomic energy. Public interest in this subject was also rising, fed by visions of a world powered by cheap electricity from nuclear reactors. To compete in this future, and turn it to U.S. purposes, the United States needed to devise and implement a clear policy on civilian reactor development. Eisenhower, a firm believer in private enterprise who was determined to

---

[1] Operation Candor was one of several ideas proposed by a disarmament advisory panel appointed late in the Truman administration and chaired by Robert Oppenheimer. The panel reported to Eisenhower in February 1953. See Richard G. Hewlett and Jack M. Holl, *Atoms for Peace and War, 1953–1961: Eisenhower and the Atomic Energy Commission* (Berkeley: Univ. of California Press, 1989), pp. 41–44. See also McGeorge Bundy (the panel's secretary), *Danger and Survival: Choices About the Bomb in the First Fifty Years* (New York: Random House, 1988), pp. 287ff. For a collection of essays on the origins and evolution of Atoms for Peace, see Joseph Pilat, Robert Pendley, and Charles Ebinger, eds., *Atoms For Peace: An Analysis After Thirty Years* (Boulder, CO: Westview Press, 1985).

shrink the federal role, shared the industry view that this should be largely a commercial undertaking. Industry participation in nuclear development and international cooperation would entail a wholesale revision of the Atomic Energy Act, which provided for a government monopoly on the ownership and control of nuclear materials and facilities and classified virtually all relevant information as "restricted data."

Combining these two strands, Eisenhower conceived the idea of an international agency that would act as a "bank" to receive contributions of fissile material from U.S. and Soviet weapons stockpiles and distribute the material to other nations for peaceful uses. Eisenhower began his UN speech with a "recital of atomic danger," cataloging the growth in numbers and explosive power of nuclear weapons since the war's end. He emphasized the decline of the U.S. nuclear monopoly: "the dread secret, and the fearful engines of atomic might, are not ours alone . . . the knowledge now possessed by several nations will eventually be shared by others— possibly all others." Then, after asserting the futility of an arms race that could bring neither side security or meaningful victory in war, Eisenhower presented the Atoms for Peace idea in terms calculated to maximize its idealistic appeal. Not only would the plan begin to reverse the arms race, but it would turn the weapons of war to the cause of peace and economic development:

> It is not enough to take this weapon out of the hands of the soldiers. It must be put into the hands of those who will know how to strip its military casing and adapt it to the arts of peace. . . . A special purpose would be to provide abundant electrical energy in the power-starved areas of the world. Thus the contributing powers would be dedicating some of their strength to serve the needs rather than the fears of mankind.[2]

As Eisenhower envisioned it, the Atoms for Peace plan was most importantly a means of reviving the U.S.-Soviet disarmament dialogue. The proposed contributions of fissile material were a deliberately modest first step that would finesse the intractable problems of inspection, enforcement, and international control that had doomed the Baruch Plan and other comprehensive approaches.[3] Yet there was also an unmistakable propaganda aspect to Atoms for Peace. It would divert world attention from the more radical Soviet disarmament proposals, while its innate appeal would make it politically risky for Moscow to reject. Moreover, the projected donations would be token and in no way detract from military

---

[2] For the text of the speech, see *Public Papers of the Presidents of the United States: Dwight D. Eisenhower, 1953*, pp. 813–22.

[3] As such, the plan would not assume Soviet goodwill or an end to Cold War tensions. AEC Chairman Lewis Strauss set out these criteria in a memo to the President, cited in Robert J. Donovan, *Eisenhower: The Inside Story* (New York: Harper & Row, 1956), pp. 187–88. On the disarmament aspect of the plan, see Henry Sokolski, *Eisenhower's Original Atoms for Peace Plan: The Arms Control Dimension*, Occasional Paper No. 52 (Washington, DC: The Wilson Center, 1983).

capabilities—especially with both countries continuing to produce fissile material. Indeed, the proposal coincided with the massive expansion of the U.S. weapons-production complex, and Eisenhower was well aware that, if implemented, it could actually increase American military superiority: "The United States could unquestionably afford to reduce its atomic stockpile by two or three times the amounts that the Russians might contribute to the UN agency, and still improve our relative position in the Cold War and even in the event of the outbreak of war."[4]

It was therefore not surprising that the Soviet Union was cool to the plan when the administration fleshed it out and presented it to Moscow in early 1954. Foreign Minister Molotov dismissed it as a deceptive public relations exercise and a smokescreen for continuing the arms race. He also noted the proliferation risks of the plan (a problem the United States had yet to face), pointing out to Secretary of State John Foster Dulles that peaceful nuclear energy production would in fact add to the world's supply of weapons-usable fissile material (since plutonium would be produced by reactors used to generate electricity). A nonplussed Dulles consulted his atomic energy advisors and learned that Molotov was correct.[5] Early on, then, the United States was forced to abandon the vision of Atoms for Peace as a way to ease Cold War tensions and help break the disarmament impasse. Although later in 1954 the Soviets agreed to participate in setting up an international agency, the idea of a fissile-material bank declined in favor of a clearinghouse organization whose main role was to facilitate nuclear cooperation. The horizontal dimension of Atoms for Peace (promoting peaceful uses) became the essence of the policy, while the vertical dimension (progressive reductions in U.S. and Soviet stockpiles) faded away.

PROMOTION VERSUS CONTROL

American policy now branched in two directions: bilateral nuclear agreements with friendly countries and multilateral talks to establish the IAEA. The Atomic Energy Act was rewritten, removing barriers to industry participation and international cooperation in civil nuclear energy development. The initial bilateral agreements provided for the transfer of small reactors for training and research purposes, together with uranium fuel enriched to 20 percent U-235—well below weapons grade. The irradiated, or "spent," fuel was to be returned to the United States for reprocessing and plutonium

---

[4] Robert H. Ferrell, ed., *The Eisenhower Diaries* (New York and London: Norton, 1981), p. 262; Dwight D. Eisenhower, *Mandate for Change, 1953–56* (New York: Doubleday, 1963), p. 254. Similarly, Eisenhower suggested to his staff that the donations "be fixed at a figure which we could handle from our stockpile, but which would be difficult for the Soviets to match." Cited in Bundy, *Danger and Survival*, p. 290.

[5] Hewlett and Holl, *Atoms for Peace and War*, p. 221–22.

recovery. These precautions minimized proliferation risks, and—equally important to the United States at this time—assured that peaceful cooperation did not impinge on the U.S. weapons program.

But nuclear power was regarded as the real political and economic payoff of Atoms for Peace, and pressures soon mounted for promoting U.S. reactors overseas. The Atomic Energy Commission argued that an aggressive foreign reactor program was necessary to maintaining U.S. technical leadership. It could also buttress U.S. military policies by facilitating access to uranium and overseas bases, and strengthening allied support for the deployment and possible use of nuclear weapons in Europe.[6] In early 1955, Eisenhower approved a National Security Council report that identified nuclear power cooperation as a key instrument of U.S. foreign policy and a vital new field of competition with the Soviet Union:

> It must be anticipated that the USSR will make the maximum use of atomic energy not only for military and industrial purposes, but also as political and psychological measures to gain the allegiance of the uncommitted areas of the world. . . . In a relatively short time the USSR may offer a small-output atomic power reactor to a country such as India, Pakistan, or Burma. If the United States fails to exploit its atomic potential, politically and psychologically, the USSR could gain an important advantage in what is becoming a critical sector of the Cold War struggle.[7]

Warning that U.S. leadership could be threatened not only by the Soviets but also by the United Kingdom "in the near future," the report called for an acceleration of U.S. reactor-development programs and "early tangible action in the international field." To support international cooperation and help get the IAEA started, it urged that the United States "make available power reactor information as rapidly as it can be declassified." Underscoring the potential foreign policy benefits of cooperation, it directed that "maximum psychological advantage should continue to be taken from the substantial actions of the United States in this field. The timing of release of declassified atomic energy information can be made a political and psychological asset to the United States."

The implications of the policy for nuclear weapons proliferation were not addressed. The only risks identified were economic and technical ones (i.e., that nuclear power might not perform up to its billing), and the issue of diversion received a single perfunctory reference at the end of a list of U.S. policy objectives in the development of peaceful nuclear energy:

> a. Maintaining U.S. leadership in the field, particularly in the development and application of atomic power.

---

[6] Hewlett and Holl, *Atoms for Peace and War*, p. 237.

[7] "Statement of Policy on Peaceful Uses of Atomic Energy," NSC 5507/2, March 12, 1955 (Secret), in *Foreign Relations of the United States (FRUS), 1955–1957, Vol. XX: Regulation of Armaments; Atomic Energy* (Washington, DC: GPO, 1990), pp. 46–55.

b. Using such U.S. leadership to promote cohesion within the free world and to forestall successful Soviet exploitation of the peaceful uses of atomic energy to attract the allegiance of the uncommitted peoples of the world.

c. Increasing progress in developing and applying the peaceful uses of atomic energy in free nations abroad.

d. Assuring continued U.S. access to foreign uranium and thorium supplies.

e. Preventing the diversion to nonpeaceful uses of any fissionable materials provided to other countries.[8]

In sum, in the first comprehensive statement of U.S. policy on peaceful nuclear cooperation, over a year after Eisenhower's UN speech, there is no suggestion that Atoms for Peace was perceived primarily—or even secondarily—as a nonproliferation strategy. The idea of the "nuclear bargain," later construed as the essence of the policy, had yet to surface.

The promotional emphasis of the Atoms for Peace policy reached a peak with the August 1955 Geneva Conference on the Peaceful Uses of Atomic Energy. The largest scientific meeting ever held, the Geneva conference brought together nuclear scientists and diplomats from around the world. In a euphoric and competitive atmosphere, massive amounts of previously classified information about nuclear power and its fuel cycle were presented, including the technology for separating plutonium from spent reactor fuel. The only significant remaining area of secrecy was uranium enrichment, which the nuclear weapon states continued to hold closely.[9] The Geneva conference served to whet appetites for the fruits of the Atoms for Peace program; U.S. delegates were approached by numerous countries seeking assistance in building and fueling power reactors. At the same time, the wholesale release of information had already begun to erode the U.S. ability to extract leverage from the supply of such assistance. This dilemma became apparent as the United States belatedly started coming to grips with the problem of controls against proliferation.

Until 1955, the United States had considered the control problem only in the most general and theoretical terms. But unlike the initial transfers of small research and training reactors, large-scale development of nuclear power overseas would create significant opportunities for producing fissile material—especially plutonium—and diverting it to military purposes. As the Soviets had pointed out from the start, Atoms for Peace could ironically end up contributing to the proliferation of nuclear weapons. Echoing the Acheson-Lilienthal report of a decade earlier, a task force of the Atomic Energy Commission (AEC) concluded that there was a

---

[8] "Statement of Policy," p. 53.

[9] See Bertrand Goldschmidt, *The Atomic Complex: A Worldwide Political History of Nuclear Energy* (LaGrange Park, IL: American Nuclear Society, 1982), pp. 257–61.

"grave military problem inescapably bound up with the advancement of the atoms-for-peace program."[10] The question then arose, if only rhetorically, as to whether the whole policy should be dropped. But a retreat from Atoms for Peace would not only have been a devastating public relations setback, it would also have abandoned the field to others, "causing the United States to default on its political and economic advantages while watching the danger arise anyway."[11]

The stimulus for the United States finally facing up to the control problem was a technical meeting on safeguards that followed the Geneva peaceful-uses conference. The meeting found the United States unprepared to offer concrete technical proposals for countering the diversion threat. The U.S. delegation, headed by physicist Isador Rabi (the chairman of the AEC's General Advisory Committee), encountered strong criticism from the Soviets and returned home shaken.[12] Rabi conveyed his thoughts to the State Department's Atomic Energy advisor, Gerard Smith, who summarized the conversation for his files:

> Rabi said that we must get these controls working before our reactors are constructed abroad. He believed that even a country like India, when it had some plutonium production, would go into the weapons business.
>
> . . . I pointed out that I believed that no thought had been given to this problem in the current design activities of American manufacturers.
>
> Rabi pointed out the sources of strength in the present American position—not only that we had a near monopoly of enriched material but also our ability to lend the technological help. Unless we see to it that controls are established during this present preliminary stage, he believes that the situation will shortly get out of control.[13]

Over the ensuing months, as planning for the IAEA progressed, the U.S. government grappled with the question of how stringent the agency's nonproliferation controls could or should be.[14] A basic question was whether the objective was merely to prevent diversion of peaceful

---

[10] Cited in Hewlett and Holl, *Atoms for Peace and War*, p. 316.

[11] Hewlett and Holl, *Atoms for Peace and War*, p. 318. In early 1955, the Secretary of Defense had seriously proposed abandoning plans for building power reactors overseas, but was told by Dulles that this would be "altogether disastrous from the point of view of foreign policy." Memorandum of Discussion, National Security Council, February 10, 1955 (Top Secret), *FRUS 1955–1957, Vol. XX*, p. 21.

[12] Hewlett and Holl, *Atoms for Peace and War*, pp. 313–15.

[13] Memorandum for the File, September 14, 1955 (Secret), *FRUS 1955–1957, Vol. XX*, p. 1981.

[14] International negotiations leading to the establishment of the IAEA began in 1955 among eight Western nations and then expanded to include the Soviet Union, Czechoslovakia, India, and Brazil. These twelve produced a draft IAEA statute in early 1956. The Agency was formally established at an 81-nation conference in September and October 1956. See Lawrence Scheinman, *The International Atomic Energy Agency and World Nuclear Order* (Washington, DC: Resources for the Future, 1987), pp. 63ff.

assistance to military uses, or actually to prevent the development of nuclear weapons by "fourth countries" (as potential proliferators were called). If the latter, then recipients of peaceful nuclear assistance should be required to renounce nuclear weapons. Gerard Smith favored a "no-weapons" pledge, pointing out that without it, IAEA assistance "would simply free the other resources of a nation to support a parallel weapons program."[15] AEC Chairman Lewis Strauss, however, argued that such a pledge was not feasible, since France and probably other nations would refuse it. Furthermore, if the United States insisted upon very strict controls, it risked facing foreign demands for reciprocal inspection rights over its own nuclear reactors.[16]

The AEC and Department of Defense were both sensitive to the linkages that might be drawn between the IAEA control system and the disarmament talks among the nuclear weapon states. Demands that nuclear weapons be renounced, and a corresponding system of comprehensive inspections, would inevitably increase disarmament pressures on the nuclear powers. These agencies therefore tended to oppose maximalist goals for IAEA safeguards and to justify their lack of zeal by downplaying the proliferation risks of Atoms for Peace. Arguing against a U.S. attempt to strengthen the modest provisions of the draft IAEA statute, Defense Secretary Charles Wilson wrote Dulles,

> The Joint Chiefs of Staff have concluded, and I agree, that the military risk of such increase in nuclear weapon potential as may be occasioned by International Atomic Energy Agency assistance in a peaceful use program is not of such significance as to require or justify an extension of the agency's functions. . . . [17]

As it had in the 1940s, then, America's reluctance to compromise its own nuclear prerogatives dampened its enthusiasm for sweeping nonproliferation plans. And, as Dulles observed, a hard-line nonproliferation policy from which the weapons states exempted themselves would not be politically viable: "It would be difficult for nations to forego permanently their right to make nuclear weapons while the U.S., USSR, and U.K. continued to make them." At best, this approach could be an interim solution for a few years, "looking toward the institution of international control of atomic energy which would apply to all countries including the present military atomic powers."[18]

By the time of the conference establishing the IAEA in the fall of 1956, chances for a strict control system had been prejudiced by a combination

---

[15] Memorandum of Conversation, State Department, February 3, 1956 (Secret), *FRUS 1955–1957, Vol. XX*, p. 309.

[16] Memorandum of Conversation, p. 308.

[17] Memorandum from the Secretary of Defense to the Secretary of State, February 24, 1956 (Secret), *FRUS 1955–1957, Vol. XX*, p. 347.

[18] Memorandum of Conversation, February 3, 1956 (footnote 13), p. 309.

of U.S. ambivalence, foreign resistance, and the rapid dissemination of information on nuclear energy. At the conference itself, nuclear safeguards were the most controversial and time-consuming topic of debate. The Agency safeguards system was to consist of inspections, measurements, and various accounting procedures by which diversions of nuclear material could be detected (and thus presumably deterred). But while the IAEA statute in principle granted the Agency sweeping access and investigative authority, in practice this authority was quite circumscribed.[19]

Opposition to tight controls was led by India and France, which regarded the very concept of safeguards as an infringement on national sovereignty. These countries fought to curtail the reach of safeguards (trying unsuccessfully to keep natural uranium free of any controls) and their duration in time as nuclear materials went through successive "generations" in peaceful programs. A key point of controversy was the Agency's degree of authority over the "back end" of the nuclear fuel cycle—the management of spent reactor fuel and its reprocessing. The United States considered this issue central to proliferation risks and sought to restrict the right to extract and stockpile plutonium under national control. But faced with adamant opposition that threatened to deadlock the conference, the U.S. delegation—at Dulles's direction—conceded the issue.[20] Other important matters were left ambiguous or deterred for later resolution. For example, the question of "critical time"—the frequency and intensity of inspections needed to provide useful warning of diversions—proved too controversial to confront rigorously, and was sidestepped.[21]

In short, the controls that emerged from the IAEA deliberations were essentially a lowest-common-denominator outcome, which the United States "regarded as minimal."[22] But U.S. officials rationalized accepting this result on several grounds: the spread of atomic information and the existence of other sources of assistance (especially Great Britain and the

---

[19] For a concise description of the system, see Scheinman, *The International Atomic Energy Agency and World Nuclear Order*, pp. 124ff. On the negotiation of the statute, see Bernard G. Bechhoefer, "Negotiating the Statute of the International Atomic Energy Agency," *International Organization*, Winter 1959. For a general discussion of the problem of control, see Arnold Kramish, *The Peaceful Atom in Foreign Policy* (New York: Harper & Row, 1963), chap. 3.

[20] Goldschmidt, *The Atomic Complex*, pp. 282–83.

[21] As one U.S. nuclear official testified, "It was clear even at this early stage that the level of inspections required for large, complex facilities would be substantial—undoubtedly extending to resident or continuous inspection in the case of large bulk handling facilities [e.g., reprocessing plants]. It was equally clear that the political climate and technical support for specifying such measures was unfavorable." Statement of Myron Kratzer in House Committee on Foreign Affairs, *The International Atomic Energy Agency (IAEA): Improving Safeguards*, Hearings, 97th Cong., 2nd sess., March 3 and 18, 1982, pp. 34–35.

[22] Scheinman, *The International Atomic Energy Agency and World Nuclear Order*, p. 75.

USSR) made it impossible and self-defeating for the United States to insist on maximum controls; the system obtained was preferable to none and could be strengthened incrementally over time; some proliferation was likely to occur regardless of the IAEA system; and proliferation on a small scale was probably manageable in light of the clear superiority of the existing weapon states.[23]

EUROPE FIRST

Already watered-down at its debut, the IAEA was further compromised by Eisenhower's decision to make support of the European Atomic Energy Community (EURATOM) the leading edge of the U.S. Atoms for Peace policy. EURATOM was conceived by the architects of the postwar European unity movement (led by the Frenchman Jean Monnet) as a key element in their integration strategy that would join France, West Germany, Italy, Belgium, the Netherlands, and Luxembourg (the six members of the nascent European Economic Community) in a common effort to develop and promote atomic energy. To Monnet and his supporters, nuclear power was a particularly auspicious field for cooperation. As a new industry, it contained fewer entrenched interests than more established economic sectors; it responded to Western Europe's need for new and secure energy supplies, given its declining coal resources and lack of indigenous oil production; and it aptly symbolized the integration movement's aim of turning Europe permanently from war to peace. Indeed, Monnet himself advocated that the renunciation of nuclear weapons be a condition of EURATOM membership.

Combining the lure of the peaceful atom and the dream of European unity, EURATOM had a potent appeal for U.S. policymakers. Eisenhower and Dulles viewed it as a potential lynchpin of Atlantic solidarity, paralleling the NATO alliance, and a new way to help knit together France and Germany—a central goal of U.S. foreign policy that had become more pressing following the collapse of plans for a European Defense Community (EDC) in 1954. Furthermore, EURATOM could stimulate foreign markets for U.S. reactor manufacturers, whose domestic prospects were as yet limited because of the relatively cheap cost of electricity in the United States.[24]

EURATOM was embraced with special fervor by the European bureau of the State Department: "It is a magic, and only partially understood, concept," a bureau policy paper declared. "But it is, we think, well understood that integration in this field could, and probably would, set in motion ancillary and concomitant developments which would lead, over

---

[23] See Sokolski, *Eisenhower's Original Atoms for Peace Plan*, pp. 27–30.

[24] Hewlett and Holl, *Atoms for Peace and War*, p. 430.

time, towards a real United States of Europe." [25] The channeling of nuclear development toward peaceful ends was an important aim of U.S. officials, who feared that otherwise atomic energy could become a rallying point for nationalist and militarist forces in Europe. France, whose rejection had doomed the EDC, was on the verge of producing plutonium in the mid-1950s—a prospect that alarmed State Department Europeanists in its own right and as a precedent for West Germany. German officials and industrialists were at this time promoting unfettered development of nuclear energy, questioning the need for special controls, and opposing any hint of discrimination against Germany in this field. [26] To EURATOM supporters in the United States, these developments signaled an approaching moment of truth. "If we do not, in the immediate future, come to some understanding with France regarding the disposition of [its] plutonium for peacetime uses," a Paris embassy official warned,

> we may assuredly expect that the French military and rightist groups will demand access to at least part of these stocks for weapons use. . . . The presence of atomic weapons in the hands of France is bound to raise problems vis-à-vis the Germans which would result in placing great if not fatal strains on the present tenuous relationship. [27]

If the French program could be co-opted into a Europe-wide peaceful venture, the prospects for limiting Germany's interest in the military uses of nuclear energy would be improved. EURATOM could thus deflect the emergence of competitive, nationally controlled programs, particularly with respect to the production of plutonium. Although the Atoms for Peace policy was later charged with complacency and negligence on this question, U.S. officials were clearly aware of the proliferation risks of reprocessing. The U.S. ambassador in Bonn, James B. Conant, framed the issue in language that anticipated the Ford and Carter policies of twenty years later.

> Germans will develop on a nationalistic basis their own atomic development in competition with the French unless some degree of European cooperation in this field is achieved. To my mind the greatest source of anxiety is that each nation will erect chemical plants for reprocessing fuel elements thereby putting production of plutonium on a national basis. Such production of plutonium would not in itself constitute manufacture of atomic weapons but

---

[25] "Peaceful Uses of Atomic Energy and European Integration," December 6, 1955 (Top Secret), FRUS 1955–1957, Vol. IV: Western European Security and Integration (Washington, DC: GPO, 1986), p. 356.

[26] The U.S. ambassador in Bonn reported that the Germans "are playing down the fact that atomic explosive material is produced as a consequence of production of atomic energy for peaceful purposes and are saying that there is no need for more control of this industry than of electricity." Telegram to the Department of State, November 4, 1955 (Secret), FRUS 1955–1957, Vol. IV, p. 346.

[27] Letter to the Assistant Secretary of State for Policy Planning (Bowie), December 27, 1955 (Top Secret), FRUS 1955–1957, Vol. IV, pp. 379–80.

would be a long and dangerous step in this direction. Therefore as a minimum of control of all six European nations a supranationally controlled chemical reprocessing plant would seem to be required.[28]

The most enthusiastic U.S. supporters of the EURATOM idea urged that the United States play its highest nuclear cards—including an offer to share American enrichment technology—to strengthen incentives for European integration. France had proposed that an enrichment project be adopted as the centerpiece of EURATOM cooperation. Only by aiding such a project, supporters of U.S. assistance argued, could the United States fully exploit the foreign policy leverage of the peaceful atom in Europe; the declassified information being shared under Atoms for Peace was too weak an inducement, "for the real binding power . . . is going to be the right to receive something which no other country or group of countries can get, that is, information which is classified."[29] "It is improbable," the State Department's European bureau argued, "that anything except cooperation in the erection of isotopic separation facilities for uranium could, today, constitute a United States initiative which would fundamentally influence the form and purpose of European development in the atomic energy field."[30]

Other U.S. officials, particularly in the AEC, were skeptical of EURATOM, however. The AEC had strong reservations about cooperating with a group entity whose security procedures would be only as reliable as those of its weakest link—assumed by the Commission to be France. (Strauss considered the French nuclear program to be riddled with "doubtful characters"; both he and Dulles had initially hoped to exclude Paris from Atoms for Peace discussions.[31]) The AEC preferred to continue with bilateral agreements, which gave the United States closer control over information security (but which integration proponents feared would undermine EURATOM). In addition, the AEC feared that EURATOM would jeopardize the United States's special nuclear relationship with Belgium, under which the United States had shared some restricted data in return for preferred access to Belgian uranium.

---

[28] Telegram to the Department of State, February 16, 1956 (Confidential), ibid., p. 414. Conant also drew a connection between plutonium production in Europe and proliferation in Africa or the Middle East.

[29] Letter to Bowie (footnote 27), p. 386. The United States had earlier blocked British assistance to France in the area of gaseous diffusion enrichment technology, invoking the 1943 Quebec Agreement. See Goldschmidt, *The Atomic Complex*, pp. 297–98. On EURATOM, French policy, and the enrichment issue, see Lawrence Scheinman, *Atomic Energy in France Under the Fourth Republic* (Princeton: Princeton Univ. Press, 1965), pp. 176–84.

[30] "Peaceful Uses of Atomic Energy and European Integration" (footnote 25), p. 357.

[31] See Memorandum of Conversation, State Department, January 25, 1956 (Confidential), *FRUS 1955–1957, Vol. IV*, p. 393; and Hewlett and Holl, *Atoms for Peace and War*, p. 218.

The Commission predictably opposed aiding Europe in the construction of an enrichment plant. While acknowledging that such a plant was a logical corollary of European atomic independence—and hence might be a potent force for integration—the Commission questioned whether this goal was in fact in the U.S. interest. Gerard Smith shared the AEC's skepticism here, noting that a European enrichment venture would end the U.S. monopoly in providing enriched reactor fuel, forfeiting a primary source of American political and technical leverage over foreign nuclear programs.[32] In the end, the United States decided against providing classified assistance to EURATOM.

While these debates proceeded in Washington, the original EURATOM concept was being steadily eroded in negotiations among the Six in Europe. In the wake of the November 1956 Suez crisis—a strong reminder of the perils of dependence on Middle East oil—France and Germany settled a number of disputes that had been blocking completion of a EURATOM treaty. Their agreement came at the expense of both integration and nonproliferation objectives, falling well short of the supranational vision of Monnet and his supporters. France kept a free hand to develop nuclear weapons, while Germany successfully resisted Community ownership of fissionable materials. EURATOM became a common agent for entering into cooperation agreements and purchasing nuclear fuel for its members, but it lacked strong central powers.[33]

Although it failed to meet the most ambitious hopes of American advocates, EURATOM proved a great boon for the promotion of U.S. nuclear exports. Indeed, the Community became a proving ground for American reactor technology, following the recommendation of the so-called Three Wise Men—a committee appointed to assess EURATOM's future energy requirements and options.[34] The group visited the United States in early 1957 and was eagerly courted by government officials who viewed support of EURATOM as a means to assert U.S. technological leadership and a public relations opportunity on the order of the Marshall Plan. United States's hopes were rewarded when the Wise Men issued their report, "A Target for Euratom," calling for a crash program of nuclear development based on the American light-water reactor (LWR) in preference to the competing gas-graphite design being pursued by Britain and France.

Seizing its opening, the United States concluded an agreement for nuclear cooperation with EURATOM in 1958. In a major concession, the administration acquiesced in EURATOM's insistence that the Commu-

---

[32] Memorandum to the Assistant Secretary of State for European Affairs, December 8, 1955, *FRUS 1955–1957, Vol. IV*, p. 361.

[33] See Lawrence Scheinman, "EURATOM: Nuclear Integration in Europe," *International Conciliation*, May 1967.

[34] See Irvin Bupp and Jean-Claude Derian, *The Failed Promise of Nuclear Power* (New York: Basic Books, 1978), pp. 26–27.

nity be allowed to safeguard its own members' programs rather than submit to outside inspections. This decision, which would later haunt U.S. efforts to negotiate the Non-Proliferation Treaty, was a severe blow to the nascent IAEA. It signaled, as the official historian of Atoms for Peace noted, that "the Americans saw the European nuclear market as more important than the safeguarding functions of the international agency, and undermined the agency's status in the eyes of the world." [35]

The United States solidified its position in the European market by offering the low-enriched fuel required by LWRs at heavily discounted prices—thereby subsidizing American reactor sales while simultaneously undercutting EURATOM's interest in building its own enrichment facility. Over the next several years, American reactor firms moved to dominate the European and world reactor market through direct sales and licensing arrangements with overseas firms. By the end of the 1960s, they were supplying 90 percent of the world market. [36]

CONCLUSION

The balance sheet on Atoms for Peace as a nonproliferation strategy is ambiguous. On the one hand, the policy can be seen as a necessary adjustment to the inevitable erosion of nuclear denial. Unable to prevent the spread of nuclear know-how, the United States sought to use cooperation to establish a degree of international control over foreign nuclear programs. In doing so, it nurtured a set of rules and institutions that provided the foundation for developing a global nonproliferation regime. On the other hand, U.S. policy stimulated interest in civil nuclear activities—and accelerated the diffusion of information and materials associated with them—to a degree that was unjustified by the near-term promise of the technology, and insufficiently sensitive to its security implications.

Despite much discussion of the foreign policy leverage to be gained from peaceful nuclear cooperation, the Eisenhower administration did not seriously attempt to use this influence to implant a rigorous system of nonproliferation commitments and controls. The "nuclear bargain" was more a post hoc construction than the essence of the Atoms for Peace

---

[35] Richard G. Hewlett, "From Proposal to Program," in Joseph Pilat, et al., eds., *Atoms for Peace: An Analysis*, p. 29. See also Jack M. Holl, "The Peaceful Atom: Lore and Myth," in ibid., pp. 154–55.

[36] Paul Joskow, "The International Nuclear Industry Today," *Foreign Affairs*, July 1976, p. 792. On U.S. penetration of the European nuclear market, see Bupp and Derian, *The Failed Promise of Nuclear Power*; and Henry Nau, *National Politics and International Technology: Nuclear Reactor Development in Western Europe* (Baltimore: Johns Hopkins Press, 1974). For an overview of the development of the world nuclear market, see William Walker and Mans Lonnroth, *Nuclear Power Struggles: Industrial Competition and Proliferation Control* (London: George Allen and Unwin, 1983), chap. 1.

policy. In the first instance, the policy was not conceived as a nonproliferation strategy at all, but rather as a field for advancing U.S. military and ideological interests in the Cold War while reaping economic benefits from the promotion of peaceful atomic uses. As the policy evolved, other interests emerged as dominant: Atlantic solidarity, European unity, and U.S. influence in the Third World. While nonproliferation was eventually recognized as a key objective, at no time did the United States elect to maximize it at the expense of these other interests.

This pattern was not simply the result of the priority of other U.S. goals, however. It also reflected a degree of fatalism, complacency, and ambivalence about proliferation itself. Although these sentiments were not uniformly shared within the Eisenhower administration, there was an overarching assumption that the spread of nuclear weapons was likely, was not inherently inimical to U.S. interests, and might in some circumstances even serve those interests. The arena in which these issues were most directly engaged was the debate over NATO nuclear strategy.

Chapter
3

Nuclear NATO: Deterrence and Nonproliferation

*T*he central issue for U.S. nonproliferation policy in the 1950s and early 1960s was the management of nuclear relations within the Atlantic alliance. As in the 1940s, the controlling objective of the policy was the containment of the Soviet Union. But whereas in the earlier period this goal had led to a strict policy of nuclear denial, it now produced a relaxation of the McMahon Act and an extensive pattern of allied nuclear weapons cooperation. Except in the case of the United Kingdom, the United States did not actually encourage or support independent allied nuclear weapons programs. It did, however, sponsor NATO nuclear arrangements that bordered on de facto proliferation, and—in the Eisenhower years—clearly placed a lower value on nonproliferation than on NATO strength. The chance that NATO cooperation might encourage the spread of nuclear weapons, as AEC Chairman Lewis Strauss put it, was "a calculated risk . . . with the greater issue of the defense of the free world on the other side of the balance."[1]

This loosening of controls flowed directly from the nuclearization of NATO strategy in keeping with the Eisenhower administration's "New Look." The new strategy created both military and political pressures for a wider dissemination of the "nuclear facts of life" within the alliance. It required that NATO forces in Europe be equipped with tactical nuclear weapons and that the allies be trained in their handling and use. At the same time, NATO's adoption of a strategy based overwhelmingly on the use of atomic weapons ensured that the allies would demand a strong

---

[1] *Amending the Atomic Energy Act of 1954*, Hearings before the Subcommittee on Agreements for Cooperation of the Joint Committee on Atomic Energy, 85th Cong., 2nd sess., p. 354.

voice in alliance nuclear decisions, and that conflict over nuclear access and control would become a central axis of Atlantic politics.

Alliance tensions over these issues grew during the Kennedy administration, which adopted a strategy calling for tighter American control of NATO nuclear forces and culminated in a harsh confrontation between the United States and Gaullist France. In a failed attempt to restore allied harmony, the United States launched the Multilateral Force (MLF) initiative for a collective NATO nuclear fleet. But the MLF, in its effort to satisfy conflicting goals and clienteles, embodied the very tensions it was supposed to soothe, and only underscored American ambivalence about nuclear sharing. By the end of 1964, when the Johnson administration shelved the MLF and turned its attention to negotiating the nonproliferation treaty, the United States had begun to resolve this ambivalence, but at a high cost in alliance relations.

THE NUCLEARIZATION OF NATO

The role of nuclear weapons in Atlantic defense was an open issue when the Eisenhower administration assumed office. The Truman legacy was mixed: Although the United States had become heavily dependent on nuclear weapons in the late 1940s, NATO had recently committed itself to massive conventional rearmament to counter Soviet military power in Europe. This development reflected a growing conviction—embodied in NSC-68, the Truman administration's basic statement of U.S. Cold War strategy—that the threat of U.S. strategic nuclear bombing was an inadequate deterrent to Soviet aggression and that containment required a strong buildup of forces across the board.

The outbreak of the Korean War strongly reinforced this belief and led to the transformation of the alliance from a simple mutual assistance pact to a full-fledged military organization. The far-reaching consequences of this change included the stationing of U.S. troops in Europe, the rearming of West Germany as the front line of NATO's "forward defense," and the setting of ambitious—and chronically unmet—allied force goals. This last trend reached its height at the Lisbon meeting of February 1952, where the allies agreed to raise 100 divisions for the defense of Europe. Ironically, this conventional overreaching in a very real sense paved the way for NATO's subsequent overreliance on nuclear weapons.

The notion of a large-scale conventional defense of Europe quickly fell victim to the economic and strategic priorities of the incoming Eisenhower administration. The new president, dismayed at the size of the defense budget he inherited, was convinced that the United States could not sustain such a level of military spending without incurring economic ruin. In addition, the Korean experience had created a profound aversion to protracted conventional wars fought on terms and territory chosen by the adversary. Nuclear weapons seemed to Eisenhower and his Secretary of State, John Foster Dulles, to be an answer to both problems. The result was the New Look policy, adopted in October 1953.

The New Look, and the strategy of "massive retaliation" that accompanied it, embraced nuclear weapons as a substitute for conventional forces and a means of regaining the initiative in the Cold War confrontation. The threat of nuclear retaliation against the Soviet Union, rather than local resistance by United States and allied ground forces, became the primary deterrent to communist aggression or expansion. "The basic decision," Dulles announced, "was to depend primarily upon a great capacity to retaliate, instantly, by means and at places of our choosing. . . . As a result it is now possible to get, and share, more basic security at less cost."[2] This emphasis, Eisenhower believed, "would justify completely some reduction in our conventional forces."[3]

For NATO, the new policies meant the wholesale nuclearization of alliance military forces. Tactical nuclear weapons—including artillery shells, mines, short-range rockets, and bombs—were developed for battlefield use and integrated with American ground and air units in Europe. "Atomic weapons," Eisenhower announced in December 1953, "have virtually achieved conventional status within our armed forces."[4] A year later, NATO officially adopted a strategy of "first use"—that is, the allies would respond to aggression with nuclear weapons regardless of whether the Soviets had used them.

To implement this strategy, the restrictions of the 1946 Atomic Energy Act—which prohibited any sharing of information on nuclear weapons—clearly needed to be relaxed. Eisenhower had long been a harsh critic of the McMahon Act, which he viewed as a foolish self-denying ordinance, damaging to alliance military and political relations, and a betrayal of the British in particular. Nevertheless, the congressional Joint Committee on Atomic Energy—Eisenhower's bête noire on nuclear policy—adamantly resisted a full abandonment of the restrictive policy. Though the JCAE gave some ground to administration preferences, it did so grudgingly and with important qualifications. Accordingly, the 1954 and 1958 revisions of the Atomic Energy Act were the equivocal outcome of an often bitter tug-of-war between the administration and Congress.[5]

---

[2] Speech to the Council on Foreign Relations, New York, January 12, 1954.

[3] Robert H. Ferrell, ed., *The Eisenhower Diaries* (New York and London: Norton, 1981), pp. 257–58.

[4] "Atoms for Peace" speech to UN General Assembly, December 8, 1953.

[5] Eisenhower disparaged the JCAE and its role in blocking allied nuclear cooperation to the end of his presidency and afterwards. In December 1960, he urged President-elect Kennedy to pursue greater nuclear sharing with the allies and described the Joint Committee as an obsolete relic of the U.S. atomic monopoly era. See Ferrell, ed., *The Eisenhower Diaries*, pp. 381–82. In 1966, he complained to Senator Henry Jackson that his efforts to increase nuclear cooperation had been repeatedly frustrated by Congress, "even though from time to time we had been successful in obtaining some minor amendments to the McMahon Act." Letter, printed in *The Crisis in NATO*, Hearings before the Subcommittee on Europe of the House Committee on Foreign Affairs, 89th Cong., 2nd sess., p. 218.

The 1954 amendments, in addition to lifting restraints on peaceful nuclear cooperation, allowed the sharing of only that information necessary for the training of allied forces and the development of joint defense plans. This essentially restricted the allies to knowledge of the external characteristics of U.S. tactical nuclear warheads. No nuclear technology or material for military applications could be transferred.

Very soon, however, pressures arose for more extensive sharing. As the European allies came to grips with the full implications of emerging U.S. strategy, they were understandably reluctant to concede to Washington a monopoly on nuclear decision making and capability. Demands for a greater voice in nuclear policy, and for access to the weapons themselves, became increasingly powerful during 1956 and 1957. Although this trend was probably an inevitable and natural consequence of the New Look policy, it was magnified by growing allied doubts about the steadiness and reliability of American support.

This loss of confidence had several sources.[6] The Suez crisis of November 1956—in which the United States failed to support, and through heavy economic and political pressure helped foil, the French and British military intervention against Egypt—was especially traumatic. For France and Britain, the crisis painfully underlined both the limits of their own capacity for independent action and the possibility of a basic divergence of security interests and perspectives between the United States and its European allies. A few months earlier, West German confidence had been severely shaken by the leak of the so-called Radford Plan—only equivocally disavowed by the Eisenhower administration—for large reductions in American forces based in Europe. Accompanying these events was a steady growth of Soviet nuclear capabilities, including the deployment of ballistic missiles targeted on Western Europe. And with the October 1957 Soviet launch of *Sputnik*—the first artificial satellite placed in Earth orbit—it became clear that the United States, too, would soon be within range of Soviet nuclear missiles.

These developments produced two allied impulses—to bind the United States more tightly and credibly to European defense, and to avoid being engulfed through decisions made in Washington and Moscow in a nuclear conflict that would devastate Europe. Though potentially contradictory, both impulses encouraged the allies to pursue, in ways that varied with the particular circumstances of each, a stronger nuclear role within the alliance.

Thus, Britain went forward with its independent nuclear force with renewed dedication, adopting its own version of the New Look. The U.K. defense White Paper of 1957 called for cuts in conventional forces, an end

---

[6] For a good summary of this period, see David Schwartz, *NATO's Nuclear Dilemmas* (Washington, DC: Brookings, 1983), chap. 3.

to conscription, and near-exclusive reliance on nuclear weapons.[7] Seeking to repair relations with the United States in the wake of Suez, Britain also accelerated its efforts to restore Anglo-American nuclear cooperation.

For France, the Suez crisis marked a watershed in nuclear and foreign policy. Following France's defeat in Indochina and the rearming of Germany, Suez crowned a devastating series of foreign policy reversals that nurtured a distrust of American policy and a determination to reassert French influence and independence. Within a few years, under President Charles de Gaulle, these attitudes would translate into a frontal challenge to American leadership of the alliance. But by the end of 1956 they had already produced a de facto decision by the Socialist government of Guy Mollet to create a French nuclear force.[8]

West Germany's situation was quite different. The 1954 agreement bringing the Federal Republic into NATO had prohibited the manufacture of nuclear weapons on German territory. While this formulation was not airtight, it was widely accepted that German acquisition of a national nuclear weapons capability would be tolerated neither by the NATO allies nor by the Soviet Union, and was therefore out of the question. But Germany was no less determined than the other allies to increase its nuclear role and influence within the alliance. Indeed, Germany's stake was in some ways the greatest of all the allies, given its geographic position (which made it the probable nuclear battlefield in the event of war) and a foreign policy based almost entirely on integration into the Western alliance and dependence on the United States. In the wake of the Radford Plan controversy, Chancellor Konrad Adenauer, who had initially failed to appreciate the implications of NATO's nuclear trend, moved quickly to adjust German policy to the realities of the New Look. Insisting on Germany's right to equality and nondiscrimination within the alliance, he and his newly appointed Defense Minister, Franz-Joseph Strauss, called for the Bundeswehr to be equipped with atomic weapons.[9]

At the December 1956 NATO meeting, the European allies requested direct access to tactical nuclear weapons. In response, the United States proposed the creation of a NATO nuclear stockpile. Under this

---

[7] Macmillan wrote that "the defence White Paper makes it clear that *all* our defence—and the economics in defence expenditure—are founded on nuclear warfare." See Harold MacMillan, *Riding the Storm, 1955–58* (New York: Harper & Row, 1971), p. 266.

[8] The weapons option had been deliberately and steadily advanced by the French nuclear bureaucracy for several years. Given this momentum, Mollet's decision was more a ratification than a new departure. On the origins of the French nuclear program, see Lawrence Scheinman, *Atomic Energy Policy in France under the Fourth Republic* (Princeton: Princeton Univ. Press, 1965); and Wilfrid Kohl, *French Nuclear Diplomacy* (Princeton: Princeton Univ. Press, 1971).

[9] See Catherine McArdle Kelleher, *Germany and the Politics of Nuclear Weapons* (New York: Columbia Univ. Press, 1975), pp. 43–49, 92–93. In 1957, Strauss held exploratory discussions with France about possible nuclear weapons collaboration; Ibid, pp. 149–51; Kohl, *French Nuclear Diplomacy*, pp. 55–61.

plan, allied troops would be equipped with their own nuclear-capable delivery systems, rather than having to rely on U.S. nuclear support groups. The actual nuclear warheads for these weapons would be stock-piled under U.S. custody and released to the appropriate allied forces in the event of hostilities. The United States would retain a veto over the firing of weapons released to the allies.

The stockpile proposal was a compromise.[10] United States military planners had considered placing nuclear warheads themselves directly in allied hands, as France had requested. But this arrangement was rejected by the Joint Committee, which opposed any further liberalization of the McMahon restrictions and whose position had gained political strength from the display of allied independence at Suez.

Developments over the next year, however, caused the administration to raise its sights and press for more ambitious sharing. The reasons were both military and political. The emerging Soviet missile threat to Europe prompted calls for a strengthening of alliance nuclear forces, including the deployment of comparable NATO missiles able to reach targets in the Soviet Union. General Lauris Norstad, the Supreme Allied Commander in Europe (SACEUR), began to lobby for such a force under his authority. Politically, nuclear sharing became viewed by the administration as a key to restoring allied confidence and preventing demoralization in the face of the Soviet nuclear threat on one side and dependency on the United States on the other. The allies, Eisenhower told a press conference in July 1957, "ought to have the right, the opportunity, and the capability of responding in kind" to a Soviet nuclear attack.[11] And Secretary of State Dulles, declaring that the allies should not be "in a position of sup-pliants . . . for the use of nuclear weapons," asserted that "We do not want to be in a position where our allies are wholly dependent upon us. We don't think this is a healthy relationship."[12]

The launch of *Sputnik* in October 1957 reinforced both allied de-mands for nuclear access and the Eisenhower administration's receptivity to them. In Europe, it exacerbated doubts about the reliability of a nuclear guarantee that, under conditions of American vulnerability to Soviet intercontinental missiles, would now carry much higher risks for the United States: Would the President carry out nuclear retaliation against the Soviet Union in response to aggression in Europe, if to do so would risk submitting American cities to nuclear annihilation?

In the United States, *Sputnik*'s political and psychological impact was even more powerful. Russia's success in space crystallized emerging anxieties about Western strength and created a virtual crisis atmosphere.

---

[10] See John D. Steinbruner, *The Cybernetic Theory of Decision* (Princeton: Princeton Univ. Press, 1974), pp. 174ff.

[11] Cited in Stephen E. Ambrose, *Eisenhower, Vol. II: The President* (New York: Simon & Schuster, 1984), p. 405.

[12] Cited in Steinbruner, *Cybernetic Theory*, p. 177.

The need to redress a rapidly deteriorating military balance was widely proclaimed. This was the theme of the Gaither Committee Report, submitted to the White House in November 1957, which called for a major military buildup including accelerated missile development, a nationwide system of fallout shelters, and the deployment of intermediate-range ballistic missiles (IRBMs) in Europe.

Eisenhower largely resisted these pressures; he did not share the general alarm over the Soviet threat and was more concerned about the economic and budgetary effects of the crash program urged by the Gaither Committee and much of Congress. But the new situation did reinforce his commitment to a greater allied nuclear role. He endorsed the IRBM proposal—which offered the quickest route to a Western missile capability against Soviet territory—and decided to press for changes in the law to allow nuclear sharing beyond the NATO-stockpile proposal. As Dulles informed the NSC prior to the special December 1957 NATO Heads of Government meeting: "We will certainly seek authorization to exchange information with our NATO allies if it is of a character that we know the Soviets already have. . . . Next we shall submit a project for the pooling of scientific knowledge with our NATO allies on nuclear energy matters, on missiles, on outer space developments, and the like." [13]

At the Heads of Government meeting, NATO officially endorsed the stockpile proposal, as well as the American offer to place IRBMs at the disposal of SACEUR. The following month, in January 1958, Eisenhower asked Congress for sweeping revisions of the Atomic Energy Act to permit more extensive nuclear cooperation with the allies. Under the amendments proposed by the administration, the United States would for the first time be able to transfer nuclear materials and equipment for military purposes, including military reactors and propulsion systems, the non-nuclear parts of nuclear weapons, and fissile materials for use in nuclear weapons and military reactors. Much broader information sharing would also be authorized, enabling the allies to participate fully in the stockpile scheme, operate nuclear weapons in wartime, and build delivery systems compatible with U.S. nuclear warheads. In the case of countries having already made "substantial progress" in the development of nuclear weapons, the United States could transfer restricted data on nuclear warhead design and fissile material production. [14]

In testimony before the Joint Committee, administration officials argued that nuclear sharing was a military imperative for NATO. Unless the allies were equipped and trained to use nuclear weapons to defend themselves, Dulles claimed, they could scarcely make an effective contribution to the alliance: "There is no use of our having soldiers in the field who even in the case of war would not be able to use what will probably be

---

[13] Briefing to NSC, December 12, 1957, in *Foreign Relations of the United States (FRUS)*, *1955–1957, Vol. IV*, p. 215.

[14] See *Amending the Atomic Energy Act of 1954*, pp. 3–11.

the only effective weapons in that war." [15] To deny nuclear capabilities to the allies would consign them to second-class status and "in effect make the U.S. a partner with the Soviet Union in imposing on [them] such an incapacity . . . that Soviet domination over Western Europe would be largely achieved." [16]

In the face of this threat, the administration suggested, nuclear proliferation was a secondary concern. While affirming U.S. opposition to the spread of nuclear weapons, Dulles did so in terms that were implicitly selective rather than absolute: "There should not be a promiscuous spread of nuclear weapons. We do not want such weapons to get into the hands of irresponsible dictators and become possible instruments of international blackmail." Moreover, he struck a decided note of fatalism about proliferation. Echoing the theme of the Acheson-Lilienthal report—but in tones of resignation rather than urgency—Dulles suggested that proliferation was inevitable unless national nuclear weapons programs were banned:

> Materials needed to make nuclear weapons are becoming increasingly available as nuclear power plants are built. The knowledge to turn these materials into weapons has been independently attained by three countries, and the scientists of many other countries have the skills to enable them to do the same. The only effective preventive is that the development of nuclear weapons should be brought under international control. [17]

Responding to congressional fears that the proposed NATO arrangements would promote proliferation, the administration predicted that sharing should, on the contrary, dampen pressures for national nuclear forces: If the allies had access to NATO nuclear weapons in the event of war, and knew how to use them, they would not need their own nuclear weapons. But this was a secondary theme, not essential to the administration's case: "Even if we are wrong," Dulles argued, "and if [sharing] should not have that deterrent effect, I still think that it is imperative to create, and to create promptly, a nuclear-capable NATO force in Europe." [18] The Assistant Secretary of State for European Affairs, C. Burke Elbrick, carried this theme even further, suggesting that proliferation might be an unavoidable, if regrettable, part of the price for Western defense:

> We have no alternative . . . but to prepare the West, to build up the West, to the point where it can meet a threat from the East. Whether this involves

---

15 *Amending the Atomic Energy Act of 1954*, p. 463.

16 *Amending the Atomic Energy Act of 1954*, p. 450.

17 *Amending the Atomic Energy Act of 1954*, p. 449. Similarly, Dulles told a May 1957 press conference in Paris: "Unless there is a definite movement to eliminate atomic weapons for everybody [the allies] want them too. . . . The only reason they can show their people they are not going into this game is because it is being called off." *FRUS 1955–1957*, Vol. IV, p. 588.

18 *Amending the Atomic Energy Act of 1954*, p. 463.

necessarily the encouragement of a fourth country to enter this field, I am not sure. It probably does. I think that perhaps in the present course of events with lack of agreement on both sides, this may be an inevitable development. But it is not our policy to encourage this.[19]

Congress did not share the administration's complacency. The JCAE was hostile to providing the allies with nuclear "do-it-yourself-kits" and greeted the administration's nonproliferation logic with skepticism. Far from mitigating pressures for allied nuclear programs, the Committee feared, sharing might only whet nuclear appetites and undercut support for maintaining conventional forces. Moreover, cooperation in actual weapons design and production, although intended for the moment only for Britain, might be extended to other countries in the future; indeed, Britain's favored treatment could encourage others to make progress on their own so as to qualify for similar U.S. help.

The outcome of this struggle was a partial victory for the administration, allowing sharing to go forward but only within fairly narrow limits. All nuclear weapons deployed in allied territory would be under strict American control. Information transfer was to be limited to that necessary for the handling and firing of NATO nuclear weapons by allied forces. Nuclear weapons parts and fissile material for military uses, as well as weapons design information, were to be shared only with countries having already achieved "substantial progress" in their own nuclear weapons programs. While the legislation itself left this phrase undefined, the report of the Joint Committee set a high threshold for eligibility, emphasizing the firm intention of Congress that only Great Britain would qualify. The report stipulated that a cooperating partner would need to demonstrate "considerably more than a mere theoretical knowledge of atomic weapons design, or the testing of a limited number of atomic weapons." It must have attained

> a capability of its own of fabricating a variety of atomic weapons, and constructed and operated the necessary facilities, including weapons research and development laboratories, weapons manufacturing facilities, a weapon testing station, and trained personnel to operate each of these facilities.[20]

Hence the American finger remained, at least in principle, firmly on the trigger of the alliance nuclear forces established in the late 1950s. The warheads assigned to NATO's tactical nuclear weapons and IRBMs (Thor and Jupiter missiles deployed in Italy and Turkey) were formally under U.S. "custody" until released to the NATO command. The United States kept a veto over their use through a "two-key" control system: firing

---

[19] *Amending the Atomic Energy Act of 1954*, p. 346.

[20] Report of the Joint Committee on Atomic Energy, 85th Cong., 2nd sess., Senate Report 1657, p. 12.

required a joint decision by the United States and the country on whose territory the particular weapon was based.[21]

In proliferation terms, these arrangements were ambiguous. Although they fell short of the sharing sought by Eisenhower, they resulted in placing massive numbers of nuclear-capable aircraft, artillery, and missiles in the hands of European allies, and especially West Germany.[22] Moreover, United States control over the use of these weapons was sometimes more tenuous in practice than in theory. Particularly in the case of quick-response forces—whose vulnerability to Soviet attack required that they be kept in a very high alert status—the concept of American custody was stretched thin. Bombs and warheads for these weapons were mated with their delivery systems rather than being stored in separate depots, and safeguards against independent allied use were primitive, as the JCAE learned to its dismay during a 1960 inspection trip:

> On the runway stood a German (or Turkish) quick-reaction alert airplane (QRA) loaded with nuclear weapons and with a foreign pilot in the cockpit. The QRA airplane was ready to take off at the earliest warning, and the nuclear weapons were fully operational. The only evidence of U.S. control was a lonely 18-year-old sentry armed with a carbine and standing on the tarmac. When the sentry at the German airfield was asked how he intended to maintain control of the nuclear weapons should the pilot suddenly decide to scramble (either through personal caprice or through an order from the German command circumventing U.S. command), the sentry replied that he would shoot the pilot.[23]

NUCLEAR SHARING AND THE ECONOMIES OF DETERRENCE

The ambiguity of the NATO sharing arrangements developed in the 1950s was not due only to the struggle between Congress and the executive branch over the easing of Atomic Energy Act restrictions. It also reflected the Eisenhower administration's own mixed policy agenda, which produced a nonproliferation policy more equivocal than those of its predecessor and successors. Indeed, proliferation per se was not seen as an urgent threat to U.S. interests. Although "irresponsible dictators" armed with nuclear weapons were a disturbing prospect, NATO allies were in a different category.

---

[21] See Irving Heymont, "The NATO Nuclear Bilateral Forces," *Orbis*, Winter 1966.

[22] See Kelleher, *Germany*, pp. 98–100.

[23] Peter Stein and Peter Feaver, *Assuring the Control of Nuclear Weapons*, CSIA Occasional Paper Series (Lanham, MD: University Press of America, 1987), pp. 30–31. This kind of situation helped create pressure for the installation of physical locking devices called Permissive Action Links (PALs) on U.S. nuclear weapons to prevent their unintended or unauthorized use. See also Steinbruner, *Cybernetic Theory*, pp. 170–71 and 182.

The dominant administration priorities were to increase NATO power in the face of growing Soviet capabilities and, equally important, to keep U.S. defense burdens as low as possible. This required some—but not too much—nuclear delegation. The administration's main objection to allied nuclear programs was that they were wasteful, duplicating the U.S. nuclear effort and diverting resources from NATO's conventional forces in Europe. By 1956–1957, the allies' failure to meet even their reduced, post-Lisbon force goals was a growing concern of SACEUR and the Eisenhower administration. Significant forces on the ground in Europe were needed to give the West some flexibility to respond to contingencies below the threshold of all-out war, to hold the line briefly against Soviet aggression before invoking nuclear retaliation (the "pause" doctrine), and to force the massing of Soviet troops so that NATO tactical nuclear weapons could be used most effectively. These forces were seen as the primary responsibility of the allies in a NATO division of labor consisting of European "shield" forces and the "sword" of American strategic retaliation.

The chronic shortfalls in NATO conventional forces threatened this concept. The problem was partly of the administration's own making, a dilemma inherent in the New Look. On the one hand, U.S. policy required that the allies play their appointed role. Indeed, that role in a sense allowed the United States the luxury of the New Look. If the allies were to emulate the all-nuclear emphasis of U.S. policy, the division of labor would be undermined.[24] On the other hand, American policy gave the allies both military and political incentives to pursue their own nuclear capabilities. As Catherine Kelleher observed, the United States was sending the allies a tacit message at variance with its explicit one, "demanding achievement of promised force levels, yet all the while brandishing the political weight of its tactical nuclear weapons as both the basis for its leadership claims and its excuse for not increasing its own conventional-force levels in Europe."[25]

The NATO stockpile and sharing proposals were an attempt to resolve this dilemma by giving the allies a stake in alliance nuclear defense. This stake would not only strengthen NATO's shield forces militarily but would, it was hoped, bolster the allies' commitment to provide those forces and reduce the appeal of national nuclear programs.

Denial of allied access to nuclear weapons could produce three possible outcomes, according to U.S. thinking, and all were undesirable. First, the allies would lack essential military capabilities and be unable to make an effective contribution to the common defense. Second, they might opt out of the alliance into neutralism. Third, they might pursue their own

---

[24] As Dulles complained when the British announced cuts in their conventional contribution to NATO, the New Look was designed for the United States, not the allies. *FRUS 1955–1957, Vol. IV*, p. 101.

[25] Kelleher, *Germany*, p. 35.

nuclear weapons programs, sapping resources needed for conventional forces. In each case the United States would be deprived, in whole or in part, of the benefits of alliance and be forced to carry a greater burden on its own.

Thus, the Eisenhower administration's determination to maximize NATO strength while minimizing the U.S. defense burden led it to steer a middle course between nuclear denial and manifold independent allied programs. Both extremes were inconsistent with the optimal division of NATO effort sought by the United States, and this middle course was inevitably unstable. Despite U.S. hopes that sharing would satisfy the allies' appetite for nuclear weapons and reconcile them to the division of labor preferred by the United States, in practice it left NATO's underlying nuclear dilemmas unresolved. Access to what Dulles called "the only effective weapons" did not encourage the allies to increase their conventional contribution to alliance defense. On the contrary, it only reinforced the allies' desire for greater influence over U.S. nuclear policy. Moreover, by keeping the control of NATO nuclear weapons in U.S. hands, the stockpile arrangement failed to address the problem of American credibility and reliability. It begged one of the critical questions of the nuclear age—whether U.S. and European interests were identical on the fateful issues of when and how the West should fight a nuclear war.

When the U.S. flexible-response strategy called the assumption of automatic nuclear retaliation into question a few years later, these unresolved issues surfaced to become the focus of a major alliance crisis. To fully understand that crisis, it is necessary to examine another key element of U.S. nonproliferation policy during this period—the American response to the independent nuclear weapons programs of Great Britain and France.

BRITAIN AND FRANCE IN U.S. POLICY

No aspect of U.S. nonproliferation policy in the 1950s was more damaging to America's broader alliance interests and goals than the unequal treatment of Britain and France in the area of nuclear cooperation. In the last years of the Eisenhower administration, the United States reestablished full collaboration with the British nuclear weapons program while rejecting de Gaulle's bid to obtain similar assistance for France. Despite strong intimations of trouble ahead, President Kennedy reaffirmed both policies in 1962. In doing so, he helped precipitate de Gaulle's veto of British entry into the Common Market and the collapse of his own "Grand Design" for Atlantic partnership.

The first steps toward resuming cooperation with Britain, including the sharing of data on nuclear-submarine propulsion, were taken following the 1954 revision of the Atomic Energy Act. But it was the Suez crisis, followed by *Sputnik*, that created the conditions for Britain to win a uniquely favored status in U.S. policy. In effect, nuclear cooperation became the chosen vehicle for renewing the two countries' "special relationship" after the trauma of Suez.

Meeting in Bermuda in March 1957, Eisenhower and Macmillan agreed to the basing of U.S. Thor IRBMs in the United Kingdom. In contrast to the terms of the subsequent offer of IRBMs to the other allies, the missiles were to be under British national control, and could be fired, as Macmillan assured Parliament, only by British personnel. Warheads would be furnished by the United States and subject to American control, but this was a provisional arrangement pending Britain's development of its own warhead.

The Thor agreement served both countries' short-term strategic interests. It allowed each to obtain an earlier missile capability against the Soviet Union than it could otherwise have had, bridging the gap that existed before Britain's own Blue Streak missile and the first U.S. intercontinental ballistic missiles (ICBMs) were available. At the same time, though, it established a linkage between the American and British weapons programs that would become an irritant both in their own relationship and in their respective relations with France. For Britain, the Thor agreement marked the beginning of a delicate balancing act—an attempt to reconcile close ties with the U.S. nuclear program, desired for both political and economic reasons, with the trappings of an independent deterrent.

Building on the Thor deal, Macmillan took advantage of America's chastened mood in the wake of *Sputnik* to pursue his primary objective—access to U.S. nuclear weapon design secrets, and particularly warhead technology. In meetings with Eisenhower and Dulles in October 1957, he obtained their promise to seek an exemption for Britain from the Atomic Energy Act. The resulting amendments, described above, opened the way for essentially unrestricted nuclear cooperation between the two countries and led to the virtual integration of British weapons development with that of the United States.[26]

A combination of motives seems to have led the administration to this nuclear favoritism towards Great Britain. One was certainly Eisenhower's personal affinity (not shared, however, by Dulles) for Britain, based on his wartime experience and his continuing dedication to the Anglo-American relationship. The postwar cutoff of Anglo-American nuclear collaboration, Eisenhower told Macmillan, was "one of the most deplorable incidents in American history, of which he felt personally ashamed."[27]

---

[26] On the U.S.-U.K. agreement for cooperation signed immediately following the passage of the 1958 AEA amendments, see Andrew J. Pierre, *Nuclear Politics: The British Experience with an Independent Strategic Force 1939–1970* (London: Oxford Univ. Press, 1972), p. 140.

[27] Harold Macmillan, *Riding the Storm*, p. 324.

Second, Britain's own nuclear progress made the denial policy less relevant and allowed the administration to argue that collaboration did not amount to fostering proliferation. Britain had tested its first atomic bomb in 1952 and a hydrogen bomb in May 1957. By the same administration logic that regarded *new* independent nuclear programs within the alliance as wasteful and duplicative, it would be wasteful *not* to assist an allied program that had become a fait accompli. Finally, cooperation between the United States and Britain was not entirely a one-way street. Although the British program undoubtedly gained more from the collaboration, the United States also benefited from access to the fruits of more than a decade of U.K. nuclear development. In addition to the exchange of scientific and technological information, the United States received supplies of plutonium in return for highly enriched uranium, under a swap arrangement instituted in 1959.[28]

Britain also had another asset to barter—its potential participation in nuclear arms control. By 1958, proposals to halt nuclear testing and the production of fissile material had emerged as a prominent subject in East-West diplomacy. Earlier in the year, the Soviets had proposed a ban on testing. To the United States, the test-ban idea was becoming more interesting both out of political necessity (the need to deny the Soviets a propaganda advantage) and because it might serve to consolidate U.S. superiority in weapons technology. Talks were to begin in September.

But Britain, although in favor of arms negotiations as a way of easing Cold War tensions, was well behind the superpowers in weapons development, and would have been severely penalized by a testing or fissile-material freeze. Thus, the price for British participation in arms control became U.S. sharing of nuclear secrets: "The British Government could only agree to an abolition of tests if the United States had amended the McMahon Act in order to allow us access to their nuclear knowledge," Macmillan later insisted. "If there was to be any question of stopping tests or a 'cutoff' of the essential material as the result of any agreement, we must be covered by the definite repeal of the McMahon Act."[29] The Eisenhower administration was sympathetic; it wanted British support of U.S. arms control proposals but had no desire to see the U.K. program set back. Nuclear sharing was a way of reconciling these two objectives.

This linkage between test-ban politics and nuclear aid to Britain was both ironic and revealing. Eisenhower's willingness to spare Britain the effects of a testing halt called into question the claim that in cooperating with Britain the United States was dealing with a firmly established

---

[28] Leonard Beaton and John Maddox, *The Spread of Nuclear Weapons* (New York: Praeger, 1962), chap. 2.

[29] Macmillan, *Riding the Storm*, pp. 464–65, 476. In June 1957 Macmillan became furious over a U.S. proposal at the UN for a halt in the production of fissile material, which would "sell us down the river *before* we have a stockpile sufficient for our needs." Ibid., pp. 300–301.

nuclear weapons program and not encouraging proliferation. Notwith-standing the "substantial progress" standard, in 1958 Britain had not yet perfected a missile warhead and could not do so in the absence of further testing without U.S. help. "If we give up now," Macmillan acknowledged, "we shall *not* have a reliable weapon."[30] In effect, the United States had undertaken to sponsor Britain's entry into the missile age.

The pattern was reinforced in the last year of the Eisenhower adminis-tration. At a Camp David meeting with Macmillan in March 1960, the President agreed to sell Britain the Skybolt missile, an air-launched ballistic missile then being developed by the Defense Department. The following month Britain canceled the Blue Streak missile, which had been intended to succeed the "V-Bomber" force as the nation's strategic deliv-ery system. Blue Streak had come under growing criticism as its costs escalated and its vulnerability to Soviet attack became apparent. Skybolt, which could be carried by the V-bombers, would extend the latters' useful life and save Britain from developing its own costly delivery system. In the future, the United States implied, Britain would also be allowed to purchase the submarine-launched Polaris missile.[31] Increasingly, the British nuclear force was becoming an appendage of America's.

France was meanwhile moving steadily forward on its own, and in February 1960 conducted its first nuclear test in the Sahara. The Eisenhower administration had treated France's early nuclear progress with a kind of benign neglect, displaying neither the solicitude it showed Britain nor the hostility of later U.S. policy toward the French nuclear program. As France began to produce plutonium in the mid-1950s and its interest in atomic weapons became clearer, the United States regarded its entry into the nuclear club as an inevitable development—not to be encouraged or welcomed, but also not worth expending much effort to prevent. The United States did hope that the European Atomic Energy Community might offer a framework for channeling French nuclear activ-ity toward civilian applications. But it distanced itself from Jean Monnet's attempt to impose a nuclear weapons ban on EURATOM members, recognizing that a direct U.S. assault on France's program would be counterproductive. "It would be most serious," Ambassador Douglas Dillon cabled from Paris, "if the French should come to believe that the United States favored their renouncing the right to manufacture atomic weapons. Such a feeling would arouse a storm of anti-American protest."[32]

Other things being equal, this essentially neutral policy toward French nuclear weapons might have spared the United States a debilitat-

---

[30] Macmillan, *Riding the Storm*, pp. 489–90.

[31] Pierre, *Nuclear Politics*, pp. 197–98. See also Harold Macmillan, *Pointing the Way, 1959–61* (New York: Harper & Row, 1972), p. 252ff. In an implicit quid pro quo, the United States acquired a Polaris base at Holy Loch in Scotland.

[32] Cable, Paris Embassy to Washington, February 3, 1956, *FRUS 1955–1957, Vol. IV*, pp. 401–2.

ing confrontation with France.[33] But the coincidental timing in mid-1958 of de Gaulle's return to power and the restoration of U.S. nuclear aid to Britain sharply altered the course of Franco-American relations for the worse. De Gaulle took control on June 1, 1958, in the wake of unrest over the Algerian war that had brought down the Fourth French Republic. Among his first acts in power, de Gaulle reaffirmed the decision to create a French nuclear force and appealed to the United States for equal treatment with the United Kingdom under the just-amended Atomic Energy Act. The negative U.S. response, given by Dulles at a meeting of the two men in Paris on July 5, reflected the determination of Congress to prevent any widening of the British precedent. Although it is not clear how far the administration itself would have been prepared to go toward meeting de Gaulle's request, congressional opposition to sharing nuclear secrets with France had made the point moot by mid-1958. The political upheaval in France, whose stability and political reliability were already viewed with suspicion by many members of Congress, only reinforced this opposition.[34]

In Dulles's talking points for the July meeting, he justified the refusal of cooperation with the familiar argument that independent allied nuclear forces were wasteful and inefficient. Alluding to France's relatively early stage of nuclear development, Dulles invoked the former U.S. denial of assistance to Britain, rather than the new policy of favoritism toward that country, as the relevant model for American treatment of France. But he also implicitly disparaged France's suitability as a partner by asserting that NATO should be strengthened "on terms that would deny nuclear power where it might be subject to possible irresponsible use."[35] This was a strong hint that the United States placed France in a different category than the United Kingdom in political as well as technical terms.

Not accepting this verdict as final, de Gaulle followed in September with an ambitious proposal for a tripartite alliance directorate consisting of the United States, Britain, and France. Under the plan, the three countries would oversee NATO political and military affairs, coordinate security policies globally as well as in Europe, and share responsibility for Western nuclear defense. France would thereby not only obtain access to American nuclear assistance but would exercise a veto over the use of U.S. nuclear weapons.[36] For several reasons, the Eisenhower administration found the plan unattractive: It would have diluted American leadership and nuclear autonomy to an unacceptable degree and, by excluding West

---

[33] See George H. Quester, "Was Eisenhower a Genius?" *International Security* 4–2, Fall 1979, p. 163.

[34] See Kohl, *French Nuclear Diplomacy*, pp. 64–67; and William Bader, *The United States and the Spread of Nuclear Weapons* (New York: Pegasus, 1968), pp. 34–35.

[35] Cited in Bader, *The United States*, p. 34.

[36] See Kohl, *French Nuclear Diplomacy*, p. 70ff.

Germany from the inner circle, downgraded the role of an ally that was in many respects more important to Washington than France. The Joint Chiefs of Staff bluntly summarized their objections to the plan:

> [It] would impose constraints on U.S. national freedom in policy determination and implementation to an extent which would have highly undesirable military implications. . . . In the free world only the United States possesses a significant atomic delivery capability. France has yet to test a nuclear device. It appears, therefore, that France is requesting an equal partnership in a world-wide nuclear organization, but can make no substantial contribution thereto. Such an arrangement is neither politically nor militarily desirable. France's primary contribution to the stability of the Free World lies in Western Europe. . . . France has no contribution to make to a world-wide nuclear organization but does have an indispensible contribution to make to NATO.[37]

As de Gaulle may well have anticipated, the Eisenhower administration rejected the proposal. Adding to the rebuff, in early 1959 the United States reneged (under pressure from Congress and Admiral Rickover) on an offer to assist France with nuclear-submarine technology.

These events marked a turning point in U.S. relations with France, setting the latter on a course of growing estrangement from NATO. In 1959 de Gaulle refused NATO tactical nuclear weapons or IRBMs unless they were under exclusive French control and accompanied by aid to the French national nuclear force. He also withdrew the French fleet from NATO's joint Mediterranean command.[38] Seven years later this process culminated with French withdrawal from the alliance military organization.

One can only speculate whether this deterioration could have been prevented by a different U.S. policy toward nuclear cooperation with France. Unfortunately, U.S. and French actions created a vicious cycle that drove the two countries further apart: U.S. rejection provoked a more independent and defiant French policy, which in turn added to American reservations about nuclear cooperation. But it seems doubtful that there was ever a firm political basis for duplicating the Anglo-American link in the case of France, even if the Eisenhower administration had energetically sought, and Congress allowed, such a relationship.[39] The divergence between U.S. and French foreign policy perspectives would have

---

[37] "French Proposal for a Tripartite World-Wide Organization," Memorandum to the Secretary of Defense, October 30, 1958. Nuclear History Project, doc. no. 414.

[38] Kohl, *French Nuclear Diplomacy*, pp. 86–87.

[39] A week before the first French test, Eisenhower hinted in a press conference that he would seek authorization to assist the French program. The administration quickly backed off, however, in the face of a storm of congressional protest. See Steinbruner, *Cybernetic Theory*, pp. 186–87; and Kohl, *French Nuclear Diplomacy*, p. 107. Eisenhower later told an interviewer that "I could have reached a satisfactory agreement with de Gaulle on the atom thing except for the law." David Schoenbrun, *The Three Lives of Charles de Gaulle* (New York: Atheneum, 1965), cited in Kohl, *French Nuclear Diplomacy*, p. 107 (footnote 57).

made it difficult for either to accept the other's terms for nuclear cooperation. Because of this divergence, the French nuclear force represented a
potential challenge to U.S. interests that the U.K. force did not.

Although the French and British nuclear weapons programs were
both motivated in large part by the desire for increased influence within
the alliance, there was a critical, if sometimes subtle, difference. For the
United Kingdom, essentially in harmony with U.S. foreign policy goals,
nuclear weapons were a means of cultivating a special relationship that
would enable Britain to share in American leadership; for Gaullist France,
devoted to national independence and aspiring to the leadership of a more
assertive Europe, they offered a platform from which to challenge American leadership and preserve France's global freedom of action. As such, it
is difficult to imagine that de Gaulle would have been comfortable for long
with the kind of "junior partner" role that Britain accepted, or with the
uneasy balancing act between dependence and independence that Anglo-
American nuclear cooperation entailed. By the same token, notwith-
standing Eisenhower's apparent desire to help France, the United States
was never likely to offer de Gaulle's nuclear effort the same encouragement and support that it gave its more sympathetic and pliant ally. As two
students of nonproliferation policy noted in 1962, "the United States will
not at present share its atomic secrets with any country which it can
imagine using them in circumstances of which it would not approve.
However the issue may be blurred by diplomacy, the Americans trust the
British far more than they trust the French."[40]

The policy of discrimination was nevertheless costly. It embittered
U.S. relations with France, which found itself in the former British role of
victim of American nonproliferation policy. And, by elevating Britain to
the new role of favored exception (later to be joined by Israel), it undercut
the credibility of that policy. The result was to reinforce France's determination to acquire nuclear weapons—both as a counter to Anglo-American
domination of the alliance and as a means of qualifying for U.S. assistance.

By rewarding independent nuclear achievement, American policy
clearly undercut the goal of discouraging national programs. But the
Eisenhower administration was largely untroubled by this dilemma and
by the potential alliance costs of giving preferential treatment to Britain.
As one official testified to the Joint Committee, "the important thing here
is not the fact that some countries may have their feelings hurt, although
that is a possibility, but the fact that the overall strength of the Western
world will be increased."[41] This complacency, while consistent with the
relatively low priority the administration attached to nonproliferation,
seems surprising in view of its hopes of using nuclear sharing to bolster
allied confidence and morale.

---

[40] Beaton and Maddox, *The Spread of Nuclear Weapons*, p. 55.

[41] *Amending the Atomic Energy Act of 1954*, p. 348.

THE KENNEDY ADMINISTRATION

The administration of John F. Kennedy marked a transition in the evolution of U.S. nonproliferation policy. More than his predecessor, Kennedy viewed the spread of nuclear weapons—particularly in the Third World—as a looming threat of major proportions. He saw nonproliferation not only as an important U.S. security interest in its own right but also as a promising field for U.S.-Soviet cooperation as the two superpowers began to pursue arms control seriously in the early 1960s.

It was in the context of alliance policy, however, that a heightened U.S. interest in nonproliferation was most clearly articulated. This interest flowed from the new strategic doctrine of "flexible response" introduced by the Kennedy administration and its Secretary of Defense, Robert S. McNamara. Flexible response was an attempt to adjust NATO strategy to the reality of growing Soviet nuclear capabilities and the consequent decline in the credibility of massive nuclear retaliation to deter communist aggression in Europe. The new doctrine called for a large increase in alliance conventional forces—enabling NATO to mount a serious nonnuclear resistance to Soviet attack—and for limited "counterforce" strikes against Soviet nuclear forces and other military targets if and when the nuclear threshold were crossed. All-out retaliation, especially against cities, was to be held back; this restraint, in theory, would give the Soviets an incentive to avoid attacks on American cities while keeping the threat of escalation in reserve (holding cities "hostage") as a source of leverage for ending the conflict on favorable terms short of total destruction.[42]

The new strategy placed a high premium on centralized control of Western nuclear operations, dictating a firm opposition to independent allied nuclear forces. McNamara gave forceful and impolite expression to this hard line in a major speech to the NATO ministerial meeting in Athens in May 1962. "The efficient use of our resources," McNamara maintained, "implies that the Alliance deterrence system have three vital attributes: unity of planning, executive authority, and central direction."[43] But the price of disunity, given the new targeting philosophy, was no longer simply inefficiency and waste, but possible disaster. It would be

intolerable to have one segment of the Alliance force attacking urban-industrial areas while, with the bulk of our forces, we were succeeding in destroying most of the enemies' nuclear capabilities. Such a failure in coordination might lead to the destruction of our hostages—the Soviet cities—

---

[42] On flexible response, see William Kaufman, *The McNamara Strategy* (New York: Harper & Row, 1964); and Alain C. Enthoven and K. Wayne Smith, *How Much Is Enough: Shaping the Defense Program, 1961–1969* (New York: Harper & Row, 1971).

[43] Cited in Schwartz, *NATO's Nuclear Dilemmas*, pp. 159–60.

just at a time at which our strategy of coercing the Soviets into stopping their aggression was on the verge of success. *Failure to achieve central control of NATO nuclear forces would mean running a risk of bringing down on us the catastrophe which we most urgently wish to avoid.*[44]

Moreover, McNamara claimed, small independent nuclear forces were ineffective even on their own terms; they were more likely to inhibit their owner from resisting pressure, or to invite preemptive attack, than to deter the Soviet Union. If actually employed, they would prove suicidal if used against Soviet cities and trivial if used against military targets. "In short," McNamara concluded bluntly, "weak nuclear capabilities, operating independently, are expensive, prone to obsolescence, and lacking in credibility as a deterrent."[45]

McNamara's stark assertion of U.S. strategic dominance within NATO contrasted sharply with the Kennedy administration's broader approach to the evolution of U.S.-European relations—the Grand Design for Atlantic partnership.[46] Here, the emphasis was on creating a more equal relationship between America and a unified Western Europe. This "twin pillar" model was intended to adapt the alliance to the economic and political revival of Europe, and particularly the formation of the European Economic Community (EEC), or Common Market; its most committed advocates were State Department officials who embraced Jean Monnet's vision of European integration. Like Robert McNamara's strategists in the Defense Department—but for different reasons—these State Department Europeanists identified President de Gaulle as a major threat to their policy. De Gaulle, contemptuous of European integration on the EEC model, represented what the architects of the Grand Design saw as a reactionary, rival vision of Europe's future—a "Europe of states," independent of the United States and under French leadership.

As their common antipathy for de Gaulle suggests, neither the strategists nor the Europeanists of the Kennedy administration desired a truly autonomous Western Europe. Nevertheless, there was a basic underlying

---

[44] Schwartz, *NATO's Nuclear Dilemmas*, emphasis added. A study prepared for the incoming administration by Dean Acheson advised that the United States seek a nonreciprocal veto over the use of allied nuclear forces: "It is vital that the major part of U.S. nuclear power not be subject to veto. It is not essential that the part of that power deployed in Europe be veto-free. It is, however, most important to the United States that use of nuclear weapons by the forces of other powers in Europe should be subject to U.S. veto and control." "NATO and the Atlantic Nations," memo for the NSC, April 24, 1964 (from National Security Archives). See also Albert Wohlstetter, "Nuclear Sharing: NATO and the N + 1 Country," *Foreign Affairs*, April 1961.

[45] Athens speech, in Schwartz, *NATO's Nuclear Dilemmas*, p. 160.

[46] Kennedy's major statement of the partnership idea was his "Declaration of Interdependence" address in Philadelphia on July 4, 1962. See *Department of State Bulletin*, July 23, 1962, p. 131. On the Grand Design, see Robert Kleiman, *Atlantic Crisis* (New York: Norton, 1964). For a good critique, see Stanley Hoffman, *Gulliver's Troubles* (New York: McGraw-Hill, 1968), pp. 461–78.

tension in their prescriptions for Atlantic relations, one seeking to reinforce American primacy and the other to moderate it. As Arthur Schlesinger wrote,

> Those concerned with the economic and political aspects of the relationship were thinking more and more in terms of a dual Atlantic partnership resting on two distinct entities, the United States and the European Economic Community. Those concerned with the military aspects were thinking more and more in terms of a single Atlantic Community based on NATO and the indivisibility of the nuclear deterrent.[47]

The inevitable clash between the two policies came with Great Britain's bid to join the EEC. This bid was a reversal of Britain's historic posture of aloofness from continental politics, and its success was central to the U.S. Grand Design. The policy required the United Kingdom to walk a fine line. Washington counted on British membership in the Common Market to help assure a compatible and cooperative European partner and to counter French influence on the continent. But in order to fulfill this role, it was necessary for Britain to establish its European credentials—especially vis-à-vis de Gaulle—and dispel the suspicion that it was simply an American "Trojan Horse." In this delicate context, the Anglo-American nuclear relationship was a clear liability.

The option of aiding the French nuclear program was weighed at the highest levels of the Kennedy administration during 1962. Harold Macmillan, anxious to placate de Gaulle, urged this course. Now supporting the French tripartite proposal, the British prime minister told Kennedy that a split in the alliance might be avoided, and the British EEC bid advanced, "if we could somehow get de Gaulle an independent nuclear force."[48] A U.S. campaign against the French bomb, Macmillan feared, could be fatal to Britain's chances. Macmillan was therefore furious at what he called McNamara's "foolish speech" at Athens: "He could hardly have done anything more calculated to upset both his French and his British allies."[49]

An opportunity to signal U.S. support for the French program came in March 1962, when General Gaston Lavaud led an unofficial "shopping expedition" to Washington in search of a variety of advanced military equipment, mostly related to the development and delivery of nuclear

---

[47] Arthur Schlesinger, *A Thousand Days* (Boston: Houghton Mifflin, 1965), p. 844.

[48] Macmillan, *Pointing the Way*, p. 351. Macmillan also considered British aid to the French program, a policy supported by his Defense Minister Peter Thorneycroft and apparently viewed by de Gaulle as a litmus test of Britain's "Europeanness." But he was not willing to proceed with Anglo-French nuclear cooperation without a U.S. blessing, and this was not forthcoming. See Pierre, *Nuclear Politics*, p. 223.

[49] Harold Macmillan, *At the End of the Day, 1961–63* (New York: Harper & Row, 1973), pp. 334–36. McNamara assured Britain, but not with great success, that his speech was not aimed at the British nuclear force, since it was coordinated with NATO.

weapons.[50] The Lavaud mission prompted a major interagency debate. Somewhat surprisingly, McNamara and the Joint Chiefs of Staff were in the camp of those who favored exploring a deal with France. Repeating arguments used in the 1940s by proponents of assistance to Britain, they saw U.S. aid as a possible lever over French nuclear policy and as a means of reversing the growing French estrangement from NATO.

The State Department was firmly opposed, however. Secretary of State Dean Rusk argued that cooperation with France would undercut U.S. nonproliferation policy without bringing compensating alliance benefits. He questioned whether it would be possible to co-opt de Gaulle, and stressed that aid to France would risk seriously alienating Germany. Among America's major allies, the Federal Republic would then become the exception to a policy of encouraging national nuclear forces, rather than the United Kingdom being the exception to a general policy of discouragement. President Kennedy took Rusk's side of the argument and reaffirmed the 1958 decision to withhold assistance from the French nuclear effort.

Kennedy also entertained the idea of ending the special U.S. relationship with Britain. Unlike Eisenhower, he worried about the precedent-setting effect of the British program and the alliance costs of U.S. discrimination in its favor. In February 1962 he wrote Macmillan privately that the British example threatened to "confirm de Gaulle in his own course and hasten the day when the Germans would demand nuclear weapons for themselves."[51]

As with France, an occasion to alter U.S. policy toward Britain soon appeared. By the end of 1962, McNamara had concluded that the Skybolt missile was highly deficient on strategic and cost-effectiveness grounds, and gained approval to cancel the program on which Britain had pinned its future nuclear delivery capability.[52] Europeanists in the State Department viewed this development as a golden opportunity to terminate the Anglo-American nuclear link (if not actually force Britain out of the independent nuclear business) and thus remove an albatross from the neck of U.S. alliance policy. As the administration debated the alternatives, this group lobbied vigorously against offering Britain the Polaris submarine-launched missile—which would extend the life of the British force far into the future—as a substitute for Skybolt. "It seems essential," a State Department letter to McNamara argued, "that we make quite clear to the British that there is no possibility of our helping them set up a

---

[50] See Kohl, *French Nuclear Diplomacy*, pp. 217–20; and Steinbruner, *Cybernetic Theory*, pp. 216–18.

[51] See Schlesinger, *A Thousand Days*, p. 856.

[52] On the Skybolt affair and the Nassau meeting, see Richard Neustadt, *Alliance Politics* (New York: Columbia Univ. Press, 1970); Kleiman, *Atlantic Crisis*; and Pierre, *Nuclear Politics*, pp. 224–43. For Macmillan's account of these events, see *The End of the Day*, chap. IX.

nationally manned and owned MRBM [medium-range ballistic missile] force."[53] Any offer to Britain, the State Department insisted, should be couched in multilateral rather than national terms and made available to the other allies on a nondiscriminatory basis.

Kennedy met with Macmillan in Nassau in December 1962 in an atmosphere of high tension. Though his initial inclination was to resist an offer of Polaris, Kennedy was finally swayed by Harold Macmillan's eloquent appeal to the special relationship, and by the firestorm of anti-American feeling the Skybolt cancellation had touched off in Britain. The two leaders drafted an agreement that, despite its ambiguity and even self-contradiction, essentially gave Britain the submarine-launched missile on a national basis. Britain agreed to assign its Polaris force to NATO, but with an escape clause allowing for independent use where "supreme national interests" required. The document also endorsed, in nonspecific terms, a future multilateral nuclear force (MLF) to which the United States and Britain would contribute forces.[54]

Against his better judgment, Kennedy had acquiesced in an outcome that was anomalous and self-defeating in terms of America's avowed alliance goals. Undercutting the McNamara Athens policy as well as the Europeanist agenda, it produced "puzzlement in the Pentagon and deep gloom in the State Department."[55] And it gave de Gaulle a perfect opening for a dramatic and devastating assault on American policy. Speaking at a press conference on January 14, 1963, the French president attacked the Nassau agreement as confirming evidence of America's hegemonic Atlantic designs and Britain's intrinsically "Anglo-Saxon" rather than European identity. He then vetoed British entry into the EEC and affirmed that France would continue with its independent nuclear policy and abstain from any integrated NATO nuclear force.[56] A week later, he raised the ante in the escalating Franco-American contest for alliance leadership by signing a Treaty of Cooperation and Friendship with West Germany.

---

[53] Cited in Schwartz, *NATO's Nuclear Dilemmas*, p. 99. Similarly, the April 1961 Acheson report to Kennedy had stated that "over the long run, it would be desirable if the British decided to phase out of the nuclear deterrent business. If the development of Skybolt is not warranted for U.S. purposes alone, the U.S. should not prolong the life of the V-Bomber force by this or other means."

[54] For a good summary and analysis of the Nassau agreement, see Schwartz, *NATO's Nuclear Dilemmas*, pp. 103–5. The meeting was poorly prepared on the U.S. side, which had underestimated the seriousness of the issue in Britain and was still preoccupied with the recent Cuban missile crisis.

[55] Steinbruner, *Cybernetic Theory*, p. 238.

[56] It is generally assumed that Nassau was more a convenient pretext than the primary cause of de Gaulle's veto. Macmillan had gained the impression at Rambouillet, and conveyed it to Kennedy at Nassau, that de Gaulle would not be offended by Britain's acquisition of Polaris. See Macmillan, *At the End of the Day*, pp. 347–48 and 356–57.

THE MULTILATERAL FORCE

American policy in Europe was suddenly in a shambles. In an effort to repair the damage, the United States elevated the Multilateral Force proposal to the top of the alliance agenda, only to see it compound the crisis and magnify the tensions between the different strands of U.S. policy.

The MLF was a novel plan for a truly integrated NATO nuclear force. It was to be a fleet of surface ships armed with Polaris missiles (25 ships carrying eight missiles each in the final version of the scheme), with crews of mixed nationality. It would be under the command of an executive body composed of representatives of each of the participating allies, who would jointly control the decision to fire the missiles. The precise control formula was unspecified beyond the proviso that the United States would—initially at least—hold a veto.

In January 1963 the MLF proposal had already been under discussion for two years, backed by Europeanists in the State Department seeking a way to counter the example of the French and British national forces and to appease West Germany's desire for greater access to nuclear weapons.[57] The sense of urgency about this problem had risen amid the controversy over the U.S. flexible-response strategy. Though intended to bolster the credibility of the U.S. guarantee of European security, the Kennedy-McNamara strategy had instead magnified allied apprehensions. To many Europeans, it looked like a weakening of nuclear deterrence and an attempt to decouple the United States from the risks of defending Europe. And by creating greater uncertainty about nuclear retaliation, the strategy gave the allies strong incentives to deny the U.S. sole discretion over the use of nuclear force. Recognizing this problem, MLF proponents questioned the political viability of McNamara's prescription for tight centralization of alliance nuclear forces under U.S. control. They came to view the collective force concept as the only realistic alternative to an untenable U.S. nuclear monopoly and an undesirable proliferation of national nuclear forces.

The MLF remained a low administration priority until 1963, however. Although Kennedy had endorsed the idea in a speech in Ottawa in May 1961 and approved exploratory discussions with the allies, he placed

---

[57] The initial proposal was drafted by Robert Bowie for the State Department as a counter to Gen. Norstad's plan for a land-based NATO missile force, and presented to NATO by Secretary of State Christian Herter in December 1960. The most thorough account of U.S. decision making and bureaucratic politics surrounding the MLF episode is Steinbruner, *Cybernetic Theory*. On the early background, see Thomas Weigele, "The Origins of the MLF Concept," *Orbis*, Summer 1968. A good critique of the plan's internal contradictions is contained in Henry Kissinger, *The Troubled Partnership* (New York: McGraw-Hill, 1965), chap. 5.

greater importance on increasing NATO's conventional forces and insisted that the initiative for a collective nuclear force would have to come from the allies. Then, in the aftermath of Nassau and de Gaulle's veto, the terms of the debate were abruptly altered and the MLF lobby unleashed. Kennedy removed his earlier preconditions and authorized the State Department to begin negotiations for the creation of a force. Suddenly the joint fleet emerged as the centerpiece of U.S. policy for dealing with NATO's political and nuclear tensions, and remained so for two years.

The allied response to what became an intense U.S. diplomatic campaign for MLF was lukewarm at best. France, the main target of the plan, was predictably hostile, viewing the force as an attempt to reassert U.S. control over alliance nuclear forces and forestall a Paris-Bonn entente. Britain agreed without enthusiasm to study the idea, which it considered bizarre from a military standpoint and doubly threatening in that it implicitly questioned the validity of the British deterrent and encouraged greater German access to nuclear weapons. To remedy these defects, Britain put forward an alternative plan for an Atlantic Nuclear Force (ANF), to be made up of national contingents from the existing allied nuclear powers. Italy and the smaller allies had reservations as well. Only West Germany, the main object of the MLF lobby's attentions, endorsed the U.S. plan with any conviction.

Given this dubious reception, Kennedy was personally skeptical whether MLF would ever see the light of day. But he remained committed to the project in public, and the State Department continued to push it with unflagging energy. When Lyndon Johnson assumed the presidency following Kennedy's assassination in November 1963, he renewed the mandate of the U.S. negotiators and, at their urging, set an end-of-1964 deadline for agreement.

As this deadline approached, the MLF became the focus of an escalating controversy. France intensified its opposition and began to exert pressure on West Germany to reject the plan, playing on a growing split between "Gaullists" and "Atlanticists" within Germany's ruling Christian Democratic party. Konrad Adenauer, who had resigned as chancellor in October 1963, now embraced the French argument against MLF and joined those urging closer Franco-German cooperation to reduce Bonn's dependence on the United States. His successor, Ludwig Erhard, who had reaffirmed German support for MLF in a meeting with Johnson in June, was caught in the middle, beset by conflicting demands from Paris and Washington and seemingly called upon to choose between the two.[58]

The constituency for MLF eroded further with the victory of Harold Wilson's Labor Party in the October 1964 British elections. The new U.K. government was even more wary than its predecessor of increasing Ger-

---

[58] See Kelleher, *Germany*, chaps. 9–10; and James L. Richardson, *Germany and the Atlantic Alliance* (Cambridge, MA: Harvard Univ. Press, 1966).

many's nuclear participation in the alliance and was concerned that MLF would block progress in arms control with the Soviet Union. Wilson revived the ANF proposal as an alternative to multilateral sharing.

President Johnson saw the hopelessness of forging an allied consensus on MLF—or even a domestic one, given growing disenchantment with the plan in Congress and the military—and decided to cut his losses. On the recommendation of a senior review committee headed by National Security Advisor McGeorge Bundy, he lifted the deadline in December 1964 and suspended the diplomatic lobbying effort on behalf of MLF.[59] He thus defused the immediate crisis without addressing its deeper causes.

In hindsight, the failure of the MLF seems inevitable. In its attempt to satisfy constituencies with widely diverging goals and interests, it embodied the contradictory impulses within American alliance policy and its ambivalence about nuclear sharing. Within the alliance, there was a common opposition to independent nuclear forces and a fear of de Gaulle's France as a political and strategic lure for Germany. But behind this essentially negative consensus lay the conflict between the strategic model of a centralized, United States-dominated Atlantic defense system and the political-economic model of a more egalitarian, "twin-pillar" Atlantic partnership. MLF awkwardly straddled the two, its ambiguity centered on the question of control. The critical issue was whether the U.S. veto was an essential and permanent feature of the plan or might be relinquished in the future in favor of a separate European nuclear force (a scenario that became known as the "European option").

For the strategists, the veto was indispensable. If the MLF had any merit—a debatable issue for the McNamara Defense Department—it was to prevent the further fragmentation of Western deterrent forces and to promote their consolidation under U.S. control. A true sharing of control, however, would subvert rather than support the McNamara strategy. The irony was that the MLF idea had a plausible strategic rationale only if it *did* give the allies a real finger on the nuclear trigger. To strengthen NATO nuclear deterrence, the threat of MLF retaliation in response to Soviet aggression would have to be more credible than the use of U.S. strategic forces—which would not be the case if the United States held a veto over the firing of MLF missiles. With a U.S. veto, MLF retaliation would be no more or less credible than the existing U.S. nuclear guarantee, and the collective force would be militarily superfluous.

Thus, only a sham MLF would satisfy the demands of U.S. strategy, while a genuine one would contradict that strategy. As one French skeptic observed of the "European option,"

A European deterrent force simply transfers to the European level the problem of the French national deterrent, but does nothing to resolve the problem. Either this European force is a mirage . . . which leaves the final

---

[59] Steinbruner, *Cybernetic Theory*; Philip L. Geyelin, *Lyndon B. Johnson and the World* (New York: Praeger, 1966).

decision in the hands of the President of the United States, or it creates a second center of decision. At that point, it is no more acceptable to the United States than the French *force de frappe*.[60]

The administration Europeanists had a different perspective, however. In their view, a European nuclear force was a logical corollary of the twin-pillar concept of Atlantic partnership, and not to be equated with national nuclear forces. They did not dispute the Pentagon's strategic logic. "In strictly military terms," Robert Bowie conceded, "it is probably true that the alliance would be best served by . . . unified control in the United States' hands."[61] But strategic premises were not the controlling ones for the most committed supporters of MLF. They viewed the force as a vehicle for advancing the cause of European integration; in this context, a devolution of nuclear control was not only acceptable but desirable.[62] Accordingly, the eventual withdrawal of the U.S. veto was critical if the MLF was to serve the Europeanists' vision. This prospect, they believed, could in fact serve as a powerful stimulus for European integration. With this in mind, George Ball considered the MLF as an "educational" exercise for the Europeans, in which the United States would play a prominent role only "for the time being."[63]

In this way, the Europeanists were led to stress precisely that aspect of the MLF that the strategists wished to minimize—its potentially "evolutionary" character. The conflict between these two versions of the plan was basic. The MLF could not, as Henry Kissinger noted, "at one and the same time satisfy demands for nuclear sharing and assuage concerns about nuclear proliferation."[64] Yet the divisions within the U.S. government and among the allies the United States wished to influence demanded that the issue be obscured. As a result, official U.S. pronouncements on MLF varied according to the spokesman and the audience, mixing hints of devolution with assurances of U.S. control.[65]

In the final analysis, the likelihood that the United States would give up its veto was always remote at best. It was very doubtful that either the Pentagon or Congress would have supported such a move, and there is

---

[60] Alfred Grosser, *La Politique Exterieure de la Ve Republique* (Paris: Seuil, 1965), pp. 134–35.

[61] Robert R. Bowie, "Strategy and the Atlantic Alliance," *International Organization*, Summer 1963. This view marks a change from the 1950s, when the Eisenhower administration portrayed wider nuclear sharing with the allies as a strategic as well as a political imperative. Bowie's article is a strong brief for the MLF by its original author.

[62] Monnet himself advocated a European nuclear force closely linked with the American deterrent. See *New York Times*, April 8, 1963, p. 1.

[63] George Ball, *The Discipline of Power* (Boston: Little, Brown, 1968), p. 61.

[64] Kissinger, *The Troubled Partnership*, p. 154.

[65] See, for example, statements made by Vice President Johnson, Secretary of State Rusk, and National Security Advisor McGeorge Bundy, *Department of State Bulletin*, December 2, 1963, pp. 853–54; 604–5.

little evidence that the White House seriously entertained the idea.[66] Thus, MLF was ultimately a kind of charade, offering the allies the appearance but not the reality of nuclear sharing. Kennedy reportedly viewed the plan this way:

> [He] considered that, so long as the United States retained its veto (and he never mentioned renunciation as a possibility, though other members of his government did) the MLF was something of a fake. Though he was willing to try it, he could not see why Europeans would be interested in making enormous financial contributions toward a force over which they had no real control.[67]

Yet this "fake" stood at the center of U.S. alliance policy for almost two years. It is ironic that the plan's most fervent supporters were wedded to the least realistic version of it, and that those in the U.S. government who were most committed to a more equal Atlantic partnership should have chosen to advance their cause in the strategic nuclear arena—precisely the sphere of alliance relations where U.S. supremacy was most pronounced and least likely to be ceded.

CONCLUSION

Despite its prominence at the time, the MLF was a detour in the evolution of American nuclear policy. It proved to be not the "first step" envisaged by its Europeanist advocates, but rather the "last hurrah" of the 1950s' liberalizing trend at a time when the tide of U.S. policy was beginning to run strongly in the opposite direction. It was as if the United States needed to flirt, if only hypothetically, with the notion of actually sharing nuclear control in order to resolve its ambivalence and confirm its growing aversion to proliferation within the alliance.

In this light, the demise of MLF marked the distance that U.S. policy had traveled since the mid-1950s. Throughout this period, the challenge had been to establish alliance nuclear arrangements that would reconcile the sometimes competing demands of strategy, political cohesion, and cost-effectiveness. For the United States, this was at bottom a process of defining acceptable terms for the American nuclear guarantee of Western

---

[66] The JCAE did not disguise its distaste for MLF, which would have required amending the Atomic Energy Act to allow the allies to share custody of nuclear weapons on MLF ships. See Steinbruner, *Cybernetic Theory*, p. 271. A change in the control formula to withdraw the U.S. veto would have required a second revision, as Rusk, testifying before the JCAE, was reminded by Chairman Pastore. The following exchange ensued:

> RUSK: We are not proposing it, and I would predict that you would not amend it.
> PASTORE: You were never more right in prediction.

Nonproliferation of Nuclear Weapons, hearings February 1966, p. 20.

[67] Schlesinger, *A Thousand Days*, p. 872.

Europe. Both the Eisenhower and Kennedy administrations supported some sharing of nuclear responsibility and opposed independent allied deterrents, but their relative priorities differed. For Eisenhower, the emphasis was on sharing, even at the risk of encouraging proliferation; the overriding goal was to get nuclear weapons into the hands of the allies. For Kennedy, the emphasis was on nonproliferation; the overriding goal was to consolidate U.S. control over NATO strategy. And while Eisenhower viewed nuclear delegation as a way to contain the economic burdens of America's security role, Kennedy viewed centralized U.S. control as essential to containing the strategic risks of that role.

These differences reflected the evolution of the nuclear balance, the growing awareness of U.S. vulnerability, and the "nuclear learning" that occurred as the United States gradually adjusted to the role of nuclear superpower.[68] This adjustment was a two-edged process, creating rifts between the United States and its alliance partners on the one hand and revealing a sphere of shared interests with the Soviet Union on the other.

Within the West, Soviet nuclear progress created conflicts over the terms and conditions of nuclear deterrence. When the United States had enjoyed overwhelming nuclear superiority, and the premise of Western strategy was virtually automatic nuclear retaliation, these conflicts remained latent. In these circumstances, any addition to Western nuclear strength could be seen as a kind of collective good, and the United States was relatively complacent about proliferation. As conditions changed, however, the risks and dilemmas of extended deterrence became more apparent, and the harmony of interests between the United States and its European allies more questionable. Alliance nuclear relations became a recurring conflict—replayed in the debates on flexible response, the MLF, and the French nuclear force—over the allocation and control of nuclear risks.[69] While the allies sought to bind the United States tightly to their defense but avoid becoming the battlefield in the event of war, the United States sought to contain any conflict below the level of strategic nuclear retaliation.

In this context, independent nuclear forces directly threatened America's ability to control the terms of its commitment to Europe. Indeed, this was an important part of the rationale for such forces: They could force the U.S. hand by acting as a "trigger" for American strategic retaliation. As the French strategist Andre Beaufre argued, the role of independent forces was to upset a superpower nuclear standoff whose growing stability had eroded the credibility of the U.S. nuclear guarantee:

---

[68] See Joseph S. Nye, Jr., "Nuclear Learning," *International Organization*, Summer 1987. The change in U.S. policy also reflects the difference between Eisenhower's preoccupation with economic constraints and the perils of U.S. overextension, and the Kennedy administration's more expansive view of the U.S. world role. (See chap. 4.)

[69] For an insightful discussion of this syndrome, see Josef Joffe, *The Limited Partnership* (Cambridge, MA: Ballinger, 1988).

French deterrence plays only a complementary role in the allied deterrent system, though a useful one because it intrudes upon a balance that is at present too stable, and because its very existence introduces a germ of instability and doubt that helps reestablish in part the deterrent strength of the entire system.[70]

By threatening to escalate a European conflict to the nuclear level, the argument went, allied nuclear forces would act as a catalyst for U.S. involvement. This would restore the presumption of automatic U.S. retaliation and thus strengthen deterrence: "Whatever may be his own true interests," General Beaufre argued, "the more powerful ally is compelled to consider the interests of the third party as if they were his own."[71]

This was of course precisely the situation the United States was determined to avoid. The "triggering" scenario gave the United States the strongest possible incentive to oppose proliferation, as Kennedy himself argued in February 1963:

> I do not believe it is in the interest of the United States to view the possession of a nuclear arsenal as a legitimate and desirable attribute of every sovereign nation. . . . If we are to be caught up in a nuclear war, should we not have a voice in the decision that launches it? Is not my first responsibility to protect the interests of the United States?[72]

Just as the risks of nuclear war introduced conflicts of interest between the United States and its allies, they also led to the discovery of common interests with the Soviet Union. This was the other side of the "nuclear learning" coin. In the vocabulary of the game theory that strongly influenced civilian deterrence theorists during this period, and in turn the thinking of Kennedy administration strategists, U.S.-Soviet relations were becoming recognized as a "mixed-motive" rather than

---

[70] André Beaufre, *NATO and Europe* (New York: Vintage, 1966), p. 85. On the "triggering" rationale for the French nuclear force, see also Kohl, *French Nuclear Diplomacy*, pp. 154–56.

[71] André Beaufre, *Deterrence and Strategy* (New York: Faber and Faber, 1965), p. 82.

[72] Letter, cited in Theodore C. Sorenson, *Kennedy* (New York: Harper & Row, 1965), p. 573. French sociologist Raymond Aron, a prominent critic of Gaullist strategy, argued that the triggering scenario would only cause the U.S. to decouple further from the risks of extended deterrence:

> Those who would like to see the Atlantic alliance replaced by an alliance of the traditional type, with each member free to use atomic weapons as it sees fit and able to rely on automatic support from its allies, have simply failed to grasp the most elementary facts of the new diplomacy. What thermonuclear weapons have rendered obsolete are not alliances as such but alliances of the traditional type. The big nations are still able to protect the small ones but will not consent to do so if the latter claim the prerogative of initiating thermonuclear war.

The Great Debate (New York: Anchor, 1965), pp. 262–63.

"zero-sum" game.[73] The superpowers' interest in avoiding mutual annihilation gave them a shared stake in stabilizing the nuclear confrontation and opened up possibilities for mutual cooperation. This cooperation might be tacit, as envisaged by Robert McNamara's "no-cities" doctrine, or explicit, as in the negotiation of arms control agreements. In either case, it implied a strong preference for nuclear duopoly.

Nonproliferation had thus emerged by the early 1960s not only as an important condition of extended deterrence for the United States, but also as a powerful shared interest of the superpowers. It was, accordingly, a natural progression when the United States turned its attention from NATO sharing to the pursuit of the Non-Proliferation Treaty after 1964. Equally natural was that this shift would be very difficult to mesh with smooth alliance relations, and that it would raise the specter of a superpower deal at Europe's expense. As U.S.-Soviet détente blossomed in the 1960s with the NPT negotiations as its centerpiece, it became clear that the MLF affair had been only one round of a continuing alliance crisis.

---

[73] See especially Thomas Schelling, *The Strategy of Conflict* (New York: Oxford Univ. Press, 1963).

Chapter
4

The NPT and U.S.
Foreign Policy

*T*he Non-Proliferation Treaty (NPT) was the main object of U.S. arms control policy from 1964 to 1968—years better remembered for the escalation of the Vietnam War. Though the war and its attendant traumas overshadowed the NPT, the latter too marked a crucial, and in many respects, wrenching passage in the evolution of postwar U.S. foreign policy. Moreover, the two policies were not unconnected, despite their superficial incongruity. The same interventionist impulse and preoccupation with communist China that fed the deepening U.S. involvement in Vietnam also helped animate the pursuit of the NPT. And the growing controversy over the war, both at home and abroad, strengthened Lyndon Johnson's stake in the treaty as a means of bolstering his image as a peacemaker and advancing relations with the Soviet Union.

The period of the NPT negotiations marked a two-fold shift in U.S. nonproliferation policy that mirrored the broader evolution of American foreign policy during the Johnson years. First, the geographical focus of concern shifted from Europe to Asia and the Third World. "No one really believes," the U.S. delegate at the NPT negotiations in Geneva argued, "that the dam which is now holding back proliferation will break in Europe."[1] Second, the effort to control proliferation became a leading rationale for, and route to, closer U.S.-Soviet cooperation.

In its role as a vehicle for superpower rapprochement, the NPT proved more controversial and disruptive than its subject alone would have suggested. The treaty's basic concept—pledges by the nuclear "haves" and "have-nots," respectively, not to transfer or acquire nuclear

---

[1] Statement by Adrian Fisher, *Documents on Disarmament, 1966*, United States Arms Control and Disarmament Agency (Washington, DC: GPO), p. 189.

weapons—was hardly a sharp break from earlier U.S. policy. But the treaty became the focus of a heated debate over U.S. priorities that set alliance-oriented traditionalists against advocates of détente and arms control. By seeming to force a U.S. choice between "NATO and Geneva," the NPT negotiations imposed severe strains on Atlantic relations, and on the U.S.-German tie in particular. "Nothing except the Vietnam War and General de Gaulle," one observer wrote, "has done so much as the negotiations on a non-proliferation treaty to drive a wedge between the United States and Europe."[2]

Another source of tension in U.S. policy remained largely submerged until late in the NPT negotiations. This was the conflict between America's desire to remain master of its overseas commitments and the demands of countries like India for security guarantees as a condition of renouncing nuclear weapons. The sharpness of this conflict grew in parallel with the controversy over Vietnam; when the U.S. Senate took up the completed treaty in the summer of 1968, the "no-more-Vietnams" sentiment pervaded the ratification debate. A negotiation that had begun in the full flowering of the most expansive phase of postwar U.S. foreign policy ended with the shattering of domestic consensus on the American global security role.

THE NPT DEBATE

United States interest in a global nonproliferation agreement rose sharply in the early 1960s. A rapid spread of nuclear weapons seemed imminent to many observers, and this prospect was increasingly seen as a major national security threat. The October 1964 nuclear test by communist China strongly reinforced these fears. The China test was especially ominous because it signaled that proliferation had broken out of the circle of advanced industrial countries.[3] It therefore not only put pressure on China's regional neighbors (especially India and Japan) to consider a nuclear option, but also stood as a precedent for other Third World countries with aspirations to greater security and prestige.

The growing sense of alarm about proliferation was crystallized in a secret government study drafted in the wake of the China test and delivered to Johnson in January 1965. The so-called Gilpatric Report painted a grim picture of global instability, heightened risks of nuclear war, and reduced American influence should proliferation continue, even among countries friendly to the United States. Arguing that the

---

[2] Pierre Hassner, "Change and Security in Europe, Part I: The Background," *Adelphi Papers* 45 (London: Institute for Strategic Studies), February 1968, p. 20.

[3] Alarm was all the greater when it turned out that China had tested a sophisticated device fashioned from highly enriched uranium—apparently produced indigenously—rather than the expected plutonium.

world was "fast approaching the point of no return" in controlling the bomb's spread, it called for much stronger U.S. efforts to deal with the threat, including negotiation of an international treaty jointly with the Soviet Union.[4]

Soviet motives for cooperation to control proliferation were also increasing at this time. To a degree, these motives paralleled American ones: the Soviets had no more interest than the United States in being drawn into a nuclear conflict by the actions of a nuclear-armed ally. After giving considerable nuclear assistance to China in the 1950s, the Soviets had pulled back, cutting off aid in 1959. Subsequently, the Sino-Soviet split and the Chinese test removed Soviet inhibitions on joining with the United States to control proliferation.[5] But Moscow also had a strong incentive to use the issue to constrain Western nuclear arrangements, and in particular West Germany's access to nuclear weapons. By enlisting the United States as a partner, the Soviet Union could limit the threat from NATO while aggravating tensions within the Atlantic alliance—a strategy that was amply rewarded in the course of the negotiations.

The NPT talks were formally centered in the UN Eighteen Nation Disarmament Conference (ENDC) in Geneva.[6] Until late 1966, they were dominated by the question of NATO nuclear sharing, as the United States sought to protect, and the Soviets to exclude, an option for some variant of the multilateral force concept. This initial phase of the negotiations was a painful denouement to the 1963–1964 MLF debate, which—it soon became apparent—had not been laid to rest by Johnson's late-1964 decision to lift U.S. pressure for the plan. West Germany continued to

---

[4] *A Report to the President by the Committee on Nuclear Proliferation*, January 1965 (partially declassified September 22, 1977). The committee was chaired by Roswell Gilpatric, a deputy secretary of defense in the Kennedy administration. For an inside account, see Glenn Seaborg, *Stemming the Tide: Arms Control in the Johnson Years* (Lexington, MA: Lexington Books, 1987), pp. 136–52.

[5] See Joseph Nye, "The Superpowers and the NPT," in Albert Carnesale and Richard Haass, eds., *Superpower Arms Control: Setting the Record Straight* (Cambridge, MA: Ballinger, 1988).

[6] The point of departure for the negotiations was a unanimous 1961 UN resolution, introduced by Ireland, calling for an international agreement by which the nuclear powers would "refrain from relinquishing control of nuclear weapons and from transmitting information necessary for their manufacture to States not possessing such weapons. . . ." The United States had abstained on essentially the same resolution the previous year. Ireland had first raised the issue in 1958, when the United States (then in the midst of the NATO stockpile and IRBM initiatives) refused to support a resolution asserting the dangers of an increase in the number of states "possessing" nuclear weapons. See William Bader, *The United States and the Spread of Nuclear Weapons* (New York: Pegasus, 1968), pp. 36–43.

On the domestic and international politics of the treaty, see George Quester, *The Politics of Nuclear Proliferation* (Baltimore: Johns Hopkins Univ. Press, 1973); Glenn Seaborg, *Stemming the Tide;* and Elizabeth Young, *A Farewell to Arms Control?* (London: Penguin Books, 1972).

insist on a "hardware" solution for allied nuclear participation, with strong backing in the State Department despite the disbanding of the MLF office. Johnson himself was anxious to avoid undercutting Chancellor Erhard, who had supported the U.S. proposal at great political risk. As 1965 began, therefore, the administration was vigorously, if disingenuously, denying the common impression that it had abandoned nuclear sharing. Dean Rusk personally assured his German counterpart, Gerhard Schroeder, to this effect.

The unfortunate result was to embroil the sharing issue in the NPT negotiations, making the Soviet Union a de facto participant in the NATO debate over allied nuclear arrangements. The Soviet strategy was to cast NATO nuclear sharing as the main obstacle to a nonproliferation agreement. Carrying its propaganda campaign against the MLF to Geneva, Moscow relentlessly invoked a "revanchist" West Germany with its finger on the nuclear trigger.[7] The Soviets insisted that the NPT ban any access to nuclear weapons on the part of nonnuclear states, including arrangements for joint ownership, use, or control of weapons, as well as their direct transfer.

The United States, defining proliferation more narrowly as an increase in the number of independent national nuclear forces, insisted that multilateral sharing and nonproliferation were compatible. But there was a widespread recognition in Washington and among the allies that a choice might have to be made between the NATO force option and progress on the NPT. Political alignments formed up accordingly. For MLF skeptics, in whose eyes the force had merit only insofar as it might dampen proliferation, the NPT offered a more direct and less ambiguous route to the same objective. But for the core supporters of MLF, who viewed the plan as a political device for placating West Germany and encouraging European unity, the NPT was by no means a substitute. They regarded a resolution of the NATO sharing question—on terms acceptable to the allies—as urgent unfinished business.

The allies also split along familiar lines. France, which was nearing its 1966 pullout from NATO as the NPT negotiations began, denounced the treaty as an instrument of superpower hegemony and did not participate at Geneva. The continental allies, led by Germany and Italy, were wary of the NPT talks and opposed to U.S. concessions at Geneva that would narrow NATO's nuclear options. Germany, seeing itself as the primary target of the prospective treaty, was the most apprehensive. By barring German nuclear weapons while legitimizing those of Britain and France, the NPT would enshrine the very discrimination that the MLF had

---

[7] The Soviets may also have feared that MLF would place pressure on them to share nuclear weapons with their Eastern European allies or other clients. On Soviet policy toward NATO sharing proposals, see Zbigniew Brzezinski, "Moscow and the MLF: Hostility and Ambivalence," *Foreign Affairs*, October 1964.

been meant to mitigate. "What is lacking in the Federal Republic," the U.S. ambassador Hillenbrand reported, "is any sense that there could be a German interest in a nondissemination agreement as such, apart from other incidental advantages which might be obtained from its inclusion in a larger context."[8] Germany was thus determined to extract a price, including a greater nuclear role in the alliance, for adhering to an NPT.

Great Britain was at the opposite pole. Eager to promote East-West détente, unenthusiastic about nuclear sharing, and not without sympathy for Soviet fears of German nuclear "access," Britain gave unequivocal priority to the NPT. While the British Atlantic Nuclear Force (ANF) proposal remained on the table, it had been largely a device for blocking the MLF and, especially after 1964, was not pushed as a serious bid for new NATO arrangements.

The nominal focus of the controversy was an issue whose practical relevance was hypothetical at best. The chances that NATO would form a collective force were remote by 1965; even more remote was the prospect that a nuclear-armed member would surrender its veto in favor of a majority-control formula for such a force—the "European clause" favored by Bonn and the American MLF lobby.[9] But while there was far more symbol than substance to these questions, the symbolism was potent. The subtext of the argument was a much broader debate over the basic premises of American policy toward Europe and East-West relations. In this setting, nuclear sharing assumed undeserved importance as a touchstone of fidelity to traditional Cold War policies, while the NPT became a rallying point for advocates of new directions.

The traditionalists—centered in the State Department—spoke for the primacy of NATO, and regarded a strong U.S.-West Germany tie as essential to American foreign policy. They argued that the reestablishment of allied confidence and unity should take precedence over new initiatives toward the Soviet Union, especially in the face of the French challenge to NATO. On East-West relations, they embraced the hard-line "negotiation from strength" approach of John Foster Dulles and Konrad Adenauer, linking a relaxation of Cold War tensions to tangible progress on postwar issues between the two blocs, including German reunification.

---

[8] "The MLF and a Possible Non-Dissemination Agreement," Cable, Hillenbrand to Rusk, October 8, 1964. National Security Archives/Nuclear History Project (hereafter NSA/NHP) doc. no. 1433. Germany's sense of being singled out for discriminatory treatment was reinforced by the likelihood that India, Israel, and other key threshold nuclear states would not sign the NPT.

[9] Officially, Germany supported a "twin-pillar" Atlantic force in which the United States and a majority-controlled European entity would both hold vetos. This concept was distinct from the Gaullist idea of a European nuclear force operated independently from the United States. See, respectively, Kai-Uwe von Hassel, "Organizing Western Defense," Foreign Affairs, January 1965; and Franz-Josef Strauss, "An Alliance of Continents," International Affairs, April 1965.

To divorce superpower détente from the resolution of these underlying conflicts, in this view, would simply reward Soviet intransigence and legitimize Europe's division.

From this perspective, the NPT was suspect. For the most part, U.S. critics of the treaty did not question the goal of nonproliferation itself. They did, however, challenge the idea of a nonproliferation treaty produced through superpower cooperation. They considered the symbolism of such cooperation dangerous and its substantive basis weak. The superpowers' common interest in nonproliferation was "more apparent than real," George Ball contended, since Moscow's main objective was to discredit West Germany and disrupt the Western alliance.[10] Moreover, since most would-be nuclear powers were friendlier to the United States than to the Soviet Union, a nontransfer pledge amounted to a unilateral Western undertaking: In return for narrowing its own future nuclear options, the West would gain nothing from the Soviet Union except a promise to refrain from doing what it would not do in any case. "We should not sacrifice community in the West," Robert Bowie asserted, "for symbolic agreements with the Soviet Union."[11]

Above all, this group believed the benefits of the NPT were unlikely to outweigh the costs of alienating West Germany from American policy. Keenly sensitive to German unease about the treaty, they sympathized with Bonn's reluctance to concede the nuclear option without compensation, and warned against overriding German preferences in pursuit of superpower détente. "Those who argue that we have been oversensitive to German desires and anxieties, and should strive for a bilateral understanding with Moscow," George Ball wrote, "are advocating a dangerous course that repeats the folly of Versailles."[12] Walt Rostow sketched an alarming scenario of what could happen if West Germans were to conclude that Washington was ignoring their interests in favor of a rapprochement with the Soviet Union:

> They will be driven to seek some independent deal with the USSR or a national or bilateral nuclear deal, which would enable them to close the gap between their position and that of the U.K. and France. The possibility of Franco-German production, on French soil, of missiles to be deployed in

---

[10] George Ball, *The Discipline of Power* (Boston: Little, Brown, 1968), p. 212. Similarly, Ball stated in a BBC interview in 1966 that "you have to be very careful in making any large generalizations about the degree of cooperation or the degree of common interest which the United States and the Soviet Union may share." *Department of State Bulletin*, October 25, 1966, p. 653.

[11] *Nominations of Robert R. Bowie and U. Alexis Johnson*, Hearings, Senate Committee on Foreign Relations, 89th Cong., 2nd sess. (1966), p. 41.

[12] Ball, *The Discipline of Power*, p. 157.

France and Germany, with French and German national crews, with the mated warheads under nominal French "custody," will grow.[13]

Arrayed against these NATO traditionalists was a countercoalition that became a kind of NPT lobby. Led bureaucratically by the Arms Control and Disarmament Agency (ACDA), this was a diverse group that drew strength from the convergence of three ascendant policy concerns during the mid-1960s: alarm about the implications of proliferation for American security, as expressed in the Gilpatric Report; the desire to dispose of nuclear sharing once and for all, which was especially strong in the Defense Department and the Joint Committee on Atomic Energy; and support for superpower arms control and détente among a growing segment of the foreign policy community. The NPT thus became a vehicle for challenging a whole range of established U.S. priorities and assumptions.

NPT advocates argued that global proliferation posed a more urgent threat to the United States than NATO's perennial nuclear discontents. If the United States allowed the allied concerns to block progress on the NPT, ACDA's Adrian Fisher argued, it would send a dangerous signal to potential nuclear powers elsewhere and might forfeit the chance to halt proliferation beyond Europe:

> If it appears that because of Alliance needs we have abandoned our efforts to prevent proliferation of national capability . . . we will in effect have given a green light to states now poised at the point of decision. . . . Our posture with respect to our allies, therefore, will materially affect the course of other potential nuclear powers.[14]

Turning Bonn's alleged nuclear ambitions against the advocates of nuclear sharing, Fisher argued that the spread of the bomb to India, Israel, and others would make the MLF irrelevant as a vehicle for containing those ambitions, since then "the Germans would not remain content with MLF participation nor even with some evolution of the MLF under the 'European Clause.'"[15]

For many supporters of the NPT, however, the main problem with nuclear sharing was not its mixed message to potential proliferators but its role as an irritant in U.S.-Soviet relations. "Our constant coming back . . . to the possible collective approach of an Atlantic nuclear force,"

---

[13] "Arms Control and the Alliance; Or How to Persuade Allies to Make Peace," Memo from Rostow (Director of Policy Planning) to Rusk, April 6, 1964, NSA/NHP doc. no. 975. Rostow succeeded McGeorge Bundy as Johnson's national security advisor in 1966. The prospect of a Franco-German nuclear entente—the nightmare of U.S. Europeanists and dream of German Gaullists—was in fact greatly exaggerated by both, since France had even less desire than the United States in seeing Germany acquire control over nuclear weapons.

[14] "Non-Proliferation of Nuclear Weapons and the MLF," Memo from Adrian Fisher (Acting Director, ACDA) to Rusk, June 15, 1964, NSA/NHP doc. no. 965.

[15] Fisher, "Non-Proliferation."

Senator Wayne Morse complained, "is bound to set us back in our relationships with the Soviet Union."[16] From this perspective, the treaty stood for a thaw in the Cold War whose value transcended its subject matter. Similarly, the MLF campaign and its excesses were seen as emblematic of the misplaced and obsolete priorities of the traditionalists. Thus, pro-NPT liberals like Senator Frank Church challenged such central tenets of Europeanist faith as deference to Bonn, support for European integration à la Monnet, and zealous anti-Gaullism.[17]

In contrast to the traditionalists, these advocates regarded an accommodation between the superpowers, with arms control its leading edge, as more important than new initiatives catering to allied preferences. "Our refusal to drop the European clause," Church argued, "seems to indicate that we have decided it is more important to bind West Germany more tightly to a truncated NATO than to improve relations with the Soviet Union. I think our priority is wrong."[18]

The argument for superpower détente was a rejection of the Dulles-Adenauer "negotiation-from-strength" approach. It held that progress on the German problem and other Cold War conflicts would come only as a consequence, rather than a precondition, of closer superpower relations. The hard-line approach, in this view, would only freeze the status quo indefinitely, blocking the settlement it was ostensibly intended to bring about. Thus, Bonn's hope of linking its NPT adherence to Soviet concessions was self-deluding. "Some in Germany," McGeorge Bundy told the Foreign Relations Committee, "have suggested that they could somehow bargain with Moscow on the topic of their nuclear restraint. I believe there is no bargain here, certainly none that Americans can support." The goal of U.S. policy, Bundy added, should be "not strength, but settlement."[19]

GENEVA, PHASE I: NPT VERSUS MLF

The ENDC turned its full attention to the NPT in the summer of 1965 amid growing evidence of Western disarray on the nonproliferation issue. The approach of the Geneva talks produced several intimations that the

---

[16] *United States Policy Toward Europe*, Hearings, Senate Foreign Relations Committee, 89th Cong., 2nd sess. (1966), p. 241.

[17] Sen. Church questioned whether a unified, nuclear-armed Europe would even be in the interests of the United States or of greater global stability: "Is it not just possible that a loose association of European countries . . . might turn out to be the safer arrangement? . . . Can we really be so confident that a United Western Europe would always remain our faithful partner?" Frank Church, "United States Policy and the 'New Europe,'" *Foreign Affairs*, October 1966, p. 53.

[18] Church, "United States Policy," p. 54.

[19] *United States Policy Toward Europe*, Hearings, pp. 6–7.

United States might concede the NATO sharing option to obtain an agreement. At the NATO foreign ministers meeting in May, Defense Secretary McNamara proposed the creation of a special allied committee for nuclear consultation at the Defense Minister level. Though not officially an alternative to the MLF approach, the idea quickly gained a following among arms control officials and members of Congress hostile to nuclear sharing.

Another straw in the wind was the article by ACDA Director William Foster in the July 1965 issue of *Foreign Affairs*. In the article, Foster identified the NPT as the most urgent business of East-West relations and called for a "reassessment of priorities" to bring the full weight of U.S. diplomacy behind it. This was widely read as a call to jettison the MLF/ANF if necessary to get a treaty, an impression that was reinforced by Foster's equanimity at the prospect of an "erosion" of Atlantic relations due to U.S.-Soviet cooperation on nonproliferation.[20] Then, on July 1, the *New York Times* leaked the story of the Gilpatric committee, reporting its advice "that a treaty to halt the spread of nuclear weapons be given priority over the establishment of an Atlantic nuclear force."[21]

Bonn reacted swiftly and angrily to these hints. At a news conference prompted by the *Times* story, Schroeder warned against taking Germany's nonnuclear status for granted and laid down two preconditions for its adherence to a nonproliferation agreement—"substantial and irrevocable steps" toward German reunification, and the prior creation of a collective NATO force:

> Some form of nuclear organization must be found which satisfies the security requirements of the non-atomically armed NATO members. . . . If this can be achieved by the establishment of a multilateral atomic deterrent force or something similar, Germany could abstain from the acquisition of her own nuclear weapons vis-à-vis her allies.[22]

The Johnson administration disclaimed official policy status for the Foster article and Gilpatric report and assured Germany that "our posi-

---

[20] William Foster, "New Directions in Arms Control and Disarmament," *Foreign Affairs*, July 1965, p. 600.

[21] *New York Times*, July 1, 1965, p. 1. The report's actual language was somewhat more hedged: "We would hope that our strong non-dissemination objectives in connection with any arrangements for Atlantic nuclear sharing would make it possible for the Soviets to join in a non-proliferation treaty despite the pendency of an MLF/ANF. This problem may not become critical until the future of MLF/ANF is known; but if it arises strongly before then, the relative priorities of the two proposals should be reviewed." *A Report to the President*, pp. 6–7.

[22] *Documents on Disarmament, 1965*, p. 276. In a clarification issued ten days later, Bonn stated that, while as a matter of national policy it had no intention of seeking its own nuclear weapons, it was not willing to assume a formal treaty obligation vis-à-vis the Soviet Union to that effect "without corresponding concessions." London *Times*, July 13, 1965, p. 12.

tion on MLF is unchanged . . . there will be no change."[23] But the awkwardness of the U.S. balancing act was apparent as Washington sought an allied mandate for Geneva at the July meeting of the NATO Council. While agreeing that a collective NATO force option should be protected, the allies divided sharply on the "European option." Britain presented treaty language that flatly ruled out the transfer of nuclear control to a joint force through the surrender of a nuclear-state veto. Bonn insisted that this possibility—which represented its only real hope of equal nuclear status with France and Britain—be explicitly kept open.

With its allies at cross-purposes, the United States produced a compromise draft treaty which it presented to the ENDC on August 17. In language crafted to accommodate both MLF and a future European force under majority control, the proposal required the nuclear states not "to transfer any nuclear weapons into the national control of any nonnuclear state, either directly or indirectly through a military alliance," or to "take any other action which would cause an increase in the total number of States and other organizations having independent power to use nuclear weapons." As explained by William Foster, the proposal would not prevent the establishment of a multilateral force "so long as such arrangements would not constitute an additional organization or entity having the power to use nuclear weapons independently of the participating nations presently possessing nuclear weapons." However, "a new organization having such power could come into existence . . . if a present nuclear nation should voluntarily turn over its entire stockpile of nuclear weapons to a collective entity and should also renounce its right of veto over the collective force." To exclude this possibility, he argued, could prejudice the ability of a future united Europe to provide for its own defense.[24]

The U.S. draft fared poorly on all sides. In Germany, then in the midst of an election campaign, the nonproliferation talks became an explosive political issue. Within days of the presentation of the American proposal, U.S. policy was denounced in widely publicized statements by the leading German Gaullists. Franz-Joseph Strauss likened the U.S. draft to the Treaty of Versailles; Adenauer pronounced it "a surrender of Europe to the Russians."[25] Erhard, who had unenthusiastically backed the U.S. draft, vigorously denied a sellout of Bonn's interests at Geneva, but took a more assertive stance on Germany's right to nuclear equality within the alliance. In a postelection speech to the Bundestag, he warned that failure to create a joint

---

[23] *New York Times*, July 25, 1965, p. 1. The message was communicated via Averill Harriman, meeting with Adenauer in Bonn.

[24] *Documents on Disarmament, 1965*, p. 347. As Foster's statement implied, this formula was meant to allow France or Britain to vest their national deterrents in a European force; it would not have allowed the surrender of the U.S. veto over forces contributed to a joint force, since there was no chance that the United States would turn its entire nuclear arsenal over to such a force.

[25] *New York Times*, August 20, 1965, p. 14, and August 27, 1965, p. 7.

nuclear force would be an "injustice" to Germany and promised "energetic efforts to ensure that no system of disarmament, relaxation or security measures is established on the concept of a divided Germany."[26]

London distanced itself from the U.S. draft on the opposite side, believing that it leaned too far toward nuclear sharing. The British disarmament minister, Lord Chalfont, told the ENDC that the United Kingdom was "irrevocably opposed to any formulations for the Western alliance which might have the effect of making the use of nuclear weapons subject to a majority vote as distinct from a unanimous vote or at least a vote in which existing nuclear countries have the power of veto."[27]

The Soviet Union depicted the U.S. draft as an attempt to legitimize German access to nuclear weapons. Moscow countered with a text that categorically banned nuclear sharing and seemed also to rule out the "two-key" arrangements governing NATO nuclear forces deployed in Europe. Emphasizing the concept of possession rather than control, the Soviet draft pledged the nuclear powers not to transfer nuclear weapons "in any form—directly or indirectly, through third States or groups of States not possessing nuclear weapons and not to accord to such States or groups of States the right to participate in the ownership, control or use of nuclear weapons."[28]

The United States continued to insist on the compatibility of its nuclear sharing and nonproliferation policies. "We don't accept the idea," Rusk told a press conference in November 1965, "that a priority, as between these two important problems, is to be accepted or acknowledged."[29] But the increasingly fractious debate within the administration belied this claim. By early 1966, the continental allies and their sympathizers in the State Department were fighting a rearguard action to preserve the sharing option, while ACDA and the Pentagon were pushing to establish McNamara's consultative formula as a substitute for a "hardware" force.[30]

---

[26] *Documents on Disarmament, 1965*, pp. 523–26.

[27] *Documents on Disarmament, 1965*, p. 360.

[28] The Soviet draft also barred the transfer of control over weapons or their "emplacement and use" to "units of the armed forces or military personnel of States not possessing nuclear weapons, even if such units or personnel are under the command of a military alliance." *Documents on Disarmament, 1965*. p. 443.

[29] *Department of State Bulletin*, November 29, 1965, p. 857.

[30] Erhard's failure to gain a public reaffirmation of MLF when he met with Johnson in December 1965 was seen as an indication that the tide was running against him. See *New York Times*, December 22, 1965, p. 10. In February 1966, the NATO Nuclear Planning Working Group met for the first time and was dominated by the dispute over sharing and the NPT. Britain urged dropping the MLF/ANF in order to unblock the Geneva talks. Italy and Germany made it clear they did not view consultation as a substitute for a joint force. As the London *Times* (February 19, 1966, p. 8) reported, they were "more interested in a meaningful solution to the NATO nuclear problem than in an arrangement designed in part to make a nonproliferation treaty possible." See also *New York Times*, February 23, 1966, p. 1.

In March, the United States offered an amended draft—summarily rejected by the Soviets—that still allowed for sharing but inched closer to banning any surrender of a nuclear-state veto. In the new version of the U.S. Article I, nuclear weapon states were forbidden to "transfer nuclear weapons into the national control of any non-nuclear-weapon State, or into the control of any association of non-nuclear-weapon States." "Control" was defined as "the right or ability to fire nuclear weapons without the concurrent decision of an existing nuclear-weapon state." The Soviets argued that the American focus on "control" was overly narrow and in fact legitimized the dissemination of nuclear weapons, "since, if these weapons did not fall into the hands of other, non-nuclear powers, the question of the veto would not arise."[31]

While the ENDC impasse continued, the bureaucratic struggle in Washington moved toward a resolution in the spring and summer of 1966. In April, the *New York Times* reported that the administration had decided to abandon all plans for a NATO nuclear force, prompting a vigorous denial from the State Department: "The United States regards the problem of nuclear sharing as major unfinished business . . . [and] has made no decision to foreclose a possible Atlantic nuclear force or any other collective approach to this problem."[32] But NPT advocates were now intensifying their efforts to break the logjam by taking the issue to the President directly. Personally engaged in the controversy for the first time, Johnson decided to give priority to the NPT. At a July 5 press conference, he signaled to both the Soviets and the State Department that the United States was prepared to give way on the NATO sharing issue:

> We are doing everything we can to reach an agreement. . . . We are very anxious to do it. We hope the Soviet Union will meet us and find an acceptable compromise in language which we both can live with. . . . We are going to do everything within the power of our most imaginative people to find language which will bring the nuclear powers together.[33]

When Johnson met with Erhard in late September, there was no public mention of NATO sharing. In October, Johnson delivered a major speech announcing a policy of "bridge building" toward the East. In it, he portrayed a Cold War thaw as the prerequisite of a European settlement rather than a reward for Soviet concessions. German reunification, he stated, "can only be accomplished through a growing reconciliation. There is no shortcut."[34] Three days later he met

---

[31] *Documents on Disarmament, 1966*, pp. 159–60, 201.

[32] *Department of State Bulletin*, May 16, 1966, p. 768.

[33] *New York Times*, July 6, 1966, p. 1. On the campaign by pro-NPT forces for Johnson's ear, see Seaborg, *Stemming the Tide*, pp. 183ff.

[34] *New York Times*, October 8, 1966, p. 12. On Germany's reaction to the speech, see "Indignation in Bonn," ibid., October 18, 1966.

with Gromyko, and the two leaders indicated that the NPT deadlock was broken.[35]

There only remained to find a face-saving formula to cover the U.S. retreat. The language was worked out in secret U.S.-Soviet talks and agreed to on December 5.[36] In the meantime, the Erhard government fell and was replaced by a "grand coalition" of the Christian Democrats under Kurt Keisinger—who became chancellor—and the Social Democrats under Willy Brandt. The change of government in Bonn eased the task of disengaging from the sharing issue, though it by no means disposed of German qualms about the treaty.

The new U.S.-Soviet text, which became Article I of the draft treaty put forth by the superpowers the following August, officially buried the collective nuclear force option: "Each nuclear-weapon State Party to this Treaty undertakes not to transfer to any recipient whatsoever nuclear weapons or other nuclear explosive devices or control over such weapons or explosive devices directly or indirectly." A companion Article II obliged the nonnuclear states not to receive nuclear explosive devices or control over them from any source, nor to "manufacture or otherwise seek to acquire" them.

The United States presented the accord to the allies at the December 1966 NATO Council meeting, which also enacted McNamara's consultative scheme by approving the creation of a permanent Nuclear Planning Group. As interpreted by the United States, Article I ruled out any force involving the joint ownership or custody of nuclear weapons, even if existing nuclear powers kept a veto over their use. It did not affect existing NATO arrangements for the transfer of delivery systems to nonnuclear allies, or the deployment of nuclear weapons on allied territory.

On the "European option," the United States maintained that the NPT "would not bar succession by a new federated European state to the nuclear status of one of its former components."[37] Bonn complained that the U.S. interpretation was overly strict with regard to the degree of political unity Europe must achieve in order to succeed to nuclear weapons, but did not press the issue. Brandt conceded that "it would be neither realistic, nor, from the German point of view, wise, to go beyond what is said in the pertinent American interpretation."[38]

---

[35] *New York Times*, October 12, 1966, p. 1; *Documents on Disarmament, 1966*, pp. 655–57.

[36] Seaborg, *Stemming the Tide*, pp. 194ff.

[37] For U.S. interpretations of the treaty's impact on alliance nuclear cooperation, see *Nonproliferation Treaty*, Hearings before the Senate Foreign Relations Committee, Pt. I, 90th Cong., 2nd sess., pp. 262–63. See also Mason Willrich, "The Treaty on Nonproliferation of Nuclear Weapons," *Yale Law Journal* 77–78 (1968), pp. 1470–77. Johnson reaffirmed the U.S. view that a united Europe would be eligible to become a nuclear power in a letter to Bonn. See *New York Times*, March 30, 1966, p. 1.

[38] *Treaty on the Non-Proliferation of Nuclear Weapons; German Attitudes and Contribution: Documentation* (Bonn: Office of Press and Information, 1969), p. 47.

GENEVA, PHASE II: ATOMS FOR PEACE REVISITED

The agreement on Articles I and II ended one phase of the NPT controversy only to open another. The negotiations dragged on for another year
and a half, prolonged by the efforts of the nonnuclear states to extract
concessions that would make the treaty a more balanced package of
"mutual responsibilities and obligations." On the whole, these efforts
were unavailing. The superpowers resisted all but a token commitment to
nuclear disarmament (Article VI pledged them to "pursue negotiations in
good faith" to end the arms race) and refused to extend meaningful
security guarantees to nonnuclear states. Within the West, the main focus
of this second phase of the talks was the treaty's impact on peaceful nuclear
development. This issue was debated in an atmosphere strongly colored
by allied resentment over the superpower fait accompli on Articles I and
II, and found the United States again cross-pressured by the competing
demands of alliance solidarity and superpower cooperation.

The European allies, joining with Japan and with civil nuclear powers
in the nonaligned world, demanded assurances that the treaty would not
adversely affect their peaceful nuclear power programs, whether by
imposing an onerous burden of inspections or by restricting their access to
fissile materials and the full range of fuel-cycle technologies. The stakes
were especially high for those countries, like West Germany and Japan,
with plans to develop plutonium-fueled fast breeder reactors. Fearing
that the treaty might prejudice their domestic energy plans, their competitiveness in world nuclear markets, and their broader technological
development, these states insisted that NPT discrimination not spill over
from the weapons field to civil nuclear development. The new German
government announced in early 1967 that this issue would now be the
litmus test of the treaty's acceptability to Bonn.[39]

Inspections under the NPT were to be far more extensive than in the
original Atoms for Peace program. To verify their compliance with the
treaty, nonweapon states were to submit their entire nuclear programs,
rather than just imported materials, to safeguards. In these circum-

---

[39] Brandt called this "the most important prerequisite" of German adherence to the treaty.
Acknowledging that "Germany is no longer a major military power," he stated that
"Germany's role and its future influence will be determined by whether or not we shall
succeed in holding the front line economically and scientifically in matters of technology
and quality, or even reaching the top. In this matter, a nonproliferation treaty must not be
an obstacle—and this is a really vital matter." See *Documents on Disarmament, 1967*, pp.
95–96. See also Lawrence Scheinman, *The International Atomic Energy Agency and
World Nuclear Order* (Washington, DC: Resources for the Future, 1988), pp. 152ff;
and Peter Pringle and James Spigelman, *The Nuclear Barons* (New York: Holt, Rinehart
and Winston, 1981), pp. 301ff. In addition to its commitment to the fast breeder, Germany
was also determined to protect its participation with Britain and the Netherlands in the
URENCO consortium for centrifuge uranium enrichment, which had been created in the
early 1960s.

stances, concern about the intrusiveness of inspections—and the resulting danger that they might lead to industrial espionage or otherwise place
nonweapon states at a commercial disadvantage—became an abiding
preoccupation of Germany, Japan, and other civil nuclear states.

For members of the European community there was another source
of misgivings. Submission under the NPT to International Atomic Energy
Agency (IAEA) safeguards, as envisaged by the superpowers, would
dilute the role of the EURATOM, which was responsible for inspecting
the nuclear programs of its member states. Germany and Italy fought this
substitution, and the United States at first accommodated them by providing, in the August 1965 draft treaty, for "IAEA or equivalent" safeguards. But the Soviet Union refused to allow what it called "self-inspection" by the Europeans, and depicted Bonn's reservations on safeguards
as a cover for nuclear weapons ambitions.[40] Moscow was again finding the
NPT negotiations a convenient forum for exploiting Western divisions.

And again the United States sided with its superpower adversary to
the dismay of its allies. By 1967 the United States was pressing for a single
system of IAEA-administered controls. Defending the shift, Rusk argued
that an exemption for EURATOM would undercut international confidence in the treaty and encourage "groupings in other parts of the world
who might wish to put together a little family group which would inspect
itself and deny outside inspection."[41] In response, EURATOM declared
the American approach a threat to the entire movement for European
unity and a violation of agreements for nuclear cooperation between the
United States and the European Community.

The safeguards dispute delayed the tabling of a complete draft treaty
for a full year, until January 1968. (The superpowers submitted a partial
draft, with the inspection article blank, in August 1967.) Over this time
the United States grew increasingly impatient with what it saw as
gratuitous allied obstructionism; privately, U.S. officials accused Germany of trying to sabotage the treaty.[42] The allies, in turn, their
suspicions and resentments heightened by U.S. pressure, protested
alleged U.S. strong-arm tactics (such as the delay of U.S. nuclear-fuel
shipments to Europe) aimed at bringing them to terms. While the U.S.
did not overtly exploit its supplier leverage, the heavy allied depend-

---

[40] In a typical statement, Soviet ENDC delegate Roshchin charged that "behind all the
alleged concern about economic needs [lies] the well-known policy of the militarist and
revanchist forces in the FRG aimed at obtaining access to nuclear weapons." *Documents on
Disarmament, 1967*, p. 144.

[41] German TV interview, in *Department of State Bulletin*, March 6, 1967, p. 360. Denying
that the treaty would inhibit commercial nuclear development, Rusk insisted that the
NPT had "nothing to do with the use of nuclear materials for peaceful purposes." On
the U.S. bureaucratic politics of the safeguards issue, see Seaborg, *Stemming the Tide*,
pp. 275ff.

[42] See London *Times*, February 4, 1967, p. 6.

ence on the American-supplied enriched-uranium fuel loomed in the background of the quarrel.[43]

The EURATOM issue was ultimately finessed; the final wording of NPT Article III required not IAEA safeguards as such, but "safeguards as set forth in an agreement" with the Vienna agency. This solution preserved a role for EURATOM inspections while making them subject to external verification by the IAEA. The details of the arrangement were to be spelled out in a future agreement between the two organizations. In effect, this postponed the hard bargaining to a later stage. EURATOM members signed the treaty with the proviso that ratification would be deferred pending negotiation of an acceptable safeguards agreement with the IAEA, a process that took until 1972 and left persistent tensions between the organizations.[44]

Another key compromise—responding to European and Japanese objections to intrusive safeguards—was an agreement to confine inspections to certain "strategic points" in the operation of nuclear facilities. The concept of strategic points was at variance with the IAEA charter's provision for safeguards access "at all times to all places and date and to any person," but was in keeping with the past practice of watering down nuclear controls to make them politically acceptable.[45]

The permissive spirit of Atoms for Peace was also honored in Article IV of the treaty, which affirmed the "inalienable right of all the Parties to the Treaty to develop research, production, and use of nuclear energy for peaceful purposes without discrimination and in conformity with Articles I and II of the Treaty." The United States assured Germany and Japan that, under this provision, civil nuclear programs could be carried into areas with direct relevance to weapons production. "Neither uranium enrichment nor the stockpiling of fissionable material in connection with a peaceful program would violate Article II so long as these activities were safeguarded under Article III," William Foster explained to the Senate; "also clearly permitted would be the development, under safeguards, of

---

[43] See *New York Times*, March 2, 1967, p. 6, and April 10, 1967, p. 1. Rusk's response to European concerns about the reliability of U.S. fuel exports hinted at U.S. leverage in this area: "There is no reason why such deliveries could not take place under a non-proliferation treaty to which EURATOM members subscribe; in fact, it may well facilitate such transactions in the future." Cited in *Documents on Disarmament, 1967*, pp. 96–98.

[44] Scheinman, *The International Atomic Energy Agency*, pp. 159–60.

[45] See Scheinman, *The International Atomic Energy Agency*, pp. 156–67. The same lowest-common-denominator approach governed the setting of criteria for safeguards effectiveness under the NPT. It proved impossible, as it had from the start of Atoms for Peace, to mandate the specific detection standards (warning times and material quantities) needed to provide confidence against diversions of fissile uranium or plutonium. As a result, the criteria established by the IAEA are treated as detection goals rather than requirements.

plutonium-fueled power reactors, including research on the properties of metallic plutonium. . . . "[46]

Article IV stopped short of establishing a legal obligation on the part of supplier countries to cooperate fully with peaceful nuclear programs. Persistent efforts, led by Italy, to write nuclear-supply guarantees into the treaty were unsuccessful. Nonetheless, the treaty did create a strong presumption of unfettered cooperation, obliging suppliers to "facilitate . . .the fullest possible exchange of equipment, materials and scientific and technological information for the peaceful uses of nuclear energy."

In sum, the NPT debates on peaceful uses produced an equivocal outcome. While they essentially reaffirmed the Atoms for Peace philosophy, they also left a concern on the part of non-nuclear-weapon states that the rules of peaceful nuclear development might be manipulated to their political and economic disadvantage. The negotiations thus set the stage for future controversies when the United States sought to tighten those rules several years later.

COMMENTARY: THE NPT AND THE ALLIANCE

As a measure of America's interest in nonproliferation, the course of the NPT negotiations represented both less and more than appeared on the surface. Less, because the treaty did not represent a basic change in the goal of nonproliferation: it was essentially a new approach to a familiar goal. More, because it linked the pursuit of that goal to a broader shift in U.S. policy toward the Soviet Union, and thus had a foreign policy significance that went well beyond the particulars of the Geneva debates.

The trauma of the gradual U.S. retreat on nuclear sharing was ironic. In the final analysis, both MLF and the NPT were nonproliferation policies, and both were attempts to contain the problem of Germany's nuclear aspirations. This basic affinity was sometimes obscured by the way the debate was framed in the United States, where the two policies were cast as symbols of competing priorities, and by the Soviet campaign against MLF. But it was recognized by Gaullists in France and Germany, who opposed both policies as attempts to reinforce Europe's subordination to U.S. hegemony. Indeed, both the MLF and the NPT were vulnerable to the criticism that they were "made-in-U.S.A" designs forced upon reluctant allies.

Beyond these similarities, though, was the crucial political difference between MLF and the NPT. The former was designed, however dubiously, to reassure Germany and promote alliance solidarity, even in the

---

[46] Cited in Scheinman, *The International Atomic Energy Agency*, p. 29. See also Charles N. Van Doren, *Nuclear Supply and Non-Proliferation: The IAEA Committee on Assurance of Supply*, Report for the Congressional Research Service of the U.S. Library of Congress (Washington, DC, October 1983), pp. 100–101.

face of strong Soviet opposition; the latter reassured the Soviet Union and promoted superpower accommodation in the face of strong German opposition. While both reflected the U.S. desire to face the other superpower in full control of the West's nuclear deterrent, the shift from MLF to NPT symbolized the difference, in Stanley Hoffmann's words, between "bipolarity as a duel" and "bipolarity as a duopoly."[47]

This shift would have been wrenching for the alliance in any event, but the U.S. handling of the NPT negotiations made it especially so. In retrospect, the failure to kill the MLF cleanly before the NPT negotiations began was a serious error. It made the MLF a political stake greatly disproportionate to its actual merits and prospects, and gave the Soviets an opening to use the negotiations to play upon NATO's divisions. The sharing issue played into Soviet hands because it was an area where the tension in U.S. policy between superpower collaboration and alliance solidarity was acute.

As the negotiations progressed, the United States was in the awkward position of going to ever greater lengths to emphasize the innocuous character of the MLF. But at the same time, the talks made it harder for the United States to drop the scheme on its merits, and to be seen as doing so. Instead, the evolving U.S. position looked like a series of concessions to the Soviet Union; when the sharing impasse was finally resolved, it was difficult to avoid the conclusion that the Soviets had been given a hand in shaping Western defense arrangements.[48] In effect, Moscow had used the negotiations to call the U.S. bluff on MLF, unmasking America's basic antipathy to meaningful nuclear sharing.

The unfolding of the negotiations thus encouraged the view that the NPT had come at the expense of the allies—that the United States had chosen "Geneva over NATO."[49] But this perception was not simply the result of clumsy U.S. tactics; it was inherent in the whole enterprise. It was inevitable that the negotiations would feed the allies' familiar nightmare of a superpower deal over their heads to keep Europe weak and divided. The NPT was especially likely to evoke these fears because both its medium (U.S.-Soviet cooperation) and its message (freezing the nuclear status quo) underscored the issues that divided the United States from its allies rather than those that unified them.

Moreover, the treaty served to reinforce allied dependence on the United States even as the process of superpower accommodation cast

[47] Stanley Hoffman, *Gulliver's Troubles* (New York: McGraw-Hill, 1968), p. 407.

[48] See Gerhard Wettig, "Soviet Policy on the Nonproliferation of Nuclear Weapons," *Orbis*, Winter 1969.

[49] See Bader, *The United States and the Spread of Nuclear Weapons*. In a statement typical of conservative criticism of the treaty, Rep. Paul Findley (R-Ill.) charged that "it has been the conscious policy of the Johnson Administration to sacrifice cohesion in the Atlantic Alliance on political and military matters in order to achieve bipolar cooperation with the Soviet Union." *Nonproliferation Treaty*, Hearings, p. 176.

doubt on the Cold War assumptions and presumed community of interests that had legitimized this dependence. As such, it raised basic questions about the meaning and purpose of NATO in an era of détente.
Expanding the terms of the earlier debates over the Grand Design and
the MLF, where the issue was the structure of the alliance, the NPT
focused attention on the question of its goals. For the allies, the Geneva
talks offered disquieting evidence that U.S. and European interests
might diverge here. Chancellor Keisinger put the matter bluntly in the
wake of the U.S.-Soviet fait accompli of late 1966:

> It is our task to find out how far American interests coincide with our own,
> with German and European interests, and how far they do not or do no
> longer coincide. At the height of the Cold War these interests were naturally
> largely identical. Since then, however, this curious, almost paradoxical situa-
> tion has developed, which apparently has not been correctly grasped by any
> diplomacy. The Alliance continues on. The antagonisms continue. But on top
> of this, a form of nuclear complicity or common nuclear responsibility has
> taken shape which forces these antagonists closer and closer together.[50]

In its more conspiratorial versions, the idea of a U.S.-Soviet "condominium" devoted to perpetuating the joint supremacy of the superpowers
was clearly overdrawn. (This theory was the leitmotif of French and
Chinese polemics against the NPT.) Nevertheless, there was some plau-
sibility to allied fears that Washington increasingly valued the alliance in
static rather than evolutionary terms—as an instrument of control and
stability rather than as a means of nurturing Europe's recovery and unity
and overcoming its East-West partition—and had come to view the ideal
European security arrangement as "a friendlier and more stable version of
the status quo."[51]

As the second phase of the NPT negotiations made clear, allied
misgivings on this score extended to the economic as well as the strategic
sphere. The debates on safeguards and peaceful uses occurred against the
background of an increasingly competitive trade environment and growing European concern about an Atlantic "technology gap." In this setting,
allied sensitivities about possible commercial discrimination or a downgrading of EURATOM under the NPT were heightened. Close to the
surface of the disputes on these issues was a European suspicion that the
United States was reassessing its interest in an economically vital and
unified European partner. As Robert Osgood observed, the allies' resentment of the NPT was strongly linked to their

---

[50] Address to CDU editors, February 17, 1967, in *Documents on Disarmament, 1967*,
p. 107.

[51] Hassner, "Change and Security in Europe," p. 15. On the evolutionary or "revisionist"
purposes of the Atlantic alliance, see Karl Kaiser, "The United States and the EEC in the
Atlantic System," *Journal of Common Market Studies*, June 1967.

growing dissatisfaction . . . with the disparity of power—technological-industrial as well as military and diplomatic—between them and the United States and their anxiety that American preponderance and wealth might consign them permanently to a second-class status. Their dissatisfaction and anxiety were aggravated by the fear that United States-Soviet cooperation, as in the proposed non-proliferation treaty, might operate in such a way as to discriminate against the allies in a whole range of military, political, and technological matters.[52]

These undercurrents of the NPT negotiations help explain why the treaty became such a focus of controversy between the United States and its allies. They are also evidence of a U.S. failure to integrate its alliance and nonproliferation policies smoothly. In some respects, the tensions between the two policies were eased by the course of events. Most important, Bonn's adoption of its own strategy of bridge-building to the East, Willy Brandt's "Ostpolitik," softened the conflict between U.S. and German approaches to détente.[53] Making a virtue of necessity, Brandt accepted the NPT as a way of reassuring Moscow and thereby "increasing our political freedom of action."[54] Placing the treaty in the context of his Ostpolitik, he described it as a step toward "lasting détente in Europe and a peace arrangement which will allow the Germans to end their separation."[55] Bonn signed the NPT in November 1969.

Nevertheless, there remained a large residue of allied resentment and distrust from the NPT negotiations. Perhaps the most costly result of America's policy at Geneva was that it encouraged the view that non-proliferation was a distinctly "superpower interest" of the United States rather than a "public interest" in which the allies also shared.

THE NPT AND AMERICAN COMMITMENTS

It was not only in promoting U.S.-Soviet détente that NPT reflected America's superpower interests. The treaty had another contextual meaning that helps explain why the U.S. pursued it with such vigor at the time that it did. It was no accident that the period of the treaty negotiations corresponded to the high-water mark of America's postwar global activism. As U.S. foreign policy entered a more expansive, interventionist

---

[52] Robert E. Osgood, *Alliances and American Foreign Policy* (Baltimore: Johns Hopkins Press, 1971), p. 58. For a discussion of the NPT in the context of the "technology gap," see Bruce L. R. Smith, "The Non-Proliferation Treaty and East-West Detente," *Journal of International Affairs* XXII-1 (1968), pp. 97–105.

[53] See Nye, "The Superpowers and the NPT," p. 172.

[54] *Documents on Disarmament, 1967*, p. 92.

[55] Statement of April 27, 1967. *Treaty on the Non-Proliferation of Nuclear Weapons. German Attitude and Contribution*, p. 16.

phase—heralded by John Kennedy's inaugural promise to "pay any price, bear any burden" to defend freedom, and epitomized by the war in Vietnam—the American stake in nonproliferation rose accordingly.

The logic echoed the case for nonproliferation within the Atlantic alliance: the spread of nuclear weapons in a region of vital interest to the United States could increase the risks of containment and threaten American access to the region. This linkage between nonproliferation and American overseas commitments was emphasized by Walt Rostow. Behind the more general arguments for nonproliferation, he argued, was "narrower American interest, rarely articulated; namely that the emergence of additional nuclear-weapons powers could weaken the structure of collective security in the noncommunist world at critical points."[56] The prospect of American security partners in Asia or the Middle East being armed with nuclear weapons posed the same risk of triggering U.S. involvement in a nuclear conflict that had spurred American hostility to de Gaulle's *force de frappe*. The feared result was a U.S. choice between maintaining a presence despite the higher risks or disengaging from the region of proliferation:

> If any state to which the United States was committed produced nuclear weapons and asserted an independent right to fire them, the United States would confront a grave dilemma: to avoid the possibility of another nation— by its own initiative—drawing the United States into nuclear war, the United States would have to dilute or withdraw its security commitment in parts of the world judged vital to the American interest."[57]

In this sense, the NPT was a global version of U.S. policy toward proliferation in Europe. It was McNamara's Athens doctrine writ large, its universalism mirroring the larger gestalt of American foreign policy in the 1960s. The prevailing definition of U.S. security interests and responsibilities in sweeping, undifferentiated terms implied an equally undifferentiated stake in preventing the spread of nuclear weapons. This resistance to establishing priorities was evident in the abstract, mechanistic notion of the proliferation threat that typified official U.S. rhetoric on behalf of the treaty. Thus, McNamara testified that "our national interests are prejudiced by the addition of every nuclear power. . . . I do not think it makes any difference whether it be Sweden or Switzerland or any other nation you claim to name."[58] And William Foster, speaking of the link between proliferation and the probability of nuclear war, argued that "with the increase in numbers, it is a straight mathematical situation."[59] While there may be an element of hyperbole in such statements, they

---

[56] Walt Rostow, *The Diffusion of Power* (New York: Macmillan, 1972), p. 379.

[57] Rostow, *The Diffusion of Power*, p. 380.

[58] *Nonproliferation of Nuclear Weapons*, Hearings, Joint Committee on Atomic Energy, 89th Cong., 2nd sess., p. 89.

[59] *Nonproliferation of Nuclear Weapons*, Hearings, p. 43.

faithfully reflect the concept of a seamless web of worldwide U.S. security interests that was the hallmark of the globalist worldview.[60]

By the same token, the urgency that policymakers attached to non-proliferation owed much to the conviction that a retrenchment from this global pattern of security commitments was unthinkable. This was an important theme of Foster's 1965 *Foreign Affairs* article, which posed a stark choice between nonproliferation and U.S. isolationism:

> In the short run we might successfully avoid involvement in, say, an Asian conflict in which nuclear weapons had a role. But any such success would, I believe, be short-lived and bought at a price that would prove unacceptable in the long run. That price would be a renunciation of our commitments and involvement all over the world—an attempt to return to isolationism at a time when the world is shrinking so rapidly as to make any such policy at best wishful thinking and quite possibly a blueprint for disaster. Despite the gloomy prospects implicit in such a policy, it is highly likely that, in a world of many nuclear powers, considerable pressure would develop—and perhaps it would prove sufficient—to force the United States in just such an isolationist direction. This possibility must surely be considered a major argument for our attempting to stop the spread of nuclear capabilities.[61]

As this passage suggests, Asia had become the immediate focus of U.S. concern about proliferation during the NPT period. Nonproliferation policy thus followed the general eastward shift of U.S. attentions in the 1960s as the European Cold War receded, the Vietnam conflict escalated, and the perceived threat from communist China grew.

The combination of China's nuclear test and the expanding American presence in Vietnam was a potent catalyst for lifting nonproliferation higher on the U.S. security-policy agenda. In 1953, the United States could with relative impunity threaten China with nuclear attack in defense of its local ally South Korea.[62] After 1964, the United States's Asian allies were exposed to the threat of Chinese nuclear blackmail, and the United States risked being embroiled in a nuclear conflict if it came to their aid. The United States thus faced a reprise of the syndrome it had earlier encountered in Europe. Like the Soviet nuclear progress of the late 1950s, the Chinese bomb threatened to increase the risks—and thus erode the credibility—of U.S. extended deterrence in Asia. At the same time, it increased the incentives for proliferation on the part of China's regional rivals and adversaries, which would further compound the risks of American involvement in the region— just at a time when that involvement was steeply rising.

---

[60] For an interesting discussion of the globalist premises of U.S. foreign policy in the Vietnam era, see Robert Tucker, *Nation or Empire* (Baltimore: Johns Hopkins Press, 1968).

[61] Foster, "New Directions in Arms Control and Disarmament," pp. 590–91.

[62] Richard K. Betts, *Nuclear Blackmail and Nuclear Balance* (Washington, DC: Brookings, 1987), pp. 31–47; see also Roger Dingman, "Atomic Diplomacy During the Korean War," and Rosemary J. Foot, "Nuclear Coercion and the Ending of the Korean War," both in *International Security*, 13–3, Winter 1988–89.

Greater U.S. emphasis on nonproliferation was in part a response to this dilemma.[63] It is notable, however, that the opposite response—encouraging proliferation on the part of Japan and India—was entertained by at least some officials. This approach, which recalled the Eisenhower-Dulles flirtation with selective proliferation in NATO, was suggested by Dean Rusk. As before, its logic was straightforward: "Why shouldn't our friends have nuclear weapons now that our enemies have them?"[64] Also underlying this approach was a worry that blanket opposition to proliferation might require the United States to assume excessive commitments for the protection of nonnuclear states.

Rusk's view, which was well outside the mainstream of policy by the mid-1960s, did not prevail and was probably not seriously considered. It did point, however, to the critical question of what the requirements of an effective nonproliferation policy might be. In particular, how far was the United States prepared to go in assuring the security of countries like India in order to dissuade them from developing nuclear weapons?

For nonaligned countries facing severe threats, security guarantees were central.[65] They were the key ingredient needed to make the NPT a package deal meeting their own interests rather than a one-sided renun-

---

[63] So, too, was the U.S. decision, announced by McNamara in September 1967, to develop a thin antiballistic missile (ABM) system—although this decision reflected a variety of motives in addition to the official one of protecting against Chinese nuclear attack. Defending the decision in the ENDC, Adrian Fisher argued that a U.S. ABM would "favor nonproliferation" because it would "provide further assurance of our determination to support our Asian friends against Chinese nuclear blackmail." *Documents on Disarmament, 1967*, p. 405. The ABM decision was not well received by the nonnuclear states. The NATO allies viewed it as further evidence of the displacement of U.S. interest from Europe to Asia; nonaligned countries assailed the superpower double standard that escalated the vertical arms race while trying to halt the horizontal one. See *New York Times*, September 14, 1967, p. 30, and September 20, 1967, p. 18; see also Robert Rothstein, "ABM and Proliferation," *Foreign Affairs*, April 1968; and Lewis A. Frank, "ABM and Nonproliferation: Related Issues," *Orbis*, Spring 1967.

In contrast, some U.S. critics of the NPT—most prominently, the physicist Edward Teller—faulted the treaty's failure to distinguish between offensive and defensive weapons, which blocked the transfer of nuclear ABM systems to U.S. allies. See Teller's testimony in *Nonproliferation Treaty*, Hearings, pp. 181ff.

[64] This paraphrase of Rusk's argument is cited in Seymour Hersh, *The Price of Power: Kissinger in the Nixon White House* (New York: Summit Books, 1983), p. 381. See also Seaborg, *Stemming the Tide*, pp. 132–40, passim. In his own memoirs, Rusk admits to being skeptical of the NPT and of the realism of a continuing U.S. nuclear umbrella over Japan and India. See Dean Rusk, *As I Saw It* (New York: Norton, 1990), p. 342.

[65] See, for example, Mason Willrich, "Guarantees to Non-Nuclear Nations," *Foreign Affairs*, July 1966. The issue was not only of interest to the nonaligned countries; West Germany sought, unsuccessfully, a guarantee of U.S. protection in the event of NATO's dissolution. See *New York Times*, July 6, 1968, p. 1, and July 11, 1968, p. 16. The United States did agree, however, that the end of NATO would be legitimate grounds for Bonn to consider withdrawing from the NPT. The Soviets were, if anything, more diffident than the United States on the issue of security guarantees. See Benjamin S. Lambeth, "Nuclear Proliferation and Soviet Arms Control Policy," *Orbis*, Summer 1970.

ciation of the nuclear option. In the aftermath of the Chinese test, there were indications that the United States understood this. Johnson promised in November 1964 that "the nations that do not seek nuclear weapons can be sure that, if they need our strong support against some threat of nuclear blackmail, then they will have it."[66]

In the final analysis, however, neither superpower was willing to accept binding obligations—beyond their existing alliances—to underwrite the security of NPT parties. Indeed, to do so could have prejudiced the very autonomy and desire to control risks that led them to oppose proliferation in the first place. As one congressional skeptic argued,

> If we get into some kind of multilateral arrangements here in which certain treaty obligations automatically are called up it seems to me we have a pretty major catalyst to get us in some kind of war. That does not seem to me to be a situation that leads to more stability. It seems to be one that leads to less.[67]

Any chance that the United States might have endorsed NPT security guarantees sank in the Vietnam quagmire. As the war dragged on, it eroded domestic consensus on the U.S. global role. Amid growing perceptions that the United States had unwisely become the "world's policeman," domestic support for overseas commitments declined precipitously; and there was scant interest in taking on new ones, even in the good cause of nonproliferation. "This is very troublesome," Rusk told a congressional committee, "because for us to give anyone . . . the kind of assurances which might give them complete comfort would involve a very far-reaching extension of American commitments."[68]

In the end, the only gesture toward NPT security assurances was a joint declaration by the superpowers and Britain in June 1968 promising to respond to nuclear aggression via the UN Security Council (and hence subject to the veto power held by the five permanent members of that body). Asked in Senate testimony whether this measure bound the United States to any responsibilities beyond those already assumed under the UN Charter, Rusk replied, "I would think not . . . both as a matter of law and as a matter of policy."[69]

CONCLUSION

The NPT negotiations straddled two major watersheds of postwar U.S. foreign policy—the onset of superpower détente and the Vietnam war. As this chapter has argued, much of the treaty's foreign policy significance

---

[66] *Department of State Bulletin*, November 2, 1964, p. 610.

[67] Rep. Craig Hosmer, in *Nonproliferation of Nuclear Weapons*, Hearings, Senate Foreign Relations Committee, part I, 90th Cong., 2nd sess., p. 94.

[68] *Arms Control and Disarmament Act Amendments, 1968*, Hearings, House Committee on Foreign Affairs, 90th Cong., 2nd sess., p. 156.

[69] *Nonproliferation Treaty*, Hearings, p. 15.

derived from its linkage to these dominating issues of the Johnson years. The congruence between the NPT and the larger foreign policy agenda of the Johnson administration helps explain why nonproliferation achieved such a high priority in the mid-1960s.

Indeed, the treaty negotiations are a rare case in which the United States was willing to pay high foreign policy costs on behalf of non-proliferation. More often, the trade-off has gone the other way when nonproliferation goals and relations with key security partners have clashed. Johnson decided to pursue the NPT, despite strong allied resistance, because the treaty served his broader interest in a relaxation of the U.S.-Soviet confrontation—an objective he sought both for its own sake (to increase stability and break out of the rigid diplomatic formulas of the Cold War), and to balance the escalating conflict in Asia. By the same token, U.S. critics of the NPT were weakened by their attachment to Cold War policies that were increasingly seen as outdated, and to an essentially fictitious nuclear-sharing option.

As in the 1940s, then, nonproliferation rose to the top of the national security agenda not because of its abstract merits but in large part because it coincided with the perceived requirements of U.S. policy toward the Soviet Union. Just as the imperative of keeping the bomb from the Soviets had driven Truman's policy of denial, the attractions of détente drove Johnson's NPT policy. In both cases, the dictates of Washington's Soviet policy overrode allied qualms. In the 1950s, by contrast (and again in the 1980s), the requirements of a strict nonproliferation policy seemed to conflict with U.S. objectives toward the Soviet Union, and the latter took precedence.

But the NPT negotiations also revealed the limits of U.S. willingness to pay high costs for nonproliferation. American diffidence on security guarantees (and on nuclear disarmament) showed that the U.S. was not prepared to surrender its superpower prerogatives in the pursuit of nonproliferation. This was hardly surprising, since the U.S. interest in nonproliferation had much to do with retaining and protecting those very prerogatives. Nevertheless, this diffidence revealed the underlying ambivalence in U.S. policy and a resulting tension within the nonproliferation regime. The superpower interests served by nonproliferation were not necessarily congruent with the steps needed to make it persuasive to potential nuclear powers.

The post-Vietnam reaction against U.S. foreign commitments compounded this problem. There was considerable historical irony here: America's global security role was an important factor in creating a strong U.S. interest in nonproliferation, and thus in bringing about the NPT; yet the domestic reaction against that role weakened the underpinnings of the treaty just as it was being completed.

The NPT was an important achievement that helped raise the political barriers against proliferation. But the tensions and conflicts that were apparent during the negotiations had a price and made the treaty only a partial success for U.S. policy. Among the industrial nations soon to emerge as leading civil nuclear powers and exporters—especially France, Germany, and Japan—support for the treaty was grudging and equivocal. Among the critical threshold weapons states—especially India and Israel—it was lacking altogether. As a result, the nonproliferation regime that emerged from the NPT talks was in important respects a fragile and incomplete one, as would become apparent within a few years of the treaty's entry into force in 1970.

Chapter
5

Geopolitics and Nonproliferation: India and Israel in U.S. Policy

*A*s a strategy for preventing the spread of nuclear weapons, the Non-Proliferation Treaty was universalistic and abstract. It posited a dichotomy between the nuclear haves and have-nots based on a convenient but greatly oversimplified standard: Nuclear weapon states were those that had exploded a nuclear explosive device prior to 1967; non-nuclear-weapon states were those that had not. Treating each group as homogeneous, the NPT recognized no gradations of nuclear capability or aspiration among the have-nots.

Similarly, considered as a U.S. foreign policy initiative, the treaty did not reflect or allow for the range and variety of American relations with nonnuclear countries. It implied, as noted in the last chapter, an un-differentiated, global U.S. stake in stopping proliferation. Nevertheless, there obviously were critical differences from one country to another. Each case presented the United States with a distinct mix of relationships, interests, and levers of influence; these in turn shaped policymakers' perceptions of the urgency of nonproliferation, the scope for pursuing it, and the possibilities for success. Just as nonproliferation had been insep-arable from broader foreign policy questions in U.S. relations with Euro-pean allies, the same was true beyond NATO. Here again the United States found that applying the general rule of nonproliferation to specific cases was a far from straightforward task that created difficult policy dilemmas and trade-offs.

This chapter looks at two of the most complex cases, tracing the U.S. response to the nuclear challenge posed by India and Israel in the 1960s and early 1970s. Both were leading "threshold" countries at the time of the NPT negotiations, with steadily growing expertise in nuclear technology and widely understood motives for acquiring nuclear weapons. They were therefore important test cases for the treaty. India, which witnessed a lively domestic debate over nuclear weapons and played a leading role in the Geneva talks, became a kind of NPT bellwether: New Delhi's decision would either crown the treaty with success or deal it a telling rebuff.[1] In Israel, where open discussion of the subject was taboo, the nuclear option was pursued behind a veil of secrecy. Both countries ultimately rejected the NPT, their abstentions marking its most conspicuous failures. Over the next few years, both moved deliberately toward weapons capabilities—Israel secretly and India in the guise of a "peaceful nuclear device" exploded in 1974. These developments, and the reactions they evoked from the two countries' adversaries in the Middle East and South Asia, remain at the heart of today's proliferation threat.

Unlike the first round of proliferators, India and Israel were neither formal allies nor Cold War opponents of the United States. While the United States enjoyed generally friendly ties with both, it also had an interest in ties with their respective regional rivals, Pakistan and the moderate Arab states. Over the period spanning the NPT negotiations and the early 1970s, U.S. relations with the two countries developed along quite different lines. While Washington established an increasingly close strategic partnership with Israel, its relations with India became fragile and strained. In each case, however, U.S. attitudes on the nuclear question evolved in a similar fashion—from alarm in the early and mid-1960s, through acquiescence as the NPT was completed, to complacency in the Nixon years.

By 1968, U.S. efforts to convert India and Israel to the cause of nonproliferation, vigorous earlier in the decade, had peaked. In the ensuing years, the Nixon administration relegated nonproliferation to a lower priority in U.S. foreign policy. American diplomacy in the Middle East and South Asia, during a critical transition in the proliferation dynamics of the two regions, suggested both inattention and indifference to the emergence of India and Israel as nuclear powers. The Indian nuclear test and other events of 1974–1975 ended this complacent phase and began a new cycle of U.S. nonproliferation activism, in which India figured as a leading scapegoat and Israel an unspoken exception.

THE PATH TO INDIA'S BOMB

By the time of its 1974 test, India had been challenging U.S. nuclear policy for decades; the new nation had established an ambitious nuclear research program even before its independence in 1947. When the

---

[1] As George Quester notes, the NPT was "drafted clearly to suggest Indian adherence." *The Politics of Nuclear Proliferation* (Baltimore: Johns Hopkins Univ. Press, 1973), p. 57.

United States launched the Atoms for Peace initiative in 1953, India's program was the most advanced in the nonindustrial world.

From the start, the purpose of the program was ambiguous. It was a centerpiece of India's economic development strategy, but was also understood—especially by Homi Bhaba, the program's founding father—to give India an option to build nuclear weapons in the future. Prime Minister Nehru, although personally opposed to nuclear weapons for India, apparently sanctioned this ambiguity and appreciated its political advantages.[2] In any event, given India's nuclear development strategy of maximizing self-sufficiency, no firm choice between an energy and a weapons focus was necessary; the requirements of the two were complementary. India's plans called for a complete and self-contained nuclear fuel cycle, including the reprocessing of spent fuel (a plant for this purpose was announced in 1958) and the recycling of plutonium fuel. Dependence on foreign suppliers, and obligations to them, were to be kept to a minimum.

New Delhi's approach to nuclear development thus clashed implicitly with the U.S. premises underlying Atoms for Peace. Whereas Atoms for Peace envisaged an expanding web of nuclear interdependence as a force for shaping and guiding recipient nuclear programs in peaceful directions, India viewed this model—and the safeguards inspections that went with it—as an icon of neocolonialism. While hostile to the philosophy of Atoms for Peace, India nevertheless recognized the value of foreign assistance, especially in the early stages of its nuclear development, and adopted a pragmatic, opportunistic policy on nuclear cooperation. Under this approach, India would accept foreign assistance as a temporary expedient, while bargaining to keep foreign controls over its program strictly limited in scope and duration. As indigenous capabilities increased and foreign dependence declined, the program would become progressively less encumbered by international controls.

India's strategy was demonstrated in the mid-1950s when it negotiated the acquisition of the CIRUS research reactor—a 40-megawatt plant fueled with natural uranium and ideal for producing plutonium—from Canada. The United States supplied heavy water to be used as the reactor's moderator material. India pledged to use the plant only for peaceful purposes but refused to allow inspections.

The United States became more closely involved with India's nuclear development when General Electric contracted in 1963 to build two power reactors at Tarapur near Bombay. The Tarapur deal, the first export

---

[2] Two useful sources on the motivations and historical development of India's nuclear program are Ashok Kapur, *India's Nuclear Option: Atomic Diplomacy and Decision-Making* (New York: Praeger, 1976); and Shyam Bhatia, *India's Nuclear Bomb* (Ghaziabad, U.P. India: Vikas Publishing House, 1979). For a good summary, see Leonard Spector, *Nuclear Proliferation Today* (New York: Vintage Books, 1984).

of power reactors to the developing world, epitomized both the ideals and the illusions of Atoms for Peace, and eventually became a major irritant in U.S.-Indian relations.[3] At the time, however, the sale was seen as an important U.S. breakthrough not only commercially but also in broader foreign policy terms. American participation in India's peaceful nuclear development, it was expected, would prove an important channel for improved bilateral relations and would help counter Soviet political and economic influence with New Delhi.

In pursuit of these hoped-for advantages, the United States acquiesced in a porous and ambiguous nuclear cooperation agreement for Tarapur. The provisions governing the safeguarding of the reactors and the reprocessing of their fuel were imprecise, sowing the seeds of bitter future disputes. On inspections, the two sides disagreed as to whether the reactors as such would be subject to safeguards, as U.S. policy required, or whether safeguards would be applied only when the plants were being operated with fuel supplied by the United States, as India insisted. This distinction was seemingly finessed by a formula whereby the reactors would be operated only on U.S. low-enriched uranium fuel, or material derived from it, during the 30-year life of the agreement.[4] Unfortunately, this formula failed to ensure that the reactors would continue to be safeguarded at the expiration of the agreement or in the event that it was terminated prematurely.

The agreement was also vague on the reprocessing of Tarapur fuel; it gave India the right to reprocess spent fuel from the reactors in its own facilities, subject to a "joint determination" by the two sides that safeguards could be effectively applied. Whether this implied a simple technical judgment or gave the United States a broader policy veto over Tarapur reprocessing was unclear. Like the issue of inspections, this ambiguity would later assume great importance amid the two countries' falling-out over nuclear policy in the 1970s. Contrary to U.S. hopes, Tarapur failed to lead to further nuclear cooperation between the two countries. India turned to Canada—whose heavy-water-moderated CANDU reactor operated on natural uranium fuel, obviating dependence on foreign enrichment services—for subsequent reactor purchases. Tarapur turned out to be a detour from the mainstream of India's peaceful nuclear development, affording the United States little influence over the course of that development.

---

[3] See Peter A. Clausen, "Nonproliferation Illusions: Tarapur in Retrospect," *Orbis*, Fall 1983. See also Roberta Wohlstetter, "'The Buddha Smiles': Absent-Minded Peaceful Aid and the Indian Bomb," Report for the U.S. Energy Research and Development Administration (Los Angeles: Pan Heuristics, 1977).

[4] The two sides' differing interpretations were formally recorded in Article VI of the agreement. See U.S. Congress, Joint Committee on Atomic Energy, *International Agreements for Cooperation*, Hearings, 88th Cong., 1st sess., September 5, 1963, and 2nd sess., April 22 and June 30, 1964, pp. 37ff.

The fecklessness of the Tarapur deal mirrored a larger failure of U.S. security policies to respond to evolving Indian nuclear weapon incentives. The fit between Washington's Cold War policies and priorities and New Delhi's assessment of its own security needs, though varying over time, was seldom close. In the 1950s, the United States was hostile to Prime Minister Nehru's foreign policy of nonalignment, and enlisted India's main adversary, Pakistan, as an ally in the extension of communist containment to Central and South Asia. India and Pakistan had been enemies since their joint independence from British rule, and had clashed militarily in 1947 over the disputed territory of Kashmir. During the Eisenhower administration, the United States forged multiple security links with Pakistan, including the supply of advanced weapons under the CENTO and SEATO treaties and a 1959 bilateral agreement. Military cooperation between the two countries—though from Washington's standpoint not aimed at India—was inevitably seen as threatening by the latter, which sought to balance the U.S. presence on the subcontinent through a policy of peaceful coexistence with its stronger communist neighbors, China and the Soviet Union.[5]

In the early 1960s, the premises of India's policy were shaken, and its nuclear weapon incentives stimulated, by the appearance of a security threat from China. The two countries fought a brief border war in the Himalayas in November 1962, in which Indian forces were routed. The shock of this defeat, followed by reports of China's progress toward nuclear weapons, produced the first stirrings of a bomb lobby in Indian domestic politics. When China exploded its first atomic bomb in October 1964, calls for an Indian response multiplied.[6] Encouraged by Homi Bhaba's announcement that India possessed the technical and economic resources to produce a bomb within eighteen months, supporters of nuclear weapons in both the ruling Congress Party and the opposition became more vocal. Although Prime Minister Shastri, who had succeeded Nehru earlier in the year, shared his predecessor's opposition to nuclear weapons, he declared that India's nuclear abstention was open to reassessment, and endorsed work on a "peaceful nuclear explosive."

Events over the next few years continued to feed Indian insecurities. September 1965 saw another Indo-Pakistani war, during which China reportedly threatened to intervene on Pakistan's behalf by opening a second front. The war ended in a stalemate, and a ceasefire was arranged on September 23. The next day, 86 members of the Indian parliament, across the political spectrum, sent a letter to Shastri demanding an

---

[5] See Raju G. C. Thomas, *Indian Security Policy* (Princeton: Princeton Univ. Press, 1986), pp. 20–24.

[6] Bhatia, *India's Nuclear Bomb*, p. 109ff. See also "Shastri Says India May Now Need Nuclear Weapons," *New York Times*, October 17, 1964, p. 12; and "Pressure Grows on India," ibid., October 27, 1964, p. 5.

immediate decision to build a nuclear force.[7] Meanwhile, Chinese nuclear progress was swift. In October 1966 Beijing tested an intermediate-range nuclear missile, and in June 1967 a megaton-yield thermonuclear (H-bomb) weapon. Thus, as the NPT negotiations moved into their culminating phase, the question of whether India would decide to become the sixth nuclear-weapon state was increasingly urgent.

This chain of events carried a double message for U.S. nonproliferation policy. On the one hand, it produced a sharp rise in U.S. concern about an Indian bomb, which loomed as a severe threat not only to the global regime Washington was trying to build, but also to U.S. security interests in Asia. On the other hand, the events increased the overlap between U.S. and Indian security perspectives in Asia. While the appearance of Sino-Indian hostility aggravated India's nuclear incentives, then, it also created the potential for closer U.S.-Indian ties that might reduce those incentives. America's new interest in bolstering India against Chinese pressure or aggression somewhat softened the earlier contradiction between U.S. Cold War diplomacy and Indian security policy. This convergence of U.S. and Indian interests produced a military assistance pact between the two countries at the time of the 1962 Himalayan war, and joint air defense exercises the following year.

After the Chinese nuclear test, the United States used both public and private channels in a campaign to persuade India of American support against Beijing. India was the main target of Lyndon Johnson's October 1964 pledge that "nations that do not seek nuclear weapons can be sure that, if they need our strong support against some threat of nuclear blackmail, then they will have it"—a pledge that was reaffirmed by the President after China's 1966 ballistic missile test.[8] In March 1965 Averill Harriman met with Shastri in New Delhi—following meetings in Israel that also featured Washington's growing alarm about proliferation—to emphasize that Beijing's nuclear capability would have no effect on U.S. readiness to back India military in the face of Chinese aggression. In effect, the United States was signaling the extension of its nuclear umbrella to cover India despite the lack of official alliance ties.

Of course, these assurances fell short of a binding commitment on Washington's part. The possibility that more explicit security guarantees—bilateral or multilateral—might be necessary to assuage India's nuclear fears had been considered by the Gilpatric committee, which urged a forthcoming U.S. response:

> While attempting to avoid all formal guarantees we should be prepared, if requested by the Indians, to offer formal or informal assurances of United States action in the event of a nuclear attack by China in exchange for an Indian commitment not to acquire nuclear weapons. We should not object if the Indian government should seek a similar assurance from the Soviet

---

[7] *New York Times*, September 24, 1965.

[8] *New York Times*, October 31, 1966, p. 1.

Union, and we should be prepared to undertake, if requested by the Indians, parallel action with the Soviets and/or the United Kingdom.[9]

However, a formal U.S. commitment to India's security confronted too many obstacles, on both sides, to be a realistic option. The United States was hesitant to expand its security obligations in Asia at a time when its involvement in Vietnam was starting to grow rapidly and to provoke a domestic political reaction against overseas military intervention.[10] On New Delhi's side, a formal security tie with the United States would have compromised its traditional nonaligned status and opposition to the American military presence on the subcontinent and the Indian Ocean. U.S. ties to Pakistan—and the latter's to China—posed an additional complicating factor.

As the NPT negotiations proceeded, India displayed ambivalence on the question of guarantees. In the period immediately following China's nuclear test and Johnson's "blackmail" statement, New Delhi did not directly approach the United States on the security issue (though Shastri did raise it with British Prime Minister Harold Wilson) and in fact downplayed its importance to nonproliferation. In the Geneva debates during 1965, India questioned the reliability of guarantees, and argued that nondiscrimination and disarmament by the existing nuclear powers were more important conditions of an acceptable treaty. These doubts were reinforced when the United States imposed an arms embargo on both parties to the September 1965 Indo-Pakistani war. While the embargo was more harmful to Pakistan than to India, it dramatized for New Delhi the risks and uncertainties of superpower patronage.

Subsequent Chinese nuclear progress apparently prompted second thoughts on the value of guarantees, however. Pointing to India's "special problem of security against nuclear attack and blackmail," Foreign Minister M.C. Chagla intimated in March 1967 that security assurances vis-à-vis China were now the key to New Delhi's NPT adherence. During 1967 India made high-level approaches to both the United States and the Soviet Union to explore the possibilities of separate or joint guarantees by the superpowers. But these soundings only confirmed the superpowers' reluctance to buttress the NPT regime with new security arrangements for nonnuclear states.[11] The United States, now torn by domestic controversy over Vietnam, was unwilling to codify Johnson's declaratory statements of support or to consider a joint undertaking with Moscow beyond the promise of a UN Security Council response to aggression—a promise,

---

[9] *A Report to the President by the Committee on Nuclear Proliferation*, January 1965 (partially declassified September 22, 1977), pp. 8–9.

[10] On the other hand, some "hawks" argued that U.S. perseverance in Vietnam, demonstrating American resolve and reliability as an ally, was essential to deter India from pursuing nuclear weapons. See Walt Rostow, *The Diffusion of Power* (New York: Macmillan, 1972), p. 496.

[11] Kapur, *India's Nuclear Option*, pp. 140–42; Quester, *The Politics of Nuclear Proliferation*, p. 64; Mitchell Reiss, *Without the Bomb: The Politics of Nuclear Nonproliferation* (New York: Columbia Univ. Press, 1988), pp. 221–22.

as Secretary of State Rusk made clear to the Senate, that imposed no new responsibilities on America.

The convergence of U.S. and Indian strategic interests in the 1960s ultimately fell short of meeting New Delhi's requirements for taking the nonnuclear pledge. But security fears were not the only—and for much of this period probably not even the primary—cause of India's refusal to renounce nuclear weapons. India had other reasons to retain its option to "go nuclear" and to oppose the superpowers' version of a nonproliferation treaty. The political value of nuclear weapons as a source of international prestige and status had been amply reconfirmed, as India could not fail to note, by reactions to the Chinese program. In addition, an unfettered nuclear program was, in India's view, a key to scientific and technological progress. Finally, the discrimination inherent in the NPT—especially in the application of safeguards and the lack of credible provisions for arms reductions by the existing nuclear powers—violated long-standing tenets of Indian nuclear policy. Given these problems, India might well have refused to consign itself formally to the status of nuclear have-not, even in the absence of the Chinese threat. The United States was not oblivious to India's nonsecurity motives for pursuing the nuclear option, but had no concerted strategy for addressing them. Ways to compensate states like India for renouncing the bomb (such as a seat on the UN Security Council or programs offering alternate paths to technological advancement and prestige), though often discussed, were not energetically pursued.

India was thus lost to a treaty that had been partly inspired, from the U.S. standpoint, by the desire to prevent an Indian bomb. Nevertheless, as the NPT was completed and opened for signature, India had made no firm commitment to build nuclear weapons, instead maintaining an ambiguous nuclear posture. Technically, the country continued to close in on a weapons capability. The Trombay reprocessing plant, in operation since the mid-1960s, had begun extracting unsafeguarded plutonium from irradiated CIRUS reactor fuel; in late 1965, the CIA estimated that India had amassed enough plutonium for a bomb and could produce one within a year.[12] And Indira Gandhi, who had become prime minister in 1966, was not opposed to nuclear weapons on moral grounds as her predecessors had been. But India held back from exploding a device, probably deterred by fears of disrupting relations with the superpowers and kindling nuclear ambitions in Pakistan. Equally important, there was no pressing security need to cross the threshold. Despite the superpowers' refusal to offer formal guarantees, their shared hostility toward China provided India a kind of "double nuclear indemnity" that helped limit New Delhi's threat perceptions.[13] With the United States's opening to China in 1970, this important condition of India's nuclear restraint would disappear.

---

[12] Richard Betts, in Joseph Yager, ed., *Nonproliferation and U.S. Foreign Policy* (Washington, DC: Brookings, 1980), p. 108, footnote 76.

[13] Thomas, *Indian Security Policy*, p. 45.

NUCLEAR ISRAEL'S CHALLENGE

If India's nuclear path remained unclear as the NPT neared completion, Israel's was all but settled. By 1968, the CIA had concluded that Israel already possessed nuclear weapons or could produce them at will.[14] This fact, and the Johnson administration's decision to treat it as a fait accompli while keeping officially silent on the issue, marked the failure of years of U.S. effort to contain Israel's nuclear progress.

Early in the nuclear age, Israel was recognized as an obvious candidate to develop atomic bombs. Surrounded by hostile Arab states that rejected its right to exist, the nation's security dilemma was clear and acute; no less apparent were the technical capabilities of Israeli scientists. Until December 1960, however, the United States lacked evidence of an active Israeli program. At that time, an American U-2 spy plane took pictures of a large nuclear plant, similar to the type used to produce U.S. weapons plutonium, at Dimona in the Negev Desert.[15] The plant, Israel acknowledged, was a large natural uranium-fueled reactor, acquired from France in a 1956 agreement that the two countries had deliberately concealed from the United States. It is now known that Israeli Prime Minister David Ben Gurion and his French counterpart, Guy Mollet, entered into an extensive web of secret nuclear dealings in the wake of the Suez crisis, involving not only the Dimona reactor but also a reprocessing plant and collaboration in the design, development, and testing of atomic weapons and ballistic missiles.[16]

Though ignorant of the scope of Israel's nuclear activities, the United States saw Dimona as a strong indication of weapons ambitions (it was "considerably larger than any need for an experimental reactor," Secretary of State Herter told the Senate Foreign Relations Committee) and

---

[14] Hedrick Smith, "U.S. Assumes Israelis Have A-Bomb or its Parts," New York Times, July 18, 1970, p. 1.

[15] John Finney, "U.S. Fears Israel Moves Toward A-Bomb Potential," New York Times, December 19, 1960, p. 1.

[16] The origins of the Israeli nuclear weapons program and its French connection were illuminated by a series of revelations in the 1980s, including those of a former Dimona technician, Mordechai Vanunu, and the reporting of French journalist Pierre Pean in Les Deux Bombes (Paris: Fayard, 1981), which has been translated into English by the U.S. Congressional Research Service. Vanunu's disclosures appeared in "Revealed: The Secrets of Israel's Nuclear Arsenal," London Sunday Times, October 5, 1986. The same paper published an interview with former French atomic energy official Francis Perrin confirming many of the points in Pean's account: "France Admits It Gave Israel A-Bomb," Sunday Times, October 12, 1986. See also Steve Weissman and Herbert Krosney, The Islamic Bomb (New York: Times Books, 1981), chap. 8. For a careful review of what is known about the Israeli program and its development, see Leonard Spector, The Undeclared Bomb (Cambridge, MA: Ballinger, 1988), pp. 164ff., and the extensive accompanying footnotes. Other analyses of the Israeli nuclear question include Paul Jabber, Israel and Nuclear Weapons (London: Chatto and Windus, 1971), and Shai Feldman, Israeli Nuclear Deterrence: A Strategy for the 1980s (New York: Columbia Univ. Press, 1982).

reacted sharply.[17] An Israeli bomb, the United States believed, would further destabilize an already volatile region—perhaps even provoking an Arab preventive war—and seriously harm American interests there. In part, this reflected the same fear of "catalytic war" (a superpower conflict triggered by a nuclear-armed client state) that worried the United States about proliferation in Europe.[18] It was also feared that a nuclear Israel would be emboldened to take a more intransigent stance in relations with the Arab states, reducing the chances for a peace settlement in the region. (Some Israeli "doves," in contrast, have argued that nuclear weapons, by making Israel more secure, should induce greater flexibility in peace negotiations.) The most immediate danger perceived by Washington, however, was that Israel's actions would stimulate Arab nuclear ambitions, including demands for assistance from the Soviet Union.[19] The result would be an escalating Middle East arms race and greater Soviet influence in the Arab world.

Israel responded to American protests with bland assurances that the Dimona reactor was intended for peaceful research and had been kept secret to prevent Arab attack or sabotage. (With probably unintended irony, Ben Gurion described the plant as similar to India's CIRUS reactor.[20]) But despite U.S. pressure, Israel stubbornly refused to place the facility under IAEA safeguards. The only concession to American misgivings that Israel was willing to offer was to permit occasional "visits"—not rigorous formal inspections—to the plant by U.S. Atomic Energy Agency scientists. In return, the United States agreed to supply Israel with several batteries of Hawk antiaircraft missiles.[21]

The 1962 Hawk deal was an important milestone in two respects. It was the first time the United States used conventional arms transfers as a deliberate strategy to counter a threat of nuclear proliferation. And it was the first departure from what had been a firm U.S. policy against military aid to Israel. This policy, motivated by the fear of alienating the Arab

---

[17] Herter's statement, made in executive session, is cited in Spector, *The Undeclared Bomb*, footnote 28, p. 388.

[18] The French, according to Francis Perrin, assumed that Israel was inspired by a Gaullist "triggering" strategy designed to force U.S. involvement, should its survival be threatened: "We thought the Israeli bomb was aimed at the Americans, not to launch it against America but to say 'if you don't want to help us in a critical situation we will require you to help us, otherwise we will use our nuclear bombs.'" See "France Admits It Gave Israel A-Bomb," London *Sunday Times*.

[19] In January 1961, Egyptian President Nasser warned that if Dimona proved to be a military plant, Egypt would take preventive action "even if we have to mobilize four million people," and would "secure atomic weapons at any cost." Cited in Robert Stephens, *Nasser: A Political Biography* (New York: Simon & Schuster, 1971), p. 317.

[20] Dana Schmidt, "Israel Assures U.S. on Reactor," *New York Times*, December 22, 1960, p. 5.

[21] McGeorge Bundy, *Danger and Survival: Choices About the Bomb in the First Fifty Years* (New York: Random House, 1988), p. 510.

states and thereby abetting Soviet influence in the region, reflected the delicate mix of American interests in the Middle East—a mix that in turn constrained Washington's perceived options for dealing with the Israeli nuclear threat.

As in South Asia, communist containment topped the hierarchy of American national interests in the Middle East. The region's economic importance as a vital source of oil for the West, and its critical geographic location, made it a key stake in the Cold War superpower competition. These considerations required the United States to maintain links and, where possible, friendly relations with the Arab world, and avoid conceding it to the Soviet sphere of influence. As such they precluded unconditional support for Israel, notwithstanding the strong American interest in Israel's survival and the close political ties between the two countries.[22] Attempts by Prime Minister Ben Gurion to obtain a formal U.S. or NATO guarantee of Israel's borders were unsuccessful—reinforcing the lesson of Suez that U.S. and Israeli interests might well diverge at critical moments. For Israel, this seemed to dictate a policy of maximum self-reliance.

In this setting, the United States waged a frustrating battle during the early and mid-1960s to contain the Israeli nuclear program and—no less important—to calm Arab apprehensions about it. The American visits to Dimona, beginning in 1962, were an apt symbol of this quixotic effort. The visits later proved to have been a deliberate exercise in deception, elaborately stage-managed by the Israeli hosts to conceal Dimona's actual operations from the American teams.[23] The deception apparently worked; the United States remained unaware of the existence of the Dimona reprocessing plant, constructed in a hidden underground chamber, which is now believed to have been producing plutonium beginning in 1965.[24] Stories leaked to the press—and undoubtedly aimed in large part at Egyptian President Nasser—reported that the U.S. teams visiting Dimona had found no evidence of weapons work.[25]

While downplaying its misgivings in public, in truth the United States strongly suspected that Israel was moving apace toward an atomic weapons capability. These suspicions were reinforced by reports of Israel's efforts to develop ballistic missiles with French cooperation. Egypt had already begun to receive deliveries of crude SCUD missiles from the

---

[22] For a historical overview of U.S. policy in the Middle East, see William B. Quandt, *Decade of Decisions: American Policy Toward the Arab-Israeli Conflict, 1967–1976* (Berkeley: University of California Press, 1977), pp. 5ff.

[23] See, for example, Seymour M. Hersh, *The Samson Option: Israel, America, and the Bomb* (New York: Random House, 1991), pp. 111–13, 131–32.

[24] Spector, *The Undeclared Bomb*, pp. 174–75.

[25] John Finney, "Israel Permits U.S. to Inspect Atomic Reactor," *New York Times*, March 14, 1965, p. 1; John Finney, "U.S. Again Reassured on Negev Reactor," *New York Times*, June 28, 1966, p. 8.

Soviet Union at this time. Israeli testing of the Jericho missile, able to deliver a half-ton payload at a range of 260 miles, began around 1965; the weapon's relatively poor accuracy suggested that it was intended to carry a nuclear warhead.[26] Another episode, though it remains murky, cast further suspicion on Israel. This was the discovery by AEC inspectors that some 200 pounds of weapons-grade uranium had disappeared from a U.S. Navy contractor's plant in Apollo, Pennsylvania. The missing material was never officially accounted for, but its diversion to Israel, with the collaboration of the plant operators, was considered a likely possibility by some U.S. officials. Meanwhile, Arab leaders portrayed an imminent atomic peril from Israel, and threatened preventive war. Nasser reportedly appealed to Moscow for nuclear weapons; though rebuffed, he obtained a Soviet promise to respond to Israeli nuclear aggression.[27]

These developments produced growing fears in the Johnson administration of an all-out Middle East arms race, and launched a series of high-level demarches aimed at brokering restraint on both sides. When Prime Minister Levi Eshkol (who had succeeded Ben Gurion in 1963) visited Washington in June 1964, the nuclear question was high on the U.S. agenda. A key U.S. objective, according to Under Secretary of State George Ball, was to "prevent stimulation of a Middle East arms race via Israeli acquisition of missiles and nuclear arms."[28] Appealing for nuclear restraint, the United States argued that Israel enjoyed clear conventional superiority over its Arab adversaries and denigrated the latters' advanced weapon capabilities. "Despite exaggerated Israeli claims," Ball asserted, "for the foreseeable future, the UAR [Egyptian] missile capability will remain primarily a psychological threat and the UAR nuclear capability nil."[29] To help gain Egyptian cooperation in mutual arms control measures, the United States sought Eshkol's "permission to inform Nasser of the peaceful nature of Israel's nuclear activities."[30]

But Israel did not share the U.S. interest in reassuring Nasser; on the contrary, its strategy was to use the provocative ambiguity of its nuclear status to keep the Arabs off balance and discourage attack. Insisting that it

---

[26] A Pentagon intelligence source in Israel, commenting on the poor accuracy of the missile, asserted that "when we need the right kind of warhead, we will have it . . . and after that, there will be no more trouble in this part of the world." Cable, Tel Aviv-Washington, March 30, 1965, in *Middle East: National Security Files, 1963–1969* (Frederick, MD: University Publications of America), reel 3. See also John Finney, "Israel Said to Buy French Missiles," *New York Times*, January 7, 1966, p. 1; and William Beecher, "Israel Believed Developing Missile of Atom Capability," *New York Times*, October 5, 1971, p. 1.

[27] *New York Times*, February 4, 1966, p. 1.

[28] "Memorandum to the President: Visit of Israeli Prime Minister Eshkol" (undated), *Middle East: National Security Files, 1963–1969*, reel 3.

[29] "Memorandum to the President."

[30] "Quid Pro Quo of Visit," State Department background paper dated May 28, 1964, in *Middle East: National Security Files*, reel 3.

must stay several years ahead of its Arab enemies in sophisticated weapons, Israel pressed for greater U.S. aid, especially advanced fighter aircraft, and demanded verified restrictions on Egyptian arms. The United States had little influence over Egypt, however. Attempts to gain Nasser's agreement to arms restrictions, with a warning that otherwise U.S. aid to Israel would increase, were unsuccessful.[31]

Unable to deliver Arab restraint or to extend a security guarantee credible to Israel, the United States turned again to conventional arms supplies as a nonproliferation lever. In February 1965, President Johnson sent Averill Harriman to Tel Aviv to discuss the first U.S. sales of offensive arms to Israel. The talks occurred against the background of two developments: growing pressure on the United States to supply arms to moderate Arab states like Jordan and Saudi Arabia (and a consequent need to assuage Israel's inevitable misgivings), and the collapse of a major pending arms agreement between Israel and West Germany.[32] But Washington's preoccupation with the Israeli nuclear program permeated the talks and helped shape the bargaining context.[33] Warning that an Israeli bomb could jeopardize the entire relationship between the two countries, the U.S. side insisted on nuclear restraint as a condition of offensive arms transfers. Israel, reversing the linkage, implicitly used its threat to go nuclear to pressure Washington for conventional arms.

Israel emerged with the better of the deal, avoiding any meaningful commitment to curtail its nuclear activities. It continued to rule out formal inspections of Dimona or to offer nonproliferation assurances beyond the enigmatic statement that Israel would "not be the first country to introduce nuclear weapons into the Middle East." This vague formula lent itself to a variety of interpretations, among them a "bomb in the basement" posture—a supply of unassembled weapon components that could be readied for use on short notice. The United States did achieve its minimum objective—a tacit understanding that Israel would not openly test or deploy nuclear weapons—though Israel might well have observed this restraint in its own interests anyway. With this slim gain, the United States reversed its policy against offensive arms sales to Israel, agreeing in 1965 and 1966 to supply several hundred tanks and 48 Skyhawk (A-4) fighter jets.

This outcome clearly etched the limits of American nonproliferation influence in the face of Israel's determination to preserve a nuclear option and Washington's competing policy interests. Anticipating the case of

---

[31] Stephens, *Nasser*, p. 457.

[32] See Jack Langguth, "U.S. Dilemma on Middle East Arms," *New York Times*, February 28, 1965, p. 1; and John Finney, "U.S. to Weigh Sale of Arms to Israel, *New York Times*, March 4, 1965, p. 1.

[33] Interview with involved U.S. official.

Pakistan two decades later, the U.S. experience with Israel also revealed the dilemmas inherent in using conventional arms sales as a tool against the spread of nuclear weapons. United States leverage was doubly constrained. First, to withhold conventional weapons because of Israel's recalcitrance on the nuclear issue risked being self-defeating; it would only increase the influence of nuclear weapons advocates within Israel by dramatizing the country's precarious security situation and its need for self-reliance. Second, the United States had a vital interest, quite apart from nonproliferation, in keeping Israel militarily superior to its Arab enemies. Though the United States strongly preferred that Israel continue to rely on European arms sources, these had dwindled by the mid-1960s; increasingly, the United States was becoming the supplier of last resort. For these reasons, as well as the unique place of Israel in U.S. domestic politics, a denial of Israel's request for arms was never seriously considered. The scope for exerting nuclear leverage narrowed accordingly, and whatever nonproliferation benefit accrued from the deal was on Israeli terms.

This pattern was confirmed over the next few years, during which probomb forces in Israel gained strength and the country probably achieved its de facto weapons capability. The 1967 Middle East war was an important catalyst in the process. On the eve of the conflict, as Egypt took a series of threatening moves, Israel appealed for American backing; Eshkol asked Johnson for a declaration that the United States would treat an Arab attack on Israel as an attack against itself.[34] Johnson, influenced by intelligence showing that Israel would easily win a conflict with the Arabs and facing strong domestic opposition to U.S. intervention, refused and pursued a United Nations solution to the crisis while cautioning Israel against preemptive attack. Israel ignored this advice, quickly defeated its adversaries, and emerged in control of the Sinai peninsula, the West Bank of the Jordan River, and Syria's Golan Heights.

This decisive victory failed to ease Israeli insecurities, however. On the contrary, the war reinforced Israel's sense of isolation (it led to a cutoff of remaining French military aid and a major resupply of the Arab states by the Soviet Union) and its perception of the United States as an unreliable ally. Also at this time, several advocates of nuclear weapons who had lost political favor earlier in the decade returned to positions of influence, among them Moshe Dayan, who became defense minister. In these conditions, the Israeli nuclear program gained momentum—a development that was noted by U.S. officials at the time.[35] The United

---

[34] See Quandt, *Decade of Decisions*, pp. 40ff.

[35] "Israel Said to Plan to Make Atom Bomb," *New York Times*, June 14, 1967, p. 16; John Finney, "Israel Could Make Atom Arms in 3–4 Years, U.S. Aides Say," *New York Times*, July 6, 1967, p. 10. See also Robert Harkavy, *Specter of a Middle East Holocaust* (Denver: University of Denver Press, 1977), p. 8.

States was effectively resigned to the Israeli nuclear capability. Based on a variety of circumstantial evidence, the CIA concluded that Israel could produce atomic weapons at any time, if it had not in fact already done so. The Johnson administration handled this estimate with extraordinary secrecy, fearing that full exposure of Israel's nuclear status would upset U.S. relations with both sides in the Middle East conflict, jeopardize the successful completion of the NPT, and increase pressures on countries like India and Japan to go nuclear.[36] The United States thus abetted Tel Aviv's policy of nuclear ambiguity, ironically becoming a partner in the deception of which it had been the original victim.

Negotiations on new arms sales in 1968 provided a further indication that the United States had come to regard Israel's nuclear capability as a fait accompli and was unwilling to exert pressure to reverse it. Officials in the State and Defense Departments hoped to use Israel's keen interest in acquiring F-4 Phantom jets as leverage on the nonproliferation issue. Assistant Secretary of Defense Paul Warnke, who led the U.S. negotiating team, gained Secretary McNamara's approval of a plan linking the F-4 sale to the Israeli agreement to sign the NPT (implying IAEA safeguards at Dimona). Also included in the proposal was an Israeli pledge to refrain, subject to U.S. inspection, from deploying aircraft and missiles equipped to carry nuclear warheads. Israeli negotiator Yitzak Rabin rejected the proposal out of hand, strongly hinting to Warnke that it was impossible to meet because Israel had already crossed the nuclear threshold. Rabin appealed to the White House, and Johnson, amid congressional pressure to expedite the sale and a backlash in Israel against alleged U.S. strong-arm tactics, ordered the deal consummated without strings.[37] The agreement, providing for the sale of 50 F-4s and 100 A-4 fighter jets, was signed in December 1968. In a bizarre footnote, Israeli agents reportedly asked—without hope of approval but no doubt confident that the request would be leaked—that the F-4s be equipped with nuclear bomb racks.[38]

---

[36] See Smith, "U.S. Assumes Israelis Have A-Bomb or its Parts" (footnote 14). At this time the United States was still unaware of Israel's reprocessing operations. According to later testimony by CIA official Carl Duckett, the judgment that Israel had achieved a bomb capability was based in part on environmental sampling indicating the presence of highly enriched uranium, and observation of Skyhawk exercises simulating nuclear bombing runs; cited in Weissman and Krosney, *The Islamic Bomb*, pp. 107–8. Another episode that fed nuclear suspicions about Israel occurred in 1968: the disappearance at sea, and apparent diversion to Israel, of a large shipment of uranium ostensibly destined for Italy. See Elaine Davenport et al., *The Plumbat Affair* (London: Deutsch, 1978).

[37] Interviews with involved U.S. officials; Smith, "U.S. Assumes Israelis Have A-Bomb or its Parts"; Quandt, *Decade of Decisions*, pp. 66–67.

[38] Smith, "U.S. Assumes Israelis Have A-Bomb or its Parts"; see also George Quester, "Israel," in Jed Snyder and Samuel Wells, eds., *Limiting Nuclear Proliferation* (Cambridge, MA: Ballinger, 1985), pp. 45–46.

NIXON'S NUCLEAR AMBIVALENCE

By comparison with its two Democratic predecessors, the Nixon administration attached far less urgency and importance to the problem of nuclear proliferation and devoted little high-level attention to it. Nixon's foreign policy priorities lay elsewhere—in strategic arms control, the opening to China, and the extrication of the United States from Vietnam. This ambitious agenda left little room for major new initiatives on nonproliferation, which seemed unnecessary in any event given the recent completion of the NPT. Moreover, Henry Kissinger, the new national security advisor, took a fatalistic view of nuclear spread; regarding it as inevitable, he was disinclined to expend American influence in quixotic efforts to prevent it.[39] Indeed, according to one account, "Nixon and Kissinger were privately hostile to the [NPT]" and directed that "there should be no efforts by the United States government to pressure other nations" to sign it.[40]

A lower priority for nonproliferation was also congruent with the larger Nixon-Kissinger foreign policy design, which emphasized the need for retrenchment from the expansive globalism of the Kennedy and Johnson years. Recalling Eisenhower after the Korean war, Nixon's goal was to reduce the costs of containment by sharing U.S. burdens more widely. The "Nixon Doctrine" called for greater self-help on the part of overseas allies and clients, and the administration's idea of a new "structure of peace" envisaged a more multipolar world order.[41] While this vision did not explicitly contemplate a devolution of America's nuclear role (the Nixon Doctrine applied to conventional defense and in fact reaffirmed the U.S. nuclear umbrella over friendly noncommunist nations), neither was it inherently hostile to proliferation. Thus, Kissinger dissented from the strict nuclear monopolism of the Kennedy-McNamara era:

> I had urged for years that it was in the American national interest to encourage a sharing of responsibilities. If the United States insisted on being the trustee of all the non-Communist areas we would exhaust ourselves psychologically long before we did so physically. A world of more centers of decision, I believed, was fully compatible with our interests as well as our ideals. This is why I opposed the efforts of the Kennedy and Johnson administrations to abort the French and if possible even the British nuclear programs.[42]

---

[39] See Michael Brenner, *Nuclear Power and Non-Proliferation: The Remaking of U.S. Policy* (Cambridge: Cambridge Univ. Press, 1981), pp. 63–64.

[40] Seymour M. Hersh, *The Price of Power: Kissinger in the Nixon White House* (New York: Summit Books, 1983), p. 148.

[41] See Osgood, *Alliances and American Foreign Policy;* and Gaddis, *Strategies of Containment.*

[42] Henry A. Kissinger, *The White House Years* (Boston: Little, Brown, 1979), p. 69. Early in the Strategic Arms Limitation Talks (SALT), the United States rebuffed Soviet proposals that Kissinger viewed as attempts to hamper the French and British programs and reinforce a superpower "condominium." See ibid., p. 548.

As Nixon's national security advisor, Kissinger reversed the long-standing policy of noncooperation with the French nuclear program. Indeed, it has been argued that he skirted U.S. law in initiating a pattern of indirect technical aid to the French program, efforts that by the mid-1980s had done much to reintegrate French nuclear weapons into NATO practice and strategy.[43]

American concern about proliferation was also dampened by the Nixon administration's downgrading of the Third World as an area of vital American interest. The developing countries, seen by the Kennedy and Johnson administrations as a decisive arena of the Cold War struggle, were disparaged by Nixon and Kissinger as peripheral players in the game of international power politics; the heart of the game, and the unswerving focus of the Nixon foreign policy, was relations among the great powers. Nixon saw the establishment of a modus vivendi, with the Soviet Union and China as the key to allowing the United States safely to reduce its direct overseas involvement. In turn, understandings among the superpowers were counted on to reduce the risks of confrontation triggered by regional conflicts involving their allies. The danger of catalytic nuclear war would thereby be lessened.

The Nixon administration's relative complacency about proliferation was accompanied by a style of diplomacy ill-suited to assuaging the motives of potential nuclear powers. This style relied heavily on secrecy, surprise, and maneuver, often deliberately creating uncertainty about U.S. intentions. The Nixon-Kissinger brand of realpolitik sometimes blurred the line between friend and foe, and suggested, as one observer noted, "a distaste for 'fixed points' of policy, an intention of pinning adversaries down without being pinned down oneself."[44] Whatever its other merits, this approach was unlikely to diminish interest in nuclear weapons on the part of insecure U.S. partners.

As a result of these priorities and predispositions, the Nixon administration was largely oblivious to the trade-offs between nonproliferation and other national interests that its predecessors had grappled with. This blind spot was particularly evident in the administration's diplomatic maneuverings in the Middle East and South Asia, which fed the momentum of proliferation in both regions.

NIXON AND THE ISRAELI BOMB

The chief goals of U.S. Middle East policy in the Nixon years were to counter the growth of Soviet influence that had followed the June 1967 war, to avoid a superpower clash in the region, and—especially after the

---

[43] Richard H. Ullman, "The Covert French Connection," *Foreign Policy*, No. 75, Summer 1989.

[44] A. Hartley, "American Foreign Policy in the Nixon Era," *Adelphi Papers* 110 (London: Institute for Strategic Studies, Winter 1974–1975), p. 8.

October 1973 war and oil embargo—to assure Western access to Arab oil. An Arab-Israeli peace settlement—including Israel's return of the occupied territories—was seen as a way to advance all these interests. In pursuit of a settlement, the administration alternated between two approaches: an "evenhanded" strategy designed to appeal to Arab interests and encourage Israeli concessions, and a pro-Israel policy aimed at convincing the Arabs to come to terms.[45]

At least until the 1973 conflict, the Israeli atomic capability seems to have played only a minor role in administration thinking, despite Nixon's frequent invoking of the danger of U.S.-Soviet nuclear confrontation in the region.[46] Seeing little scope for influencing Israeli nuclear policy (and perhaps disinclined to try, given its relatively tolerant view of that policy), the White House effectively dropped the issue from the agenda of U.S.-Israeli relations. American visits to Dimona were discontinued in 1969 after complaints by the United States team that it could no longer attest to the absence of weapons work at the facility. To continue the visits under these conditions might have forced an unwanted showdown on the nuclear issue.[47]

In its first year, the Nixon administration followed an evenhanded Middle East policy, seeking to improve relations with Israel's principal enemies, Egypt and Syria, and to encourage Soviet restraint in the region. But in early 1970 the Soviet Union sharply increased its flow of arms and military advisors to Egypt, underwriting Nasser's proclaimed "war of attrition" against Israel; the latter responded with bombing raids against Egypt. As the sporadic fighting intensified, the United States fended off Israeli appeals for new aircraft deliveries—hoping to elicit reciprocal Soviet restraint—and attempted to broker a cease-fire. Only when convinced that Egypt was flouting the cease-fire and installing new Soviet surface-to-air missiles along the Suez Canal did the United States begin to tilt toward Israel.[48] This shift was reinforced in September 1970 when Jordan (the most moderate of Israel's adversaries) was threatened by a radical Palestinian takeover backed by Syria with, Nixon assumed, Soviet approval. Jordan's King Hussein appealed to Israel for support against invading

---

[45] See Quandt, *Decade of Decisions;* and Seyom Brown, *The Crises of Power: An Interpretation of United States Foreign Policy During the Kissinger Years* (New York: Columbia Univ. Press, 1979), p. 73.

[46] For example, Nixon likened the September 1970 Jordanian crisis to "a ghastly game of dominoes, with a nuclear war waiting at the end." *RN: The Memoirs of Richard Nixon* (New York: Grosset & Dunlap, 1978), p. 483. As noted below, the October 1973 U.S. nuclear alert may have been indirectly related to Israel's nuclear capability.

[47] See Spector, *The Undeclared Bomb*, p. 392 (footnote 51).

[48] It was at the height of this crisis, as Nasser visited Moscow to appeal for more Soviet aid, that CIA Director Richard Helms briefed the Senate Foreign Relations Committee on Israel's nuclear capability. The briefing was quickly reported in the press (see footnote 14)—a leak that one account views as "a clear warning to the Soviets." See Pringle and Spigelman, *The Nuclear Barons*, notes, p. 525.

Syrian forces, and the United States in turn promised to cover Israel should it decide to intervene. In the end, Jordan defeated the Syrian and Palestinian forces on its own and reestablished domestic control.

Prompted by these events to abandon the evenhanded strategy, the United States turned to a Middle East policy founded on building up Israeli strength. Arms sales to Israel increased massively, rising from $30 million in fiscal year 1970 to $545 million in 1971 and about $300 million in each of the next two years.[49] The United States also increased aid to Jordan and other moderate Arabs, but ceased trying to court Egypt and Syria. The intended message to these states was that their hopes for reclaiming the occupied territories lay in U.S. influence with Israel rather than in reliance on Moscow. Until they absorbed and acted on this message, the United States would keep Israel militarily supreme and not press Tel Aviv to come to the peace table. This policy seemed vindicated when Anwar Sadat (who had succeeded Nasser after the latter's death at the time of the Jordan crisis) broke with Moscow in July 1972 and expelled Soviet advisors from Egypt. But the breach was only temporary; fifteen months later U.S. policy premises were confounded by the Egyptian-Syrian surprise attack against Israel.

The October 1973 war and Arab oil embargo transformed the Middle East conflict and forced renewed attention to the question of Israel's nuclear status.[50] From the outset, the United States was determined that neither Israel nor the Arabs should gain a decisive victory, and—as in the 1970 crisis—Nixon and Kissinger again attempted to use arms leverage to shape the two sides' incentives. In the first days of the war, the U.S. delayed resupplying Israel, pressing Golda Meir to accept a cease-fire-in-place. After rallying to turn back the Arab forces, Israel agreed to a cease-fire, but now Sadat temporized. The United States reacted by speeding the flow of aid to Israel. Finally, when Israel crossed the Suez Canal and encircled Egypt's isolated Third Army Corps, the United States applied strong pressure to halt its advance. As the Arabs invoked the oil weapon and the Soviets threatened to intervene, Kissinger warned that the United States would not back Israel against Soviet resupply efforts aimed at rescuing the Third Army.[51] The crisis peaked on October 24 when the United States placed its nuclear forces on worldwide alert, apparently in response to signs that the Soviets were preparing to intervene and might be moving nuclear weapons into the region.[52] The next day, all sides accepted a UN call for a cease-fire, and the fighting ended.

---

[49] Quandt, *Decade of Decisions*, p. 163.

[50] See London Times Insight Team, *The Yom Kippur War* (New York: Doubleday, 1974).

[51] Quandt, *Decade of Decisions*, pp. 197–98.

[52] On the U.S. alert, see Scott D. Sagan, "Nuclear Alerts and Crisis Management," *International Security*, Spring 1985, pp. 122ff.

There is much speculation but little hard evidence of the role that Israel's nuclear capability played in the calculations of the various actors during the October 1973 war. *Time* magazine later reported that in the first days of the Arab attack, Israel was prepared to use nuclear weapons and actually deployed a number of warheads on missiles or aircraft.[53] Seymour Hersh reports that the Israelis actually put their nuclear weapons on alert twice during the 1973 war.[54] Others have surmised that Israel may have used the nuclear threat, explicitly or tacitly, to blackmail the United States into expediting new arms deliveries.[55] It is certainly plausible that knowledge of Israel's nuclear potential could have influenced U.S. conduct during the war; but Kissinger's ultimatum in the last stage of the conflict suggests that this factor did not give Israel decisive leverage over U.S. actions. On the other hand, one account of the U.S. alert states that Kissinger saw Moscow's threat to intervene as a possible attempt to deter Israeli use of nuclear weapons against Egypt.[56] If true, this suggests that the Israeli bomb gave Tel Aviv indirect leverage— through U.S. fear of Soviet reactions to it—over Washington.

In the altered Middle East landscape following the October war, the Israeli nuclear issue assumed new prominence. The war experience strengthened Israel's commitment to maintaining a nuclear option. As in 1967, doubts were raised about U.S. reliability; Kissinger's tactics at the close of the war were especially resented.[57] America's isolationist public mood as the Vietnam war ended, and the rise of Arab influence in the West as a result of the oil embargo, added to Israeli unease. The October war also raised U.S. consciousness on the question of Israel's nuclear capability, making it more difficult to ignore as a factor in the equation of Middle East—and potentially superpower—relations. Kissinger reportedly paid closer attention to the problem in the wake of the conflict, and the possible merits of the Israeli bomb were publicly debated by U.S.

---

[53] "How Israel Got the Bomb," *Time* magazine, April 12, 1976. According to Leonard Spector, U.S. officials have confirmed the general thrust of the *Time* account. See *The Undeclared Bomb*, p. 177.

[54] Hersh, *The Samson Option*, p. 233.

[55] See Helena Cobban, "Israel's Nuclear Game: The U.S. Stake," *World Policy Journal*, Summer 1988, pp. 424–25.

[56] Marvin Kalb and Bernard Kalb, *Kissinger* (Boston: Little, Brown, 1974), p. 493. Kissinger's own memoirs provide no clue as to the impact of Israeli nuclear weapons on his thinking or actions. Experts differ on how the Israeli bomb figured in Arab calculations during the conflict. Some believe it was a powerful restraining factor in Arab military decisions, while others discount its role. See Barry M. Blechman and Douglas M. Hart, "The Political Unity of Nuclear Weapons: The 1973 Middle East Crisis," *IS* 7, no. 1, Summer 1982, pp. 132–56.

[57] Of Kissinger's demand that Israeli forces halt their advance against the Third Army, Moshe Dayan complained, "The U.S. denied us the fruits of victory. It was an ultimatum—nothing short of it." Cited in *New York Times*, January 26, 1975.

foreign policy experts.[58] A new CIA estimate in 1974 flatly stated that "we believe that Israel has already produced nuclear weapons," and later the same year Israeli president Ephraim Katzir went well beyond the official line in signaling the nation's nuclear status: "It has always been our intention to develop the nuclear potential," he told a group of science writers; "We now have that potential."[59]

Yet the effect of these developments on U.S. policy was scarcely visible. Otherwise, the United States continued its pose of benign ignorance, unwilling either to confront Israel on the nuclear issue or to tailor its foreign policy in the region to dampen the country's nuclear incentives. The top American priority in the Middle East was now to achieve an Arab-Israeli settlement and prevent another conflict that could destroy the economic well-being and political unity of the West. To achieve a settlement, the United States would need to maintain Israeli goodwill while dramatically improving its relations with Egypt and the other Arab states—a balancing act that left little room for confronting the nuclear question forthrightly.

This subordination of nonproliferation to diplomatic expediency was most apparent in Nixon's offer, during his Middle East tour in June 1974, to sell nuclear power reactors to Israel and Egypt. The proposal was not tied to either country's acceptance of the NPT or its safeguards regime. (As such, it represented a retreat from the policy of the Johnson administration, which had explored peaceful nuclear cooperation with the two countries conditioned on their agreement to comprehensive IAEA inspections.[60]) When the Israelis protested the offer to Egypt, demanding that it be subject to U.S. supervision, Kissinger reportedly advised them not to raise the issue, because the United States would then be forced to ask for inspection rights at Dimona. At this point, "the whole matter was taken off the agenda. The Israeli leadership went out of its way to calm the Israeli public about the Egyptian nuclear reactor, arguing that after all it was better that the reactor should come from the United States than the

---

[58] See Harkavy, *Specter of a Middle East Holocaust*. One prominent advocate of Israeli nuclear weapons was Robert W. Tucker. Tucker predicted a growing divergence of Israeli and U.S. interests as the United States pursued a Mideast settlement and attempted to placate the Arabs. See "Israel and the United States: From Dependence to Nuclear Weapons?" *Commentary*, November 1975, p. 29. See also Steven Rosen, "Nuclearization and Stability in the Middle East," in Onkar Marwah and Ann Schulz, eds., *Nuclear Proliferation and the Near-Nuclear Countries* (Cambridge, MA: Ballinger, 1975). Other analysts were more sanguine about the chances for a peace settlement providing guarantees of Israeli security. See, for example, Richard Ullman, "Alliance with Israel?" *Foreign Policy*, no. 19, Summer 1975, and Zbigniew Brzezinski et al., "Peace in an International Framework," *Foreign Policy*, Summer 1975.

[59] Cited in Spector, *The Undeclared Bomb*, pp. 397–98 (footnote 63).

[60] See Hedrick Smith, "U.S. Studies a Plan to Bar Israeli-UAR Atom Race," *New York Times*, February 28, 1966, p. 1. The plan foundered on the Dimona issue, as did separate efforts to negotiate U.S. cooperation with Israel on a nuclear desalination plant.

Soviet Union."[61] But the Nixon administration plan provoked strong opposition in Congress, newly sensitized to the proliferation issue by India's nuclear test, and the proposal was subsequently withdrawn.

NIXON AND THE INDIAN BOMB

The Nixon years were bracketed by India's rejection of the NPT and its May 1974 test of a nuclear device. During this time, the decision to proceed with a "peaceful nuclear explosion" (PNE) was taken by the government of Indira Gandhi and clearly signaled to the outside world. But the Nixon administration barely registered the impending challenge to U.S. nonproliferation policy and made no serious effort to deter it. Neither in the sphere of peaceful nuclear cooperation nor in that of high foreign policy did U.S. relations with India reflect a strong priority for nonproliferation. In the former area, the United States sheltered the Tarapur deal from the growing nuclear strains between the two countries. In high foreign policy, U.S. interests on the subcontinent were dominated by the Nixon-Kissinger rapprochement with China. The perceived dictates of the China diplomacy combined with the outbreak of another India-Pakistan war to place the United States in a stance of outright hostility toward India.

During 1970–1971, the Indian government became increasingly explicit about its plans to conduct a nuclear test. These signals were a cause for U.S. concern on two grounds: a test by India would directly challenge the fledgling NPT regime (which made no distinction between PNE's and nuclear weapons), and it was likely to involve plutonium produced in the CIRUS reactor for which the United States had supplied the initial charge of heavy water. Fearing that American-supplied material might thus be implicated in a foreign nuclear explosives program, the United States advised India in November 1970 that such a test would violate the peaceful-use assurances under which it had assisted the CIRUS project.[62] India rejected the U.S. position as a retroactive attempt to tighten its commitments under the CIRUS agreement; a year later it dismissed a similar Canadian warning against using CIRUS plutonium in an explosive test. But neither the United States nor Canada pursued the matter further.

With the United States treating the PNE issue as an "agreement to disagree," cooperation on the Tarapur reactor project went forward undisturbed. The reactors became operational, fueled with U.S. low-enriched

[61] Matti Golan, *The Secret Conversations of Henry Kissinger: Step-by-Step Diplomacy in the Middle East* (New York: Quadrangle/The New York Times Book Co., 1976), pp. 214–16. See also Kissinger, *The White House Years*.

[62] U.S. aide-memoire to the Indian Atomic Energy Commission, cited in Spector, *Nuclear Proliferation Today*, p. 32.

uranium, in early 1969. At about the same time, India announced its plans to build a facility for reprocessing Tarapur fuel and was assured that the United States foresaw no problems with the "joint determination" required under the 1963 agreement. Like most such agreements, Tarapur remained the province of nuclear bureaucrats in the AEC and the State Department, attracting little notice from senior foreign policymakers. The United States thus did not attempt to link Tarapur to the two nations' larger policy differences over NPT adherence and PNEs. American nuclear officials believed, probably correctly, that the reactor project provided little leverage for pressing India on these broader issues. (In addition, linkage lacked a firm legal basis, since the Tarapur deal was a self-contained agreement, and India's compliance with it was not in question.)

Nevertheless, in theory the United States could have cited the NPT as grounds for reassessing its nuclear cooperation with India and other abstainers from the treaty. Continued nuclear assistance to countries refusing the comprehensive, "full-scope" safeguards required of treaty signatories undercut the NPT regime by allowing nonsigners to receive assistance on more lenient terms than signers. To avoid this perverse situation, the United States (and other supplier states) could have ceased nuclear cooperation with countries that would not join the NPT or submit to comparably rigorous safeguards. But this course, though later adopted by the United States in the 1978 Nuclear Non-Proliferation Act, was deliberately rejected at the time the NPT came into effect—largely so as not to jeopardize existing U.S. cooperation with EURATOM and Japan, whose early adherence to the NPT could not be assumed.

While U.S.-Indian peaceful nuclear cooperation proceeded on its own track, a growing estrangement characterized the two nations' broader political relations. In strategic terms, the Nixon administration attached only marginal importance to the Indian subcontinent; indeed, the main U.S. goal in the region was simply "to avoid adding another complication to our agenda," according to Kissinger.[63] Nixon was predisposed to be more sympathetic to the anticommunist military government of Pakistan than to nonaligned India, and this tendency was reinforced by the administration's opening to China, in which Pakistan served as the key channel of communication. The new China policy thus had the effect of drawing the United States closer to both of India's main adversaries.

The impact of this shift on Indian security perspectives became clear during the Indo-Pakistani conflict of 1971. The crisis originated in the Pakistani elections of December 1970, which brought advocates of regional autonomy to power in East Pakistan. In March 1971, the central government under President Yahya Khan moved to quash the separatists and establish military rule over the East. A bloody civil war ensued, with Pakistani troops brutally suppressing the population of the East, stimulating a massive flow of refugees into India.

---

[63] Kissinger, *The White House Years*, p. 848.

Nixon's response to the crisis was shaped almost entirely by the nascent U.S. dialogue with China.[64] Secret contacts between the two governments, with Pakistan as the intermediary, had by early 1971 prepared the way for Kissinger to visit Beijing that summer. To protect this link, Kissinger wrote, "the U.S. had every incentive to maintain Pakistan's goodwill."[65] Even more decisive in the administration's calculus was the need to demonstrate to China, Pakistan's ally, that the U.S. was a reliable partner and "took seriously the requirements of the balance of power."[66]

Guided by these wider concerns, the President refused, against the advice of the State Department and strong domestic criticism, to condemn Pakistani actions in the East or pressure the Khan government for restraint. Taking China's view of the conflict, the White House defined the main threat as the possibility that India, supported by the Soviet Union, would intervene on behalf of East Pakistan. China might then feel compelled to enter the conflict in turn. Should that scenario materialize, the State Department recommended U.S. support of India, but, in Kissinger's words, "nothing more contrary to the President's foreign policy could be imagined."[67] After his return from Beijing, Kissinger warned the Indian ambassador that the United States would not aid New Delhi if it became embroiled with China as a result of the fighting in Pakistan.[68] Three weeks later, India and the Soviet Union signed a Treaty of Friendship. Though it was not a security alliance and gave India no assurance of military backing, the treaty was seen by Nixon and Kissinger as a hostile act, encouraging Indian intervention against Pakistan and making the subcontinent rivalry in effect a Sino-Soviet conflict by proxy.

In December, large-scale fighting broke out between India and Pakistan. While the United States remained officially neutral, Nixon ordered a "tilt" toward Pakistan, culminating in a major exercise in gunboat diplomacy. Reacting to intelligence that alleged an imminent invasion and dismemberment of West Pakistan by India, Nixon ordered the aircraft carrier USS *Enterprise* into the Bay of Bengal as a warning

---

[64] See Kissinger, *The White House Years*, pp. 852–66; and Nixon, *RN: The Memoirs of Richard Nixon*, pp. 525–31. For critical assessments of White House policy premises during the crisis, see Christopher Van Hollen, "The Tilt Revisited: Nixon-Kissinger Geopolitics and South Asia," *Asian Survey*, April 1980; and Hersh, *The Price of Power*, pp. 444–64.

[65] Kissinger, *The White House Years*, p. 853.

[66] Kissinger, *The White House Years*, p. 918; see also Hersh, *The Price of Power*, p. 458, quoting Kissinger NSC aide Winston Lord.

[67] Kissinger, *The White House Years*, p. 865. The policy split, according to Kissinger, "hinged on the geopolitical perspective of the White House as against the regional perspective of the State Department, and on the relative weight to be given to China and India in the conduct of our foreign policy." Ibid., p. 897.

[68] Hersh, *The Price of Power*, pp. 451–52.

signal to New Delhi and Moscow. But the war soon ended in a decisive Indian victory, with East Pakistan gaining independence as the new state of Bangladesh.

Like Israel in 1967, India emerged from war with its enemy routed but its insecurities heightened. The sea change in U.S. China policy reduced Beijing's superpower adversaries by half, undermining a basic premise of Indian security policy. Although China had not intervened in the subcontinent war, it might be less restrained in the future, confident that its new friendship with the United States would deter Soviet counteraction on behalf of India. On a more symbolic level, the *Enterprise* episode was an affront to Indian national pride that left a lasting imprint on the country's security thinking. These factors reinforced the momentum of India's nuclear program.[69] Gandhi had probably made the final decision to proceed toward a nuclear test by early 1972, leading to a 15-kiloton underground explosion in the Rajasthan desert on May 18, 1974.

The initial U.S. reaction to India's test was mild.[70] The Nixon administration deliberately played down the event, hoping to deny India a prestige victory and to avoid inflating the importance of proliferation. Also, with the Israeli case in mind, the administration did not want to set a precedent for action against proliferators that might force its hand in the future. Accordingly, the White House vetoed any form of sanctions against India, whether in the area of nuclear cooperation or economic aid. Fuel shipments for Tarapur were held up briefly, but resumed in the fall of 1974 after India gave assurances that no plutonium derived from this fuel would be used in explosive devices. (Canada, in contrast, halted assistance to India's nuclear energy program in the wake of the Rajasthan test.) Only later, as Congress became aware that U.S. heavy water had figured in the test, and other developments brought the proliferation issue to the forefront, did India become the target of a revived U.S. campaign against the spread of nuclear weapons.

CONCLUSION

India and Israel epitomize both the U.S. concern about nuclear proliferation that helped inspire the NPT and the powerful constraints—both external and self-imposed—on effective action to deal with the problem. In different ways, the two cases illustrate a failure to mesh nonproliferation with competing foreign policy interests, and a resulting gap between

---

[69] See Sumit Ganguly, "Why India Joined the Nuclear Club," *Bulletin of the Atomic Scientists*, April 1983, pp. 30–33; Raju G. C. Thomas, "India's Nuclear and Space Programs," *World Politics*, January 1986, p. 326.

[70] See Brenner, *Nuclear Power and Non-Proliferation*, pp. 68–71; and Spector, *Nuclear Proliferation Today*, pp. 35–37.

rhetoric and reality in America's response to the spread of nuclear weapons.

In the case of Israel, the United States seemingly enjoyed a strong position from which to bargain for nuclear restraint. But the mix of American interests in the Middle East deterred the United States from fully exploiting the potential leverage afforded by Israel's political, economic, and military dependency. Indeed, the very closeness of U.S. ties to Israel made Washington reluctant to employ this leverage. Although conventional arms deliveries were seen as contributing to nonproliferation, this was generally a derivative goal, secondary to maintaining a conventional balance of power in the region and—especially in the Nixon years—influencing Israeli, Arab, and Soviet incentives with regard to a peace settlement.[71]

In the final analysis, Washington was not prepared to force an open breach over the nuclear issue; doing so could have cost the United States a valued strategic partner while probably aggravating the insecurities that drove Israel's nuclear program. On the other hand, American interests in the Arab world precluded the kind of unconditional support for Israel—through an alliance or unlimited conventional arms sales—that might have assuaged those insecurities. As a result, both the positive and negative levers for obtaining Israeli nuclear restraint were weak in practice. Ironically, America's stake in Israel proved strong enough to persuade the United States to retreat from a firm nonproliferation policy, but not strong enough to persuade Israel that it could safely do without a nuclear option.

In these circumstances, the United States settled for the best it could get—an undeclared Israeli nuclear capability with a tacit understanding barring overt testing or deployment. This "solution," though damaging to the credibility of U.S. nonproliferation policy, essentially made a virtue of necessity. As with Great Britain, there were plausible grounds for granting Israel a favored status in U.S. policy—its special relationship with the United States, its relatively stable and democratic domestic politics, and the belief that it was likely to use nuclear weapons only if its survival were directly at stake. Furthermore, Israel's "bomb in the basement" was not without potential benefits to U.S. interests: it might encourage Arab and Soviet restraint in the Middle East and make Israel feel more amenable to withdrawing from the occupied Arab territories as part of a peace settlement. As a last-resort guarantee of the nation's survival, the Israeli nuclear capability could be seen as a substitute for a stronger American commitment, freeing the United States to pursue an evenhanded policy in the region.

---

[71] The effectiveness of U.S. arms transfers to Israel as a diplomatic lever is also questionable. See Thomas R. Wheelock, "Arms for Israel: The Limits of Leverage," *International Security*, Fall 1978; and Andrew Pierre, *The Global Politics of Arms Sales* (Princeton: Princeton Univ. Press, 1982), pp. 159–60.

The Indian case intersected U.S. interests quite differently. Here, U.S. nonproliferation leverage was limited not by the closeness of relations but by their tenuousness. Whereas Israel's nuclear option was motivated almost entirely by security concerns, India's motivation was a more subtle mix of economic, political, and security factors. Treating India as only marginally important in strategic terms, the United States did not come to grips with the challenge it posed to the nascent NPT regime. American foreign policy during the period of the treaty negotiations and the ensuing Nixon years offered India little incentive to moderate its pursuit of a nuclear capability. And in a context of generally distant and often cool relations between the two countries, the Tarapur link gave the United States no real leverage over Indian nuclear policy.

The U.S. failure to take India seriously was most apparent when the American opening to China coincided with the 1970–1971 Pakistani crisis. Viewing the conflict on the subcontinent through the prism of superpower geopolitics, the Nixon administration encouraged the perception that its new China policy came at the expense of India, and virtually consigned the latter to the Soviet camp. In doing so, it helped confirm India's march toward the 1974 explosion.

At the same time, the shift in the American China policy implicitly altered the U.S. stakes in Indian proliferation. The initial U.S. alarm about an Indian bomb was in part a function of American enmity toward China and the assumption that India was, in a de facto if not a formal sense, a U.S. security responsibility. Following the 1964 Chinese test, India had been classed with Japan as a friendly country whose emulation of China threatened to increase the risks of the U.S. security role in Asia. But this concern diminished as the United States established ties with the People's Republic and increasingly regarded India as a Soviet client. In terms of realpolitik, containing the Indian bomb now became more a Soviet than an American problem.

Chapter
6

U.S. Policy Revised and Embattled: The Ford and Carter Administrations

*T*he Indian nuclear test was one of a series of developments in the mid-1970s that signaled a blurring of the line between the peaceful and military uses of nuclear energy. The oil crisis following the October 1973 Middle East war was another: dramatizing the risks of energy dependency, it boosted plans for nuclear power development and reinforced interest in plutonium-fueled "breeder" reactors. These promised a renewable source of nuclear power but, unlike conventional reactors, would give countries direct access to nuclear weapons material. In addition, U.S. dominance in the commercial nuclear market was eroding as European countries began to compete for reactor exports and develop their own uranium-enrichment facilities. The dangers of predatory export competition became obvious when France and West Germany agreed to supply the most sensitive nuclear technologies—those needed to produce bomb-usable uranium and plutonium—to Third World customers.

These disturbing trends raised the proliferation issue from its lowly place on the U.S. foreign policy agenda and provoked a rethinking of the basic assumptions inherited from the Atoms for Peace and NPT periods. The result was a revision of U.S. nonproliferation policy and law, aimed at restoring the separation between the peaceful and military use of atoms through new restrictions on nuclear trade and development. The policy shift began under President Ford and became a central theme of Jimmy Carter's candidacy and administration.

The Ford-Carter initiatives were in a sense anomalous. They broke the historical pattern by raising the priority of nonproliferation efforts at a time of U.S. retrenchment from overseas military involvement. America's more reticent post-Vietnam security posture, combined with declining nuclear market power and conflicts among foreign policy goals, hampered U.S. effectiveness on nonproliferation. The new policies encountered strong and, to a considerable degree, successful resistance from industrial allies and Third World nations, who saw them as threatening to their energy security and development. And, as debates on civil nuclear power and trade raged, proliferation continued. Pakistan moved steadily toward a nuclear weapons capability, evading repeated U.S. efforts to frustrate its progress.

At the close of the decade, the Soviet threat returned to dominate U.S. foreign policy calculations. In the wake of the Iranian hostage crisis and the Soviet invasion of Afghanistan, the Carter administration found it hard to reconcile a firm nonproliferation policy with the requirements of countering the Soviet threat. Nonproliferation gave way, most visibly in South Asia, to what National Security Advisor Zbigniew Brzezinski called "more fundamental national security interests."[1]

THE FORD TRANSITION

Gerald Ford's brief tenure as President was a bridge between Nixon-era complacency on nuclear proliferation and Jimmy Carter's crusade on the issue. The events of 1974–1975, and the congressional pressures they produced, caused the Ford administration to challenge traditional nuclear premises along two fronts—the rules governing nuclear exports by the Western industrial countries and plans for domestic nuclear power development in the United States.

On exports, the United States launched a diplomatic effort to stop the incipient flow of sensitive technology to the Third World. These nuclear exports held the danger that they would be ruled strictly by calculations of commercial and diplomatic advantage—magnified in the climate of economic insecurity and pessimism brought on by the oil crisis—and that nonproliferation controls would come unraveled. In particular, the newly competitive supply market would tempt reactor exporters to sweeten their offers by adding sensitive fuel-cycle technologies into the bargain. This was precisely what West Germany had done to win the nuclear "deal of the century"—an agreement to sell Brazil eight nuclear reactors as well as uranium-enrichment technology (ostensibly for making low-enriched reactor fuel, but with the potential to produce bomb-grade levels of uranium 235) and a reprocessing plant (for extracting plutonium from used, or "spent," reactor fuel).[2]

---

[1] Zbigniew Brzezinski, *Power and Principle: Memoirs of the National Security Advisor, 1977–81* (New York: Farrar, Straus & Giroux, 1983), p. 145.

[2] See Norman Gall, "Atoms for Brazil, Dangers for All," *Foreign Policy*, Summer 1976; and William Lowrance, "Nuclear Futures for Sale," *International Security*, Fall 1976. On the general problem of supplier competition leading to deteriorating nonproliferation standards, see Steven Baker, "Monopoly or Cartel," *Foreign Policy*, Summer 1976.

The United States tried to stop this trend by convening the so-called London Suppliers Group in 1975. The group brought together the leading Western nuclear exporters, including France, which, as a nonparty to the NPT, had not participated in earlier supplier efforts to coordinate policies.[3] Although it adopted more rigorous standards for safeguards inspections on exported technologies, the London group failed to agree to the ban on enrichment and reprocessing sales sought by the United States. Nor did it forbid nuclear cooperation with countries refusing to sign the NPT or to accept equivalent comprehensive ("full-scope") safeguards; such a prohibition would have ruled out sales to several of the potentially lucrative markets for nuclear exports, including Brazil, Argentina, India, and Pakistan.

The Ford administration addressed the most egregious Third World nuclear developments through bilateral approaches to the countries involved. These efforts were successful in the cases of Taiwan and South Korea, but unavailing with Pakistan and Brazil—a mixed record that reflected America's waning ability to dominate the nonproliferation regime and foreshadowed the frustrations of the Carter administration.

In East Asia, Korea and Taiwan had become interested in nuclear weapons in the early 1970s in response to multiple signs of a declining U.S. security commitment to the region—the Vietnam debacle, the Nixon doctrine, and the reversal of Washington's China policy. Both countries hoped to acquire reprocessing technology, which would give them access to plutonium produced in nuclear research or power reactors. Taiwan, whose earlier attempts to purchase a reprocessing plant in the United States and Europe were blocked by the Nixon administration, had by 1975 created a plutonium-extraction lab on its own. When U.S. intelligence learned of this and other weapons-related activities, the Ford administration intervened forcefully and imposed a secret agreement on Taiwan to dismantle the plutonium unit and desist from weapons work.[4]

United States strong-arm tactics also prevailed in South Korea, which, according to later revelations, had launched in the early 1970s a vigorous secret effort to obtain equipment for a nuclear weapons program. Washington became suspicious when Korea contracted with France to buy a reprocessing plant, as there was no apparent energy rationale for the facility (no Korean power reactors were yet operating). The Ford administration also suspected that Seoul's reluctant 1975 ratification of the NPT

---

[3] In deference to France, the initial London meetings were held in secret. See Michael Brenner, *Nuclear Power and Non-Proliferation: The Remaking of U.S. Policy* (Cambridge: Cambridge Univ. Press, 1981), pp. 93ff.

[4] Leonard Spector, *The Undeclared Bomb* (Cambridge, MA: Ballinger, 1988), pp. 346–47 (footnote 24); interview with involved U.S. official. American leverage was magnified by Taiwan's ambitious nuclear power program and its total dependence on U.S. low-enriched uranium to fuel its reactors. Because Taiwan had become a "nonstate" following the reversal of U.S. China policy, and had lost its membership in the IAEA, no other supplier could have stepped in if the United States had cut off its nuclear fuel supply.

had been more a tactic to gain access to Western technology than a sincere renunciation of nuclear weapons. Dealing from a position of commanding strategic leverage, the United States threatened to cut military sales credits to its highly dependent client state, and persuaded Korea to cancel the purchase in early 1976.[5]

With Pakistan, however—another customer for French reprocessing technology—the United States had a weaker hand to play. Pakistan's quest for nuclear weapons began in early 1972 at the instigation of Prime Minister Zulfikar Ali Bhutto, who had assumed power in the wake of the country's defeat and dismemberment by India the previous fall.[6] Bhutto apparently planned to obtain plutonium for an atomic bomb by reprocessing spent fuel from Pakistan's KANUPP reactor, and he negotiated a deal with Paris for the necessary facility during 1973 and 1974. France, hopeful of gaining future reactor and military aircraft orders from Pakistan, accepted the latter's implausible claims that the plant was intended for peaceful energy uses, though it did press for strict IAEA inspection rights at the urging of the United States.

The Ford administration, recognizing Pakistan's acute sense of insecurity, tried to divert it from the nuclear path with conventional military aid. In 1975 the United States lifted its arms embargo dating from the 1965 Indo-Pakistani war. The following August, Henry Kissinger met Bhutto in Islamabad and offered 110 A-7 attack planes as an inducement to cancel the French reprocessing contract. The offer was controversial because it violated American policy against transfers of advanced offensive weapons to the subcontinent, and would have caused serious concern in New Delhi. But Bhutto rejected the bargain despite Kissinger's warnings that the reprocessing issue could undermine U.S.-Pakistani relations.[7] Kissinger was equally unsuccessful in persuading Paris to withdraw from the reprocessing deal.

Ford and Kissinger also took aim at the German-Brazilian nuclear extravaganza, but again without success. Their efforts here were handicapped by the conviction in Bonn and Brasilia that U.S. opposition was commercially motivated. Westinghouse, the supplier of Brazil's first nuclear plant, had competed for the multireactor order and lost out to

---

[5] Spector, *The Undeclared Bomb*, p. 341; Mitchell Reiss, *Without the Bomb: The Politics of Nuclear Nonproliferation* (New York: Columbia Univ. Press, 1988), p. 93; and Leslie Gelb, "Nuclear Proliferation and Arms Sales," *New York Times*, August 11, 1976, p. 3.

[6] See Steven Weissman and Herbert Krosney, *The Islamic Bomb* (New York: Times Books, 1981), pp. 40ff; and Ashok Kapur, *Pakistan's Nuclear Development* (London: Croom Helm, 1987). As Foreign Minister in the 1960s, Bhutto had lobbied for a Pakistani bomb program to keep pace with India's nuclear progress. His views were rejected and Pakistan's atomic program remained dedicated to peaceful ends, although Islamabad did follow New Delhi in rejecting the NPT.

[7] Weissman and Krosney, *The Islamic Bomb*, p. 163; Gelb, "Nuclear Proliferation and the Sale of Arms"; James Markham, "U.S.-Pakistani Rift on Atom Fuel Grows," *New York Times*, May 8, 1977, p. 9.

Germany, in part because U.S. companies were barred from offering the sensitive technology desired by Brazil. In addition, the Nixon administration had undercut the competitiveness of U.S. firms by a clumsy and shortsighted attempt to privatize the American uranium-enrichment industry in the early 1970s. To further this plan, the Atomic Energy Commission had revised its contract provisions in a way that artificially inflated the demand for enrichment services. Then, pointing to a projected shortage of enrichment capacity, the AEC abruptly closed its order books in July 1974 and reclassified some 45 existing contracts—including two held by Brazil—as "conditional." The inevitable result was a devastating loss of confidence in the United States as a nuclear supplier.[8]

Though not the main cause of Brazil's opting for German reactors, the enrichment contracts fiasco helped ratify that decision and accelerated the broader erosion of U.S. primacy in the nuclear market that the Germany-Brazil deal exemplified. In these circumstances, U.S. arguments against the agreement were too easily dismissed as a case of "sour grapes." In Brazil, the nuclear agreement, already a potent symbol of the country's great-power ambitions, was embraced all the more fervently as it emerged as a symbol of defiance toward Washington. Both parties rejected the U.S. plea to remove enrichment and reprocessing from the agreement, stressing the rigor of the IAEA safeguards to be applied to these technologies. Seeing a lost cause and unwilling to strain relations with Germany over the issue, the Ford administration muted its protests. To ease tensions with Brazil, it signed a February 1976 agreement for semiannual high-level political consultations between the two countries.[9]

Domestic nuclear power development was the second front of Ford's nonproliferation drive. In its final months, the administration began to question the entrenched wisdom guiding nuclear energy policy in the United States and the rest of the industrial world. The target of this reappraisal was the "closed" nuclear fuel cycle. Under prevailing plans, spent fuel from nuclear plants would be reprocessed to separate and recover plutonium from the irradiated fuel elements. The plutonium would be recycled in new fuel rods for use either in existing reactors or in the fast-breeder reactors then under development. The latter would in turn "breed" new plutonium (in a natural uranium blanket surrounding the reactor core), producing more fissile material than they consumed in the process.

This vision of the nuclear future had long been treated as dogma on energy and economic grounds. The anticipated rapid growth of nuclear power would deplete world uranium reserves; as uranium became scarcer and more expensive, the shift to a "plutonium economy" would become compelling. The 1973–1974 oil crisis reinforced the argument by drawing

---

[8] See Brenner, *Nuclear Power and Non-Proliferation*, Part I; and Edward Wonder, *Nuclear Fuel and American Policy* (Boulder, CO: Westview Press, 1977).

[9] See William Courtney, "Brazil and Argentina: Strategies for American Diplomacy," in Joseph Yager, ed., *Nonproliferation and U.S. Foreign Policy* (Washington, DC: Brookings, 1980), pp. 377–80.

attention to the energy security benefits of the closed fuel cycle, which promised to reduce the dependence of energy-poor countries on foreign uranium and enrichment services. The nuclear orthodoxy also held that reprocessing and plutonium recycle were necessary for the safe disposal of nuclear reactor wastes.[10]

In the mid-1970s, government and outside analysts belatedly started addressing the proliferation dangers of this transition to plutonium fuel. In many respects, their analysis closely paralleled that of the Acheson-Lilienthal report of thirty years earlier. In a plutonium economy, they warned, countries would be able to edge very close to a weapons capability under the guise of a legitimate nuclear power program. The presence of large stocks of readily available plutonium would facilitate the diversion of weapons material from civilian nuclear programs, creating a tempting pathway to proliferation that would swamp the monitoring capabilities of the international safeguards system.[11]

By mid-1976, the Ford administration was being pressed from several directions to address these concerns. Congressional interest in proliferation was mounting; Jimmy Carter was promoting the issue in his presidential campaign; and the first U.S. commercial reprocessing plant (at Barnwell, South Carolina) was nearing completion. In response, Ford ordered an interagency study of plutonium policy that posed the first official challenge to conventional nuclear wisdom. Known as the Fri study, the review led Ford to an important policy statement on the eve of the 1976 election. In it, he emphasized the international security implications of U.S. domestic nuclear policy, and announced that the United States would no longer regard reprocessing and plutonium recycle as a "necessary and inevitable step in the nuclear fuel cycle." Calling for a rethinking of nuclear trade and development premises, he argued that the plutonium transition "should not proceed" without stronger assurances that the world community could manage its associated proliferation risks.[12]

---

[10] For a thorough discussion of these issues, see the Report of the Nuclear Energy Policy Study Group, *Nuclear Power Issues and Choices* (Cambridge, MA: Ballinger, 1977). Generally known as the "Ford-MITRE" report, this study was an important influence on the Carter administration nuclear policies.

[11] The most influential statement of the argument was a report prepared for the Arms Control and Disarmament Agency: Albert Wohlstetter et al., *Moving Toward Life in a Nuclear Armed Crowd?* (Los Angeles: Pan Heuristics, 1976). Anticipating the Carter policy line, the report made a strong case against plutonium on economic as well as nonproliferation grounds. See also Albert Wohlstetter, "Spreading the Bomb Without Quite Breaking the Rules," *Foreign Policy*, Winter 1976–1977.

[12] Statement on Nuclear Policy, October 28, 1976, *Public Papers of the President*, 1976, p. 2763. The statement also called for a three-year moratorium on sales of sensitive fuel-cycle facilities (enrichment and reprocessing). The Fri study was named for its chair, Robert Fri, who was deputy director of the Energy Research and Development Agency (the successor agency to the AEC, which Congress abolished in 1974, and precursor of the Department of Energy, which was created by Carter in 1977). On the Fri study and Ford statement, see Brenner, *Nuclear Power and Non-Proliferation*, pp. 101–15.

When the Ford administration ended, the further defining and implementing of this new direction remained up in the air. So, too, did the fate of U.S. atomic-energy law, which Congress had begun to revamp during Ford's tenure. In June 1976, Congress passed the Symington amendment, which barred U.S. foreign economic and military assistance to countries importing enrichment technology and refusing to accept NPT-type full-scope safeguards. (A companion measure covering reprocessing, the Glenn amendment, was adopted the next year.) And a far-reaching overhaul of U.S. nuclear-export procedures—designed to tighten non-proliferation controls and curtail executive-branch discretion in nuclear sales—was pending as President Carter took office in January 1977.[13]

THE CARTER NONPROLIFERATION CAMPAIGN

The Carter administration assumed power with nonproliferation near the top of its foreign policy agenda.[14] Only in Truman's efforts to retain the U.S. atomic monopoly, and Johnson's on behalf of the NPT, had the United States previously accorded the issue such priority. In contrast to these earlier peaks of presidential interest, however, Carter approached nonproliferation less as a traditional U.S. national security interest than as part of an emerging cluster of "world order" problems. These revolved around the theme of global economic interdependence, which—in the wake of the energy crisis and a trend toward politicization of trade and resource issues—was widely seen in the mid-1970s as displacing the classic Cold War foreign policy agenda. Superpower détente and the growing prominence of relations between the industrial and the less-developed nations (the "North-South dialogue") furthered the sense of an important shift in the focus of world politics. Thus Cyrus Vance, Carter's Secretary of State, criticized the Nixon-Kissinger strategy for being "too narrowly rooted in the concept of an overarching U.S.-Soviet 'geopolitical' struggle":

> New crises unrelated to competition with the Soviet Union had and would occur around the globe with increasing frequency. . . . Not only had the bipolar focus of the postwar period given way to a more complicated set of

---

[13] Congressional activism on the issue had been spurred by several developments, including the revelation that U.S. heavy water had figured in the Indian nuclear test; Nixon's offer of reactors to Israel and Egypt; and rising public concerns about the safety and environmental risks of nuclear energy. For an exhaustive treatment of the reform of U.S. nonproliferation legislation, see Robert L. Beckman, *Nuclear Non-Proliferation: Congress and the Control of Peaceful Nuclear Activities* (Boulder, CO: Westview Press, 1985).

[14] In an early interview, Secretary of State Vance stated that, of the problems facing his department, he "assigned the highest priority to prevention of the spread of nuclear weapons and coordination of that policy with control over sales of conventional weapons." *New York Times*, February 11, 1976, p. 11.

relationships in which power was more diffuse, but also it had become essential for the United States to grapple with the North-South issues. . . . Global interdependence, once a fashionable buzzword, had become a reality, and our future was inextricably entwined with the economic and political developments of a turbulent Third World.[15]

Nuclear proliferation, like the oil crisis, became an exemplar of this new class of global problems facing America.

Proliferation also connected squarely to another central theme of the Carter foreign policy—its pronounced idealistic, antimilitarist thrust. A hallmark of the administration was its repudiation of the alleged cynicism of the Nixon-Kissinger realpolitik and its declared intention to restore a firm moral foundation to U.S. foreign policy. This moralism was manifest in Carter's campaign for human rights, his abolitionist instincts regarding nuclear weapons, and his determination to curb the international arms trade. It strongly colored the administration's nonproliferation initiatives.

Against this reformist, world-order focus, however, the Carter administration also embodied a more traditional set of priorities. National Security Advisor Zbigniew Brzezinski was the chief spokesman within the administration for Cold War geopolitics, with an emphasis on military power and the Soviet threat. The tension between the two worldviews—personified by the rivalry between Vance and Brzezinski—became an increasingly debilitating source of friction and incoherence in the Carter foreign policy.[16]

Nonproliferation policy suffered from this tension and from being largely identified with the idealist/world-order agenda. As a result, the issue became detached from the traditional agenda of U.S. national security policy. Loosening its previous anchor in this agenda, nonproliferation acquired a fragile quality and—despite the high priority initially assigned to it—lost "weight" as a vital U.S. national interest.

---

[15] Cyrus Vance, *Hard Choices: Critical Years in America's Foreign Policy* (New York: Simon & Schuster, 1983), p. 27. A good collection of articles capturing the new attention to interdependence and North-South issues at this time is Richard Cooper, ed., *A Reordered World* (Washington, DC: Potomac Associates, 1973). Contemporary academic analyses contrasting the "world order" and "power politics" foreign policy agendas are Joseph Nye and Robert Keohane, *Power and Interdependence* (Boston: Little, Brown, 1977); and Stanley Hoffman, *Primacy or World Order* (New York: McGraw-Hill, 1978). President Carter's classic statement of the new agenda was his commencement address at Notre Dame University in May 1977, in which he rejected the "inordinate fear of communism" as the guiding principle of U.S. policy and affirmed the primacy of world order concerns. See *Public Papers of the President*, 1977, p. 954.

[16] See, in addition to the two protagonists' memoirs, Gaddis Smith, *Morality, Reason, and Power: American Diplomacy in the Carter Years* (New York: Hill & Wang, 1986). A good discussion of the tension between liberal and conservative worldviews in the Carter years is Michael Mandelbaum and William Schneider, "The New Internationalisms: Public Opinion and American Foreign Policy," in Kenneth Oye, Donald Rothchild, and Robert J. Lieber, eds., *Eagle Entangled: U.S. Foreign Policy in a Complex World* (New York and London: Longman, 1979).

(Brzezinski considered it essentially a "humanitarian" issue, a case of "good intentions."[17]) The implications of this detachment were obscured while U.S.-Soviet détente lasted, but they became obvious late in the decade when the reassertion of Cold War priorities caused nonproliferation—along with other "world order" issues—to be largely jettisoned by the administration.

In substance, the Carter nonproliferation policy built on the Ford reforms. It stressed tighter controls on peaceful nuclear cooperation, and urged supplier countries to embargo sales of sensitive facilities and require their customers to accept full-scope safeguards. On domestic fuel-cycle policy, Carter went beyond the Ford pause to declare—in an April 7, 1977, nuclear policy statement—an indefinite deferral of U.S. plans for commercial reprocessing and plutonium recycling. He called for the termination of the Department of Energy's fast-breeder reactor demonstration project at Clinch River, Tennessee, and a redirection of U.S. breeder research and development toward a search for alternative, "proliferation-resistant" technologies. In the meantime, the U.S. nuclear power industry would continue to rely on the "once-through" fuel cycle, with spent reactor fuel being stored as such (either at reactor sites or in new central storage facilities) rather than reprocessed. The other industrial countries were asked to reassess their own plans for an early transition to plutonium power and to defer commitments to new reprocessing facilities.

Tactically, the new U.S. policy relied heavily on supply leverage—on the U.S. ability to reshape the incentives and program choices of its nuclear fuel and reactor customers. This was especially true of the Nuclear Non-Proliferation Act (NNPA), a major reform of U.S. law on peaceful nuclear cooperation, that emerged from Congress in May 1978 with the Carter administration's qualified support. The NNPA imposed stricter criteria for U.S. nuclear exports, and called for the renegotiation of existing agreements to bring them in line with the new conditions. It required the termination of U.S. cooperation with countries embarking on weapons programs, assisting others to do so, or—after a two-year grace period—failing to submit their nuclear programs to full-scope safeguards inspections.

In addition, the NNPA created an exacting new standard for U.S. consent to the reprocessing of American-origin nuclear fuel. While U.S. veto rights had been a standard feature of American agreements for cooperation—with the important exception of the agreement with EURATOM—the presumption had been that the United States would

---

[17] Brzezinski, *Power and Principle*, pp. 129ff. An exception to this tendency was the school of thought represented by Albert Wohlstetter, who combined hawkish Cold War views with a hard-line, alarmist analysis of the proliferation threat (see footnote 11). This mindset was relatively rare in the Carter administration, but was characteristic of Pentagon officials like Fred Ikle and Richard Perle under President Reagan (see chap. 7).

routinely approve reprocessing. Under the NNPA, however, approvals were subject to a finding that the reprocessing would not result in a "significant increase in the risk of proliferation." This risk was defined mainly in terms of the United States having "timely warning" of any diversion of plutonium—that is, warning well in advance of the time it would take the diverter to fabricate a nuclear explosive. Taken literally, the "timely warning" standard would virtually rule out reprocessing and plutonium use in non-nuclear-weapon states. The NNPA also required the United States to renegotiate its nuclear agreement with EURATOM in order to obtain veto rights over the reprocessing of U.S. fuel exported to the European community.[18]

In both spirit and practice, the Carter reforms suggested a partial reversion from the Atoms for Peace philosophy to a denial-based non-proliferation strategy. But even as it sought to restrict and abridge the traditional nuclear bargain, the Carter administration was also trying to bolster foreign perceptions of the United States as a "reliable supplier" of fuel and reactors. Indeed, such confidence was critical to the success of U.S. efforts to discourage plutonium use abroad. This duality risked making U.S. policy self-defeating: the use of fuel leverage to force others away from plutonium commitments could undermine confidence in U.S. supply, thereby increasing incentives for foreign countries to develop their own fuel-cycle capabilities in order to escape dependence on the United States.[19]

CONSTRAINTS AND CONTRADICTIONS

The Carter nonproliferation agenda was ambitious and diplomatically tricky. It required, for example, that the United States treat its closest allies both as part of the problem and part of the solution—challenging their domestic nuclear energy programs while soliciting their support in curtailing exports to the Third World. Moreover, the international environment of the 1970s was not hospitable to a major U.S. campaign against nuclear proliferation. Even at the height of its post-war power, of course, the United States had not been able to dictate the terms of the non-

---

[18] On the issue of consent rights (officially called "subsequent arrangements"), see Victor Gilinsky, "Plutonium, Proliferation, and the Price of Reprocessing," *Foreign Affairs*, Winter 1978–1979. On the NNPA, see Frederick Williams, "The Nuclear Non-Proliferation Act of 1978," *International Security*, Fall 1978. Though the Carter administration supported the bill overall, it had misgivings about attaching the full-scope safeguards requirement retroactively to existing agreements and argued for flexibility in applying the "timely warning" standard to foreign reprocessing. See Beckman, *Nuclear Non-Proliferation*, pp. 307–46.

[19] A good critique of this weakness in U.S. policy is Thomas Neff and Henry Jacoby, "Nonproliferation Policy in a Changing Nuclear Fuel Market," *Foreign Affairs*, Summer 1979.

proliferation regime. But by the 1970s it was fast losing two critical supports of its earlier regime building—its hegemonic security role in the noncommunist world and its near-monopoly position in nuclear markets. The diffusion of economic and military power and rising interdependence constrained U.S. influence, increasing both the incentives and the ability of other nations to resist the Carter policies.[20] The result, on nonproliferation and other global issues, was a wide gap between the ends and means of U.S. policy.

Compounding these external obstacles to the Carter nonproliferation campaign were internal tensions and conflicts within the administration's broad foreign policy agenda. Partly by inclination and partly in response to the increasingly complex global environment, the Carter administration launched an unusually large number of high-profile policy initiatives. In many cases these clashed—directly or indirectly—with the administration's nonproliferation objectives.

Perhaps the most obvious case was that of energy policy, which Carter declared to be the "moral equivalent of war." The Carter challenge to plutonium power was widely regarded overseas as perversely out of phase with the imperative of increased energy security and reduced oil dependence in the wake of the OPEC crisis. Though the United States made a cogent economic argument that the trade-off between energy security and nonproliferation was more apparent than real, the argument was politically unpersuasive to allies whose energy vulnerability far exceeded America's.

A second area of discontinuity was the traditional security realm. Here, the post-Vietnam retraction of American power remained a source of unease and provided potential nuclear incentives for American Cold War allies, especially in Asia. The Carter administration, while avoiding an isolationist stance, followed its Republican predecessors in seeking to lower America's direct overseas military involvement. In contrast to the Kissinger era, though, this retrenchment was colored by a moral aversion to military intervention and covert action in the cause of Cold War anticommunism. Similarly, Carter broke with previous U.S. policy in seeking to impose sharp limits on conventional arms sales abroad. In May 1977 he announced that arms transfers would become an "exceptional instrument of foreign policy" and established several qualitative and quantitative guidelines intended to reduce U.S. activity in this area. Strictly observed, this policy risked sacrificing a potentially useful nonproliferation lever in some parts of the world. Although in practice the

---

[20] See Joseph Nye, "Maintaining a Nonproliferation Regime," in George Quester, ed., *Nuclear Proliferation: Breaking the Chain* (Madison: University of Wisconsin Press, 1981), pp. 19–20. A study of the market for low-enriched uranium reactor fuel found that "as of 1980, the combination of excess capacity and Soviet exports is such that it would be physically possible for *all* non-U.S. demand to be satisfied by non-U.S. sources." Neff and Jacoby, "Nonproliferation Policy," p. 1134.

new guidelines were repeatedly stretched and evaded, the policy added to the perception of a weakening of U.S. security links with traditional partners.[21]

A third area of friction was North-South relations. An important theme of the Carter foreign policy was the need for a sympathetic and forthcoming U.S. response to Third World demands for a more equitable global economic order. The case for taking the less-developed countries (LDCs) seriously was both moral and pragmatic, given their growing ability to threaten Western economic and security interests.[22] Yet the attempt to curtail Third World access to nuclear technology through the London Group and unilateral U.S. pressure was inevitably perceived as a neocolonial suppression of the "have-not" countries' development aspirations—a perception that alienated far more LDCs than the few that were directly affected by restrictive U.S. nuclear policies. Similarly, these policies clashed with the goal of cultivating closer U.S. ties with emerging Third World regional powers having potential nuclear ambitions, such as Iran and Brazil. Nixon and Ford had regarded such countries as important stabilizing forces and surrogates for U.S. power (often amply supplied with U.S. arms) in key regions. The Carter administration was more ambivalent: Brzezinski supported the previous policy, while others wished to distance the United States from regimes that were often antidemocratic.

Human rights was yet another area in which the Carter nonproliferation strategy was intersected and complicated by the pursuit of other goals. Many targets of U.S. nonproliferation policy—including Argentina, Brazil, Pakistan, South Africa, and South Korea—were also targets of the human rights campaign. By antagonizing these countries on the rights issue, the United States risked strengthening their resistance to its nuclear policies. Furthermore, sanctions imposed in response to human rights violations, such as restrictions on economic and military aid or multilateral bank loans, would constrain U.S. flexibility to use carrots and sticks to influence nuclear behavior.[23]

---

[21] On the Carter arms transfer policy, see Andrew Pierre, *The Global Politics of Arms Sales* (Princeton: Princeton Univ. Press, 1982), pp. 52–62; and Seymour Weiss, *President Carter's Arms Transfer Policy: A Critical Assessment* (Coral Gables, FL: Advanced International Studies Institute, 1978). On U.S. practice under Nixon and Ford, see Leslie Gelb, "Arms Sales," *Foreign Policy*, Winter 1976–1977. On arms sales as a nonproliferation tool, see Richard Burt, "Nuclear Proliferation and the Spread of New Conventional Weapons Technology," *International Security*, Winter 1977; and Lewis Dunn, "Some Reflections on the 'Dove's Dilemma,'" in Quester, ed., *Nuclear Proliferation*.

[22] See, for example, C. Fred Bergsten, "The Threat from the Third World," *Foreign Policy*, Summer 1973, reprinted in Cooper, ed., *A Reordered World*.

[23] As with arms transfers and nonproliferation itself, the Carter administration in practice pursued its human rights campaign unevenly and selectively, often sacrificing it to geopolitical expediency. See Sandra Vogelgesang, *American Dream, Global Nightmare: The Dilemma of U.S. Human Rights Policy* (New York: Norton, 1980).

TWO EARLY MISPLAYS: BRAZIL AND SOUTH KOREA

Amid this multiplicity of sometimes competing objectives, the Carter administration's typical style was to compartmentalize issues. This tendency produced a "disaggregative approach to foreign policy" in which priorities were not clearly established and the trade-offs and linkages between issues were not explicitly addressed.[24] One result was that while nonproliferation was declared a paramount objective, it was often not clear how this goal meshed with others. Two early controversies—the German-Brazilian nuclear deal and the withdrawal of troops from South Korea—underscored the problem of keeping the various strands of U.S. policy coherently aligned.

Brazil, occupying an important role on several of the administration's agendas, epitomized the complexity of the Carter foreign policy challenge. It was a traditionally close U.S. hemispheric ally, an emerging Third World power and potential nuclear weapon state, and a dubious respecter of human rights. It was also highly dependent on OPEC oil. Moreover, the administration was divided on which of these attributes should take precedence in U.S.-Brazilian relations. As a candidate, Carter had portrayed Brazil as one of the anticommunist military dictatorships from which the U.S. should distance itself. To human rights and nonproliferation officials in the administration, it was important to confront Brazil on these issues. Brzezinski, on the other hand, sided with Latin America bureau officers in the State Department in favoring Kissinger's policy of courting Brazil as a "regional stabilizer."[25]

In fact, the nuclear issue became the center of U.S.-Brazil relations at the outset of the new administration. Prior to the inauguration, Germany notified Carter officials that it planned to issue export licenses for the transfer of reprocessing technology under the 1975 deal. This triggered an immediate confrontation on the issue, with the United States trying to prevent the transfer lest it preempt Carter's nonproliferation initiatives. Rebuffing high-level administration demarches (Vice President Mondale to Bonn and Deputy Secretary of State Christopher to Brasilia), the two countries flatly refused to alter the deal, and charged Washington with interference in their sovereign affairs.

Brazil had numerous reasons to resist Carter's efforts, as it had Ford's. In addition to being an emblem of emerging national power and status, the German deal was the centerpiece of Brazil's energy policy. With its burgeoning energy requirements and dependence on imports for 80

---

[24] Kenneth Oye, "The Domain of Choice: International Constraints and Carter Administration Foreign Policy," in Oye, Rothchild, and Lieber, eds., *Eagle Entangled*, pp. 19–20. This failing, Oye argues, "fostered equivocation on the fundamental question of adaptation to the reality of declining power and expanding interests" (p. 20).

[25] Smith, *Morality, Reason, and Power*, pp. 129–30; Brzezinski, *Power and Principle*, p. 128.

percent of its oil, Brazil looked to the eight German reactors to provide a quarter of its energy by the year 1990. Similarly, it considered enrichment and reprocessing technologies necessary to avoid reliance on foreign enriched uranium, which, a government white paper stated, would simply "replace one form of dependence with another."[26] Brazilians saw Carter's opposition to the deal as an effort to perpetuate U.S. nuclear hegemony and frustrate their country's development and independence; the anti-American backlash was compounded by the release of a State Department human rights report critical of Brazil. This double-barreled U.S. assault provoked Brazilian president Geisel to cancel the two countries' 1952 military assistance agreement.[27]

In April, Germany issued licenses for the export of reprocessing technology, marking the Carter administration's failure in the first test of its nonproliferation policy. Unfortunately timed and clumsily handled, the episode was an inauspicious debut, damaging to U.S. credibility and to relations with Germany and Brazil.

South Korea illustrated the other side of the problem of integrating nonproliferation and foreign policy. Whereas the nuclear issue had been allowed virtually to drive U.S. relations with Brazil in early 1977, it was largely neglected in the making of policy toward Korea. Carter's Korean policy was dominated by his determination to reduce the U.S. military role in that country. As a presidential candidate, he had promised to withdraw American ground forces from Korea. In March 1977 he announced that all 30,000 U.S. troops—accompanied by some 1,000 tactical nuclear weapons—would be brought home by 1982. The plan was in keeping with the existing trend toward U.S. disengagement from Asia; Nixon had earlier removed close to half the U.S. forces stationed in Korea at the start of the decade. But Carter's move also reflected antipathy toward the Seoul regime on human rights grounds and the backlash produced by the 1976 "Koreagate" revelations of wholesale bribery of U.S. officials by Korean agents.[28]

The withdrawal plan was strongly opposed by South Korea as well as Japan and other Asian allies, who saw it as a sign that the United States was abandoning the region. A U.S. pullout, they feared, would tip the Asian balance of power toward the Soviet Union and dangerously weaken deterrence of attack by the numerically superior (albeit qualitatively weaker)

---

[26] Cited in Jonathan Kandell, "Brazil Bitter at U.S. Effort to Impose Nuclear Curb," *New York Times*, March 28, 1977, p. 1.

[27] "Brazil Cancels Military Aid Treaty Over U.S. Report on Human Rights," *New York Times*, March 12, 1977. The action was mainly symbolic since Brazil's arms dependence on the United States was negligible. Ironically, the nuclear controversy had the effect of rallying domestic opponents of the Brazilian regime to the government's cause, thus alienating potential U.S. allies on the human rights question.

[28] Richard Halloran, "Carter Sees Pullout from Korea by 1982," *New York Times*, March 10, 1977, p. A1.

North Korean army. These misgivings were shared by the U.S. military; General John Singlaub publicly called the plan an invitation to war (thus inviting his own dismissal by Carter), and the Joint Chiefs advised against it. Carter's foreign policy advisors also questioned the wisdom of withdrawal. According to Vance—whose East Asia bureau strongly dissented from the policy—only Brzezinski supported the president.[29]

The possible impact of the pullout on South Korean nuclear ambitions apparently did not figure in Carter's original decision. Amid the ensuing controversy, proliferation was a frequently mentioned but secondary theme. Korean officials hinted during the spring of 1977 that the country would have no choice but to develop a nuclear weapons program if the United States left it to face the threat from the north alone.[30] A Congressional Budget Office analysis of the troop question noted that "there seems to be little doubt that the withdrawal . . . could substantially increase South Korea's incentives to acquire nuclear weapons."[31] Nonproliferation officials in the administration warned of this risk, but there is little evidence that their arguments weighed heavily in the thinking of the President, who was determined to carry out his campaign pledge. Carter's seeming complacency on the point was doubly surprising in light of his strong interest in nonproliferation and Korea's very recent history of nuclear weapons activities. The episode was a striking example of Carter's tendency to compartmentalize issues, and it underscored the potential conflict between nonproliferation and the scaling back of U.S. security burdens.

In mid-1979, however, following a visit to Seoul in which he was persistently lobbied by South Korean president Park, Carter reversed himself and suspended the troop withdrawal. The catalyst for the shift was the leak of a new and more alarming CIA estimate of North Korean armed forces, which gave administration opponents of the pullout an opening to reargue their case.[32] While the Korean nuclear threat may have influenced Carter's decision (and was probably deliberately used by the Park regime for leverage on the troop issue), it was almost certainly not decisive.[33] Rather, the

---

[29] Vance, *Hard Choices*, p. 129; Drew Middleton, "Carter Military Plans for Asia Raise Strategic Issues," *New York Times*, April 5, 1977, p. 3; Bernard Weinraub, "General Brown Explains Korea Pullout View," ibid., July 15, 1977, p. 18. In a largely unsuccessful attempt to cushion the blow of the pullout decision, Carter reaffirmed the U.S. security commitment and increased military assistance to South Korea—in effect exempting it from the administration's arms transfer and human rights policies. See Bernard Gwertzman, "U.S. Cuts Foreign Aid in Rights Violations; South Korea Exempt," *New York Times*, February 25, 1977, p. 1.

[30] "Official Hints South Korea Might Build Atom Bomb," *New York Times*, April 1, 1977, p. 4; "Habib to Visit Seoul for Talks on Pullout," ibid., April 9, 1977, p. 5.

[31] Cited in Reiss, *Without the Bomb*, p. 85.

[32] Vance, *Hard Choices*, p. 130; *New York Times*, July 21, 1979, p. 3.

[33] Cf. Mitchell Reiss, who suggests, but does not show, that Park's manipulation of the nuclear threat, which might well have been a bluff, was the key to Carter's reversal. *Without the Bomb*, pp. 85–86.

shift reflected a broader rethinking of the strategic stakes at a time when the administration was reawakening to the Soviet threat.

THE PLUTONIUM DEBATE

The central drama of nonproliferation policy in the first half of the Carter administration was the debate between the United States and its industrial allies over the nuclear fuel cycle. In Western Europe and Japan, opposition to the Carter policy on plutonium fuels was widespread and emphatic. To the allies, the campaign against plutonium was reckless and irresponsible in view of the energy crisis, and a dismaying abdication of America's historic role in sponsoring nuclear power development. More directly, it posed a threat to the allies' domestic energy plans: consent rights over the disposition of U.S.-origin fuel gave Washington a powerful lever against reprocessing and plutonium use, since most reactors in Europe and Japan were still fueled with U.S. low-enriched uranium.

Japan was particularly vulnerable to this leverage, since it had recently signed contracts to ship spent reactor fuel to France and Britain for reprocessing and was on the verge of starting up a pilot reprocessing plant of its own, at Tokai Mura. Both activities would require U.S. approval. Several European countries outside EURATOM also needed U.S. consent to have their fuel reprocessed. While the members of EURATOM were exempt from this requirement under the existing cooperative agreement with the United States, the NNPA required the U.S. to seek veto rights in a renegotiated agreement; failure to agree to talks on the issue would subject EURATOM to a U.S. fuel embargo. In addition, Britain and France had a large stake in U.S. policy, since they were making major investments in reprocessing plants whose profitability depended on servicing U.S.-controlled fuel from Japan and other overseas customers.

The Carter administration was divided over how firmly the United States should exercise its control over foreign reprocessing. "Purists" and their allies in Congress favored a hard line, maximizing U.S. leverage in an effort to strangle the fledgling plutonium industry; "realists" saw a need to tread more cautiously in the interests of allied unity. To use U.S. leverage to the maximum, they feared, would not only damage U.S. relations with Europe and Japan but would hasten the decline of U.S. nuclear influence by driving customers to other suppliers.[34]

---

[34] See Brenner, *Nuclear Power and Non-Proliferation*, pp. 122ff., and Nye, "Maintaining a Nonproliferation Regime," p. 23. The antiplutonium hard-liners were dominant in the National Security Council (where Jessica Tuchman was the responsible staffer) and the Council for Environmental Quality, and had pockets of strength in the Energy Department and Nuclear Regulatory Commission. The pragmatic line was ascendant in the State Department and the U.S. Arms Control and Disarmament Agency.

The purists showed early signs of being ascendant, but in his April 7 statement and remarks afterwards, Carter expressed benign tolerance of European and Japanese plutonium plans, and said the United States had no intention of trying to block them. Weeks later, however, the hard line again appeared to prevail. The administration announced that reprocessing of U.S.-origin fuel would be approved only as a last resort, upon a clear showing of physical need—that is, if the reactor in question had no available storage space for spent fuel and was at risk of being shut down as a result. The United States would retain a veto over any use of the separated plutonium. The new criteria were presented by Joseph Nye, Carter's top nonproliferation official, at an IAEA conference in Salzburg that became a forum for bitter attacks on U.S. policy.

The intensity of opposition to the United States stemmed from several sources.[35] Governments in Europe and Japan saw the antiplutonium campaign as a threat to the economic and political viability of their nuclear power programs, which in turn were central to energy security strategies aimed at reducing oil dependence. Resentment of the Carter policy was compounded by the differential energy vulnerability of the United States and the other Western industrial nations. The United States, generously endowed with domestic reserves of oil, coal, and uranium, could do without plutonium; Europe and Japan, it was argued, could not. (In 1977, the United States imported only about 40 percent of the oil it consumed; for Japan, Germany, and France, import dependence was over 95 percent.) The United States's motives were also suspect: aborting the transition to a plutonium economy would undermine the allies' reprocessing and breeder-reactor programs—which were farther advanced than America's—and prolong dependence on low-enriched uranium fuel, where the United States remained dominant.

Underlying these arguments were deeper political grievances—the legacy of Western divisions over the NPT and the oil crisis. The Carter policies were accused, especially in Bonn and Tokyo, of reneging on U.S. assurances during the NPT negotiations that nonweapon states would have full access to nuclear fuel-cycle technologies.[36] Critics argued as well that the United States, by questioning whether plutonium fuel cycles could be adequately safeguarded against diversion, was undercutting the credibility of the whole NPT/IAEA system.

---

[35] For European perspectives, see Karl Kaiser, "The Great Nuclear Debate: German-American Disagreements," *Foreign Policy*, Summer 1978; and Pierre Lellouche, "International Nuclear Politics," *Foreign Affairs*, Winter 1979. On Japan, see Richard Lester "U.S.-Japanese Nuclear Relations: Structural Change and Political Strain," *Asian Survey*, May 1982.

[36] At the height of the plutonium controversy, according to one report, Japan threatened to withdraw from the NPT if the U.S. "persisted in trying to dictate world nuclear energy policy from Washington." London *Financial Times*, November 5, 1977, p. 12, as cited in Beckman, *Nuclear Non-Proliferation*, p. 353.

Lingering resentments from the oil crisis, and the alliance strains that it spawned, also played into the nonproliferation debate. In this context, the assault on plutonium was part of a larger pattern of U.S. acts of omission and commission that were seen as damaging to allied energy security. United States's support of Israel had helped trigger the Arab oil embargo, and rising U.S. oil imports in the early 1970s had helped create the conditions for OPEC's drastic price increases. Then, in the wake of the crisis, Washington had pressured the industrial consuming nations to form a united front against OPEC—a posture that many feared would increase their energy risks and that France openly challenged.[37] In short, U.S. policies across a range of energy-related issues seemed to be placing Europe and Japan in harm's way, and this perception fed opposition to the Carter nuclear initiatives. As time went by, the U.S. failure to implement a coherent domestic energy policy, despite Carter's call to arms on the issue, further undercut U.S. leadership on nuclear policy.

Faced with this strong resistance to its policies, the Carter administration tried to temper the controversy by building consensus around a new middle ground. The effort was uneven and precarious, given the splits within the administration. State Department pragmatists, led by Joseph Nye and Gerard Smith (the former champion of the Multilateral Force and now Carter's ambassador-at-large for nonproliferation), had to steer a path between foreign critics and the U.S. nuclear establishment on one side and administration purists and their congressional allies on the other. In essence, they tried to define an approach to nuclear development that would avert the worst dangers of plutonium while being responsive to European and Japanese energy concerns.

The U.S. goal was to narrow the grounds for plutonium separation and use, defer large-scale plutonium operations, and confine them to the advanced industrial states. This approach would accommodate allied research and development on breeder reactors while drawing a line against early breeder commercialization and the recycle of plutonium in existing reactors. (Called "thermal recycle," this practice would create a broad precedent for plutonium use by any country with a nuclear program.) Reprocessing as a means of managing nuclear wastes would also be discouraged. Basic to the argument was the idea that a transition to plutonium was premature in market terms (breeders were far from being commercially competitive), so that a go-slow, "evolutionary" approach was compelling on economic as well as nonproliferation grounds.[38] To

---

[37] On these questions, see Robert J. Lieber, "Economics, Energy, and Security in Alliance Perspective," *International Security*, Spring 1980; and Frans R. Bax, "Energy Security in the 1980s: The Response of U.S. Allies," in Donald Goldstein, ed., *Energy and National Security* (Washington, DC: NDU Press, 1981).

[38] See Joseph Nye, "Nonproliferation: A Long-Term Strategy," *Foreign Affairs*, April 1978, and "Balancing Nonproliferation and Energy Security," Speech to the Uranium Institute, London, July 12, 1978.

promote its efforts at nuclear consensus-building, the United States devised an elaborate two-year study known as the International Nuclear Fuel Cycle Evaluation (INFCE). Although formally designated a technical assessment and not a diplomatic negotiation, INFCE became the forum for an often politicized airing of differences between the United States and its critics.[39]

The administration also wielded the lever of reprocessing consent rights gently. Prior to the onset of INFCE, the United States negotiated an interim agreement allowing Japan to operate its Tokai Mura plant, and Gerard Smith assured Paris and London that the United States would not interfere with their reprocessing services during the course of the study—a concession that was key to obtaining French participation. In mid-1978, the United States received two requests from Japan to ship spent fuel to Europe for reprocessing. One met the administration's "physical need" standard but the other did not. After intense debate, the issue went to the White House, and Carter approved new criteria under which the United States would consent to reprocessing under any contracts signed prior to 1977. Testifying before Congress, Nye defended the approval in terms that echoed the allies' complaints about U.S. policy. Denial, he said, would "create a sense of injustice, of inequity, that we had come along to change the rules of the game governing the nuclear fuel cycle in midstream, causing great difficulty for countries who had large investments, who had regarded this as essential to their energy security."[40]

By the end of the Carter administration, though the United States had given considerable ground on the plutonium question, its efforts had not entirely failed. Predictably, the INFCE reports did not endorse the U.S. preference for the "once-through" fuel cycle. But they validated the principle that proliferation risks should be weighed seriously in designing nuclear power programs, and suggested a more circumscribed plutonium economy than the previous conventional wisdom had anticipated. For example, INFCE concluded that the economic benefits of thermal recycle were marginal, that reprocessing was not a necessary step in nuclear waste disposal, and that breeder reactors made sense only in advanced industrial countries with large nuclear programs.

At the same time, the sharp downturn in U.S. nuclear power growth in the late 1970s—especially following the 1979 Three Mile Island accident—lent support to U.S. arguments for a stretch-out of commitments to plutonium fuel. The downturn meant that uranium would be much cheaper and more abundant than forecast, and that fuel cycles involving

---

[39] See Peter Clausen, "Nuclear Conference Yields Potential New Consensus," *Arms Control Today*, June 1979.

[40] *Nuclear Fuel Transfer for Reprocessing: Pending Cases*, Hearings before the House International Relations Committee, Subcommittee on International Economic Policy and Trade, October 3, 1978, p. 79. On the debate on this issue, see also Gilinsky, "Plutonium, Proliferation, and the Price of Reprocessing."

plutonium separation and recycle could not compete with conventional nuclear plants. In the 1980s, allied breeder programs slipped steadily behind schedule; market realities had largely produced the victory over plutonium commercialization that had eluded the Carter administration. On the other hand, Japan and others continued to have spent reactor fuel reprocessed abroad for lack of publicly acceptable alternatives for managing nuclear waste. A long-term solution on the exercise of U.S. veto rights over this reprocessing (and the use of the resulting plutonium) was unfinished business left to the Reagan administration.

The Carter administration met with similarly mixed success on the issue of nuclear export policies. Germany stood firm on its deal with Brazil but announced a moratorium on further reprocessing exports, and France canceled its sale of this technology to Pakistan in 1978. Here, the United States benefited from several advantages it had lacked in the German case: an opportunity to pursue the matter through quiet diplomacy, strong evidence of Pakistan's nuclear weapons aims, and the relatively modest French economic stake in the sale.[41] Where supplier stakes were higher, the U.S. appeals for restraint were less persuasive. Thus France and Italy entered into questionable export deals with Iraq, a major oil supplier to Europe and (despite nominal NPT membership) would-be nuclear power.[42] Another suspect state—non-NPT member Argentina—obtained a reactor and heavy-water plant from Germany and Switzerland, despite refusing to accept full-scope safeguards on its nuclear program. The United States protested, but its nonproliferation arguments were no match for the logic of oil dependency and commercial advantage that drove these deals.

CARROTS AND STICKS IN SOUTH ASIA

In the second half of the Carter administration, the speculative dangers of the nuclear power fuel cycle gave way to the immediate threat of bomb programs in South Asia as the focus of U.S. nonproliferation policy. Pakistan and India became ill-timed and unwanted test cases of two basic strands of that policy—the use of economic and military aid (under the Glenn-Symington amendments) and nuclear fuel supply (under the NNPA) for leverage on foreign nuclear programs. But U.S. assistance was a weak lever against the growing dynamic of nuclear rivalry on the

---

[41] Since late 1976, France had been gradually moving toward suspending the deal and in general taking more seriously the proliferation dangers of sensitive nuclear technology exports. See Pierre Lellouche, "France in the International Nuclear Energy Controversy," *Orbis*, Winter 1979.

[42] France sold Iraq a large research reactor fueled with highly enriched uranium—the Osirak plant later destroyed by an Israeli air strike (see chap. 7). Italy provided "hot cells," laboratory-scale facilities for plutonium separation. For background on Iraq's nuclear program and its links to European suppliers, see Weissman and Krosney, *The Islamic Bomb*.

subcontinent, and the policy failed both tests; it was finally abandoned in 1980 when the Soviet invasion of Afghanistan pushed rapprochement with Pakistan and India ahead of nonproliferation on the scale of Carter administration priorities.

Carter had inherited the U.S.-Pakistani impasse over Bhutto's drive toward a weapons capability. In July 1977, Bhutto was overthrown in a military coup led by General Mohammed Zia ul-Haq, who proved equally dedicated to the Pakistani bomb. Early U.S. approaches to Zia were unsuccessful in stopping the reprocessing deal with France, and U.S. aid was suspended under the Glenn amendment. A year later, when Paris itself reversed the deal, the aid ban was lifted. There ensued a debate within the administration over the prospects for "buying out" Pakistan's nuclear ambitions with advanced conventional weapons. Nye and others fought to resubmit Kissinger's offer of A-7 attack planes, which were highly valued by the Pakistani Air Force. But Carter, citing the A-7's range and capabilities, vetoed the plan as contrary to his policy of restricting arms transfers. Instead, the United States offered to sell the less-advanced F-5 fighter, which Zia spurned as inadequate to counter the threat from India.[43]

Against this background, Pakistan's nuclear efforts persisted, diverted but not thwarted by France's pullout from the reprocessing deal. Early in 1979, the United States learned of a centrifuge enrichment project at Kahuta, supported by an elaborate clandestine scheme for acquiring the necessary components of a facility.[44] The Carter administration regarded the project as conclusive evidence of a weapons program, and again cut off foreign assistance, this time under the Symington amendment.[45]

The administration imposed sanctions without enthusiasm or much hope of success. The amount of bilateral economic aid involved was token (about $40 million in 1979 and $45 million in 1980), and Pakistan's military needs were mainly supplied by France and China. Pakistan would suffer little deprivation from the cutoff and could not be expected to reverse its nuclear policy as a result. Similarly, attempts by the supplier nations to frustrate further technology acquisition by Pakistan might slow its program but were unlikely to stop it.[46]

---

[43] Don Oberdorfer, "Arms Sales to Pakistan Urged to Stave Off A-Bomb There," *Washington Post*, August 6, 1979.

[44] The effort was conceived and managed by A. Q. Khan, who had obtained plans for a centrifuge plant while working for the Urenco enrichment consortium in the Netherlands. Using deceptive documentation and exploiting gaps in the supplier countries' export control systems, Khan had by 1979 obtained many of the necessary components and materials for the facility. See Weissman and Krosney, *The Islamic Bomb*, pp. 174ff.

[45] Richard Burt, "U.S. Aid to Pakistan Cut After Evidence of Atom Arms Plant," *New York Times*, April 7, 1979, p. 1.

[46] See the testimony of Assistant Secretary of State Thomas Pickering in *Nuclear Proliferation: The Situation in Pakistan and India*, Hearings, Senate Governmental Affairs Committee, Subcommittee on Energy, Nuclear Proliferation, and Federal Services, 96th Cong., 1st sess., May 1, 1979.

Furthermore, the political costs of a showdown on the nuclear issue were considered high. The Kahuta affair came at a particularly bad time: Following a Soviet-backed coup in neighboring Afghanistan in mid-1978, and the Iranian revolution a few months later, the United States was growing concerned about its deteriorating position in South Asia. Pakistan was seen as an important pillar of Western influence amid the regional upheaval, and the Carter administration had been carefully trying to maintain friendly ties with the Zia regime. (Its reaction to the regime's execution of Bhutto in early April had been deliberately muted.) The termination of aid at this juncture risked surrendering what small leverage the United States had with Zia, and was seen by some administration officials as counterproductive. But Pakistani nuclear activities were too blatant to overlook. They were an unavoidable test of Washington's resolve on nonproliferation; failure to carry out U.S. policy in this case would signal acquiescence in Pakistan's nuclear program, undercut U.S. credibility on the issue elsewhere, and seriously prejudice U.S. relations with India.

While reluctantly employing the rather short stick of sanctions, the administration also looked for carrots to lure Pakistan off its nuclear course. It promised civilian nuclear cooperation and diplomatic support for a regional nuclear-free zone (long advocated by Pakistan but opposed by India) if Islamabad would submit its program to international controls, and renewed the offer of F-5 jets. A task force under Gerard Smith considered offering much more capable F-16 fighter-bombers, but this was rejected as too provocative to India.[47] The latter, meanwhile, threatened to accelerate its own nuclear program in response to the Kahuta revelations.

To add to its pessimism, the administration was simultaneously moving toward a moment of truth in U.S. nuclear relations with India. Under the 1978 Nuclear Non-Proliferation Act, American fuel exports for the Tarapur reactors would be prohibited after March 1980 unless India agreed to full-scope safeguards on its civil nuclear program. The approach of this deadline ironically acted as a spoiler in what otherwise might have been a warming trend in U.S.-Indian relations. Carter had taken office with hopes of healing the strains of the Nixon-Kissinger period and weaning India away from the Soviet Union. In New Delhi, Indira Gandhi had been succeeded as Prime Minister by the more dovish Moraji Desai. Desai announced that India would not repeat the 1974 nuclear test or proceed with a weapons-production program, but he was adamant against reversing India's historical rejection of the NPT and its safeguards provisions. A confrontation over the Tarapur fuel question was thus inevitable.

Bilateral talks, including an exchange of state visits by Carter and Desai in 1978, confirmed the bleak outlook for a compromise settlement

---

[47] Richard Burt, "Pakistan is Offered a Choice on A-Arms," *New York Times*, April 17, 1979, p. 3; "U.S. Will Press Pakistan to Halt A-Arms Project," ibid., August 12, 1979, p. 1.

of the issue. India reiterated its traditional argument on the discriminatory nature of the NPT/IAEA system and demanded far-reaching superpower arms control (including a comprehensive test ban and deep reductions in nuclear forces) in return for accepting full-scope safeguards. The NNPA, India maintained, constituted a unilateral, retroactive change in the 1963 agreement for cooperation and was unacceptable. (Carter administration officials, who regretted the NNPA "guillotine clause," were not without sympathy for this complaint, but were constrained by the clear intent of the legislation.) In addition, India claimed that U.S. termination of fuel exports would free it to abrogate safeguards at Tarapur, which, under New Delhi's interpretation of the 1963 agreement, were linked directly to the fuel-supply provisions.[48]

Fuel shipments for Tarapur were narrowly approved in 1978 and 1979 on the grounds that negotiations, however unpromising, were still in progress.[49] But the already slim hopes for an accommodation became even slimmer after the Pakistani enrichment project was exposed. India's bargaining position hardened in the face of the new threat from Pakistan. While standing firm against the NNPA conditions, New Delhi also rebuffed U.S. soundings on a nuclear-free zone on the subcontinent, to be guaranteed by the United States, the Soviet Union, and China.[50] In keeping with its traditional policy, India rejected any nonproliferation formula that would equate it with Pakistan while legitimizing China's right to nuclear status. The situation deteriorated further when Desai lost power in mid-1979 and the new caretaker government declared his disavowal of weapons development and testing to be under reconsideration. As the year wore on, the Carter administration became increasingly fatalistic about the chances of averting a nuclear arms race in South Asia.[51]

The last two months of 1979 saw the Iranian seizure of the U.S. embassy staff in Tehran and the Soviet invasion of Afghanistan. These shocks produced an upheaval in U.S. foreign policy, rearranging the Carter administration's priorities and radically altering the context of its

---

[48] The U.S., in contrast, argued that India's safeguards obligations at Tarapur would remain in force regardless of the fate of the U.S.-Indian fuel link.

[49] In the 1978 case, the NRC vote was split 2-2, thus failing to approve the export. Carter overrode this outcome by issuing an executive order authorizing the shipment. The NRC commissioners opposed to the export argued that because a termination of nuclear cooperation was likely at the end of the NNPA grace period, and India threatened to abrogate Tarapur safeguards at that time, U.S. fuel deliveries during the grace period would simply add to the nuclear material at risk of diversion in the future. See *Export of Nuclear Fuel to India*, Hearings and Markup, House International Relations Committee, 95th Cong., 2nd sess., May 23, June 8 and 14, 1978. In the 1979 case, the NRC approved the shipment by a 3-2 vote.

[50] "Curb on Atom Arms in South Asia Urged," *New York Times*, May 27, 1979.

[51] Richard Burt, "Fears Rising in Washington that an India-Pakistan Nuclear Race Is Inevitable," *New York Times*, August 24, 1979, p. 4.

nonproliferation efforts in South Asia. The Soviet threat immediately ascended to the top of the Carter agenda, ratifying the triumph of Brzezinski's hard-line geopolitical views over Vance's more conciliatory approach. Brzezinski argued, and Carter agreed, that the Soviet action posed an immediate threat to vital American interests; military domination of Afghanistan would put Moscow in a position to dismember Pakistan and Iran and expand its control to the Indian Ocean and the Persian Gulf.[52] United States influence in Southwest Asia—already eroded by the revolution in Iran—would crumble, and the West's access to oil would be jeopardized. To counter this threat, Carter imposed a range of sanctions against the Soviet Union, including a grain embargo, and committed the United States to defend the Persian Gulf against outside aggression (the so-called Carter Doctrine). In acknowledgment of the Cold War's revival, he requested that the Senate suspend consideration of the Strategic Arms Limitation Treaty (SALT II), whose chances for ratification were now nil.

In South Asia, the mending of frayed relations with Pakistan and India became of paramount concern, and nonproliferation sanctions were a luxury the United States could no longer afford. To secure stronger security ties with Pakistan, the administration was prepared to seek a waiver of the Symington amendment to permit a resumption of aid to that country. Brzezinski made a highly publicized visit to the Pakistan-Afghan border, and, with Defense Secretary Harold Brown, pressed for a large, long-term military-assistance package. But a combination of budget constraints, worries about India's reaction, and congressional distaste for the Zia regime pared the U.S. offer down to only $400 million, split evenly between economic assistance and military sales. Equally important, though it reaffirmed the 1959 U.S.-Pakistan bilateral security agreement (aimed at the Soviet Union), the United States was not willing to give the additional guarantees against India that Islamabad wanted. In these circumstances, Zia dismissed the administration's offer.[53]

India, too, assumed new importance in U.S. strategy in the wake of the Afghan crisis. The Carter administration was anxious to keep New Delhi—with Indira Gandhi once again in power—from siding with the Soviet Union, and hoped to solicit its public opposition to the invasion. An early-1980 mission headed by Clark Clifford failed to obtain the latter

---

[52] See Brzezinski, *Power and Principle*, pp. 426ff.

[53] Brzezinski, *Power and Principle*, pp. 448–49; Steven J. Baker, "Nuclear Proliferation," in Hoyt Purvis and Steven J. Baker, eds., *Legislating Foreign Policy* (Boulder, CO: Westview Press, 1984), pp. 146–47; Bernard Gwertzman, "White House Seeks Longterm Aid to Bolster the Defense of Pakistan," *New York Times*, February 1, 1980, p. 1. See also the testimony of Assistant Secretary of State Peter Constable in *India-Pakistan Nuclear Issues*, Hearings, Senate Foreign Relations Committee, 96th Cong., 2nd sess., March 18, 1980.

objective, or to alleviate India's concerns about the possible resumption of U.S. military aid to Pakistan. Soon afterwards, U.S. fears of expanding Soviet influence in India were aggravated when the two countries signed a $1.6 billion arms agreement. In this setting the administration came to regard the Tarapur fuel link as one of the few potential channels of cooperation with India, and began to look for an escape from the impending NNPA-mandated cutoff.

In May, the Nuclear Regulatory Commission unanimously rejected export licenses for the next scheduled shipments of fuel to India. Carter then overruled the NRC and issued an executive order authorizing the exports—an action permitted by the NNPA but subject to reversal by a joint congressional resolution. These developments set the stage for a major debate on the issue. The President finally prevailed—aided by the intense lobbying efforts of former Senator Edmund Muskie, who had succeeded Vance as secretary of state—when the Senate upheld his order by a two-vote margin. Arguing for the shipments, the administration depicted the consequences of a cutoff in dire terms, and—in ironic contrast to the premises of both Atoms for Peace and the NNPA—left little doubt that the Tarapur link had given India more leverage than it had the United States. Deputy Secretary of State Warren Christopher told the Senate that "Tarapur has become a crucial indicator to the Indians of the seriousness with which we view our relationship with them." "India expects us to act on these applications," he warned, "and if we fail to act, we do so at our very considerable peril."[54] Significantly, the administration rejected the notion of a trade-off between nonproliferation and broader foreign policy interests, arguing that continued fuel shipments served both objectives: a cutoff would not only undercut U.S. interests in closer relations with India (and thus "play into the hands of the Soviet Union," as Ambassador Robert Goheen argued[55]), but would carry proliferation risks, given India's threat to terminate safeguards at Tarapur and reprocess the accumulated spent fuel there.

Opponents of the export argued that it was an illusion to suppose that the United States would gain significant foreign policy benefits from

---

[54] *The Tarapur Nuclear Fuel Export Issue*, Joint hearings, Senate Foreign Relations and Governmental Affairs Committees, 96th Cong., 2nd sess., June 19, 1980, pp. 81 and 97. The administration tried to square its position with the NNPA by arguing that the shipments should be considered to fall within the grace period, since India had expected them to occur before the cutoff date. But a clear subtext of administration arguments was that the NNPA attempt to impose full-scope safeguards retroactively had been both politically and legally dubious. "If we were to cut off our fuel shipments," Christopher testified, "India could plausibly ask whether the United States is a country that abides by its commitments." *Resolutions of Disapproval Pertaining to the Shipment of Nuclear Fuel to India*, Hearings and Markup, House Committee on Foreign Affairs, 96th Cong., 2nd sess., June 26, July 23, and September 10, 1980, p. 24.

[55] Robert Goheen, "Problems of Proliferation: U.S. Policy and the Third World," *World Politics*, January 1982, p. 200.

continuing to supply fuel (citing the India-Soviet arms deal as evidence of India's true leanings), and dismissed the nonproliferation argument as acceding to Indian blackmail. In reality, the proliferation risks of a cutoff were probably overdrawn by the administration. An alternative supplier of fuel (the Soviet Union being the most likely) would have insisted on continued safeguards at Tarapur—stricter, in all likelihood, than those contained in the 1963 U.S. agreement. Proponents of the export recognized the Soviet option, but defined it as a further political risk of U.S. termination rather than a means of reducing the proliferation risks of such action—strong evidence of the primacy of anti-Soviet foreign policy considerations over nonproliferation in Carter's decision to continue fuel supplies.[56]

At the end of Carter's term, U.S. nonproliferation efforts in South Asia were in disarray. On behalf of what were defined as overriding strategic imperatives, the United States had pulled back from a strict implementation of its nuclear policy and law toward both India and Pakistan. Yet it had little to show for its retreat—no Pakistani aid package, no Indian support against the Soviet Union, and no significant influence over either country's nuclear policies. This disappointing outcome was not surprising, however, because in both cases the United States was dealing from a position of strategic weakness that was in part of its own making.[57] Successive U.S. administrations had taken South Asia seriously only intermittently and as a function of U.S. preoccupations with the Soviet Union and China. Three times between 1965 and 1980 the United States had banned assistance to Pakistan and later reversed itself. This zigzag course, Washington's parsimonious approach when it did offer aid, and its manifest inability to save Pakistan from disaster in 1971, gave the United States no firm basis from which to induce or enforce Islamabad's nuclear restraint. In the final analysis, probably only a firm alliance with Pakistan against India would have persuaded Zia to abandon his nuclear program. This option was not only politically unthinkable, but it would also have

---

[56] See McGeorge Bundy, "Ship the Fuel to India," *Washington Post*, June 13, 1980. Bundy rhetorically questioned whether Soviet substitution for U.S. fuel supply would be "a gain for the good cause." In nonproliferation terms, though, the switch probably would have been a net gain. A stronger case for the proliferation risks of a cutoff existed if India were to reprocess Tarapur fuel and fabricate its own plutonium fuel for recycle in the reactors, rather than turn to an alternative outside supplier. Even in this case, though, India would have had strong disincentives to a safeguards abrogation. Furthermore, India had ample unsafeguarded stocks of weapons-usable plutonium elsewhere in its nuclear program. As Sen. Glenn argued, "The real Indian threat is not the removal of safeguards from Tarapur, it is the lack of safeguards at its other facilities." John Glenn, "No Fuel for Tarapur," *Washington Post*, September 22, 1980. See also Peter Clausen, "Nonproliferation Illusions: Tarapur in Retrospect," *Orbis*, Fall 1983.

[57] See Richard Betts, "India, Pakistan, and Iran," in Joseph Yager, ed., *Nonproliferation and U.S. Foreign Policy*, pp. 353ff.

forfeited any U.S. influence over India and stimulated the latter's nuclear weapons program.

CONCLUSION

United States nonproliferation policy aimed very high and inevitably fell short of its early aspirations. On the positive side, the Ford and Carter administrations succeeded in raising international consciousness about the proliferation dangers of overly permissive nuclear-export policies and a wholesale rush to commercialize plutonium fuels. In effect, the United States argued that the world was no longer safe for the Atoms for Peace philosophy—that developments both within and outside the realm of nuclear relations demanded a more cautious approach to nuclear development and trade. To a considerable degree, these arguments were assimilated into a new conventional wisdom among the industrial countries. On the other hand, the United States experienced painful limits on its ability to translate a much higher declaratory priority for nonproliferation into effective action. The United States was regularly frustrated by two related problems—conflicts between nonproliferation and other objectives, and the general decline of American influence.

The first problem reflected both the external reality of the decade's complex foreign policy agenda and an internal U.S. failure to integrate the nuclear issue into the larger national security picture. This failing gave nonproliferation more of an abstract quality than it had had in earlier periods of high priority for the issue. Truman's interest had been directly linked to the emerging conflict with the Soviet Union; Kennedy's and Johnson's derived largely from the imperatives of nuclear strategy and U.S. global interventionism. But Ford and Carter raised the issue at a time of U.S. retrenchment and superpower détente. For them (and especially Carter), proliferation was a generalized world-order problem. It was no less urgent because of this, but was vulnerable to being traded off against more concrete interests when these made their claim on U.S. attentions.

The problem was aggravated by the decline of U.S. influence due to post-Vietnam inhibitions, the diffusion of power, and the rise of economic interdependence and energy security as central issues of world politics. In this setting, the United States found it difficult to make its preferences carry weight with other governments. (South Korea and Taiwan, where America's residual Cold War clout still held sway, were exceptions.) Unable to relieve its allies' energy vulnerabilities (and indeed, suspected of contributing to them), the United States was handicapped in its campaign against plutonium fuel cycles. Unable to guarantee security for India or Pakistan (and perceived by both at various times as part of their problems), the United States had little real leverage against their nuclear programs. The Carter administration finally judged the costs of an un-compromising nonproliferation policy to be excessive in terms of alliance relations and the South Asian security balance. In the end, the traditional priorities of U.S. foreign policy—Western alliance solidarity and Third World communist containment—drove nonproliferation diplomacy from the field.

Chapter
7

Nonproliferation Eclipsed: The Reagan-Bush Era

With the 1980 election of Ronald Reagan as president, U.S. foreign policy became devoted to reasserting American power in the world, ushering in a reinvigorated Cold War against the Soviet Union and its dependents. Three years into the Bush presidency, the United States continued to seek to reassert its world leadership in a fundamentally changed, "post–Cold War" world.

Reagan's first priority was to counter the expansion of Soviet influence and to reverse what the new administration saw as a steady deterioration in the East-West balance of power during the 1970s. The keys to this strategy were increased arms spending, aggressive opposition to Third World communism, and unequivocal support for anticommunist U.S. client states.

Nuclear nonproliferation occupied a subordinate position in this scheme. Although Reagan did not entirely discard the Ford-Carter policies, he reduced the priority and visibility that the issue had assumed in the previous several years, and repudiated some of the basic premises of his two predecessors' "revisionist" approach. Reagan's anti-Soviet strategy dictated a closer embrace of several near-nuclear nations whose ties with the United States had been strained over nuclear and human-rights issues. Pakistan became one of the largest recipients of U.S. military aid and, exploiting Washington's failure to link this aid to meaningful nuclear restraint, moved with impunity over the threshold of an atomic-weapons capability. In Latin America, southern Africa, and the Middle East, the United States also subordinated strict nonproliferation efforts to Cold War imperatives.

In the realm of nuclear trade and development, Reagan abandoned

155

the Carter crusade against plutonium and stressed peaceful cooperation rather than denial as the preferred nonproliferation strategy. The administration championed a return to U.S. commercial leadership in nuclear power and aggressively promoted nuclear exports. On the other hand, it continued efforts through the Suppliers Group to impede the flow of technology to Pakistan and other would-be proliferators, and established new constraints on the spread of ballistic-missile technology. In addition, the drying up of nuclear-export markets in the 1980s, and the sharp decline in nuclear power growth in the industrial countries, limited the practical effect of Reagan's declaratory shift to a more promotional policy. As a result, there was more continuity in U.S. nonproliferation policy from Carter to Reagan than might have been predicted from the latter's initial rhetoric.

In the late 1980s, the foundations of the postwar world shifted. With Mikhail Gorbachev's rise to power in Moscow and the collapse of the Soviet empire in Eastern Europe, the Cold War revival of the early Reagan years gave way to East-West reconciliation. Superpower competition was no longer the defining premise of American policy toward Third World conflicts, and new possibilities for U.S.-Soviet cooperation arose. The Persian Gulf crisis that ushered in the 1990s—and refocused international attention on the proliferation threat—made apparent both the risks and the opportunities of this post–Cold War world.

REAGAN, AMERICAN POWER, AND NONPROLIFERATION

A handful of basic tenets guided the Reagan administration foreign policy.[1] America's world standing had dangerously eroded during the 1970s, not as a result of inexorable global changes but largely because of mistaken policies. The three administrations of that decade had erred in seeking an accommodation with Moscow. Taking advantage of America's misplaced interest in détente and arms control, its declining defense budget and post-Vietnam diffidence about overseas intervention, the Soviet Union had gained the upper hand in the superpower military balance and the global competition for influence.

These premises offered both a simple explanation for U.S. frustrations and setbacks, and a prescription for reversing them. American reticence

---

[1] Analyses of the Reagan foreign policy include Coral Bell, *The Reagan Paradox: American Foreign Policy in the 1980s* (New Brunswick, NJ: Rutgers Univ. Press, 1989); David E. Kyvig, ed., *Reagan and the World* (Westport, CT: Greenwood Press, 1990); William G. Hyland, ed., *The Reagan Foreign Policy* (New York: New American Library, 1987); and Kenneth Oye, Robert Lieber, and Donald Rothchild, eds., *Eagle Resurgent? The Reagan Era in American Foreign Policy* (Boston: Little, Brown, 1987). The most useful memoir, though it covers only the first 18 months of the administration, is Alexander Haig, *Caveat: Realism, Reagan, and Foreign Policy* (New York: Macmillan, 1984).

and Soviet expansion were the problem; a reassertion of U.S. power was the solution. Notions of complexity, interdependence, and the diffusion of power that had influenced policymakers in the 1970s were now unfashionable. The Carter world-order focus and interest in North-South relations, already in eclipse at the end of his term, were scorned by the incoming Reagan administration, which viewed global issues and regional conflicts through the single prism of the Soviet threat. The new adm.nistration placed top priority on massive increases in defense spending, a major nuclear buildup, and military support for anticommunist governments and rebel movements abroad (the so-called Reagan Doctrine). The United States, untempted by arms control and unfettered by qualms about military intervention and the human-rights credentials of U.S. partners, would reengage the Soviet threat on a global basis and roll back Moscow's recent gains.

In practice, this ideological design was sometimes tempered by pragmatic flexibility.[2] Despite his harsh anti-Soviet rhetoric (most memorably, his characterization of the Soviet Union as an "evil empire"), Reagan discontinued Carter's grain embargo against Moscow. After a serious clash with European allies, he also dropped efforts to prevent the transfer of Western oil-pipeline technology to the Soviets. And he resumed superpower arms control talks, initially as a political maneuver to outflank a growing U.S. antinuclear movement, but eventually—after Gorbachev's rise to power in 1985—in earnest.

In the Third World, however, the administration's policies were largely faithful to its Cold War convictions. The United States sponsored anticommunist rebel movements in Afghanistan, Nicaragua, and Angola, and used military force directly in Lebanon, Grenada, and Libya. Carter-era criticism of human rights abuses by anticommunist authoritarian governments was muted in favor of an emphasis on combating international terrorism, which the Reagan administration viewed as largely inspired and supported by Moscow. Finally, the sale of conventional arms to U.S. allies and clients was elevated to the status of a leading foreign policy tool—"perhaps *the* major instrument for action overseas," one expert noted, "short of the direct use of U.S. armed forces."[3]

This set of priorities and goals left little room for an aggressive nonproliferation policy. The Reagan administration disagreed with both the prominence and the substance of the policies it inherited. It believed that Carter's strong emphasis on the problem had needlessly antagonized American allies and handicapped the domestic nuclear industry—toward

---

[2] See, for example, Bell, *The Reagan Paradox.*

[3] Andrew J. Pierre, *The Global Politics of Arms Sales* (Princeton, NJ: Princeton Univ. Press, 1982), p. 68. A July 1981 administration statement on conventional arms transfers rejected Carter's moralistic policy of restraint and—echoing the administration's "realist" line on nuclear proliferation—announced that the U.S. would henceforth "deal with the world as it is rather than as we would like it to be."

which Reagan was far more sympathetic than Carter had been. In addition, Reagan shared some of the Nixon-Kissinger fatalism about the spread of nuclear weapons. Though as president he disavowed a campaign statement that the problem was none of America's business, his administration was not inclined to spend much political capital in a campaign against it. This was especially true since the targets of such a campaign were likely to be partners in the contest against Moscow—the critical litmus test for befriending or challenging Third World regimes. Too scrupulous a regard for nonproliferation (or for human rights or arms restraint) would weaken the anti-Soviet coalition the administration was determined to forge. Thus, in sharp contrast to the Kennedy-Johnson era, when an expansive and interventionist approach to American power prompted increased concern about nuclear proliferation, the Reagan revival consigned the issue to the background.

Significantly, however, the Reagan administration did not admit to a trade-off between nonproliferation and its Cold War strategy. On the contrary, it argued that a reassertion of American power would serve the cause of nonproliferation by reducing the security incentives for acquiring nuclear arms. Here the administration stressed the political and security dimensions of proliferation—the problem of motives—in contrast to Carter's emphasis (misplaced, in the Reagan view) on technical capabilities. Revitalized alliances, arms sales, and a stronger overall defense posture would reassure potential nuclear powers whose confidence had been shaken by the vacillations and inhibitions of U.S. foreign policy after Vietnam. If successful, this approach promised to narrow the gap between nonproliferation and national security policy that had hampered U.S. initiatives in the 1970s. At the same time, it begged the question of whether the regional and domestic sources of proliferation would yield before a revival of U.S. power directed at the Soviet threat—particularly if the United States did not impose on its partners a choice between security backing and nuclear weapons. As discussed below, the policy failed its key test in the case of Pakistan.

The Reagan administration also saw a close correlation between U.S. power and nonproliferation influence in the area of peaceful nuclear cooperation and trade.[4] It placed great importance on restoring American leadership in the nuclear market and foreign confidence in the United States as a "reliable supplier" of nuclear fuel and technology. Responding to the nuclear industry's complaints about the restrictive trend of the preceding years, the administration stressed cooperation rather than denial as a means of influencing other nations' nuclear policies. In this, it harked back to the logic of the original Atoms for Peace "bargain," and the historical link between the U.S. market dominance of the 1950s and 1960s

---

[4] The following pages draw on Peter Clausen, "The Reagan Nonproliferation Policy," *Arms Control Today*, December 1982.

and the rise of the nonproliferation regime. James Malone, a senior State Department nuclear official, argued that

> United States influence has played a key role in raising international aware-
> ness about nuclear proliferation. . . . It is important to realize that the
> critical factor in enabling the U.S. to make such a contribution has not in the
> first instance been the correctness of our position but rather the influence we
> were able to muster by virtue of our role as a technology and trade leader in
> international nuclear commerce.[5]

Deputy Energy Secretary Kenneth Davis evoked a similar nostalgia for the era of U.S. primacy: "We used to be the leader in the world, developing the safeguards, developing international agencies, developing the whole process. We were the leaders because we were the leaders in international trade related to nuclear power. We lost a substantial part of our leadership in technology under the previous administration."[6] As this statement implies, the administration's view of nuclear trends paralleled its larger critique of U.S. power in the 1970s in attributing U.S. decline to policy errors rather than to structural trends like the rise of competing suppliers and the diversification of the nuclear market. On the other hand, Reagan officials acknowledged this diversification as a fact of life, and often cited it as an argument against unilateral U.S. attempts (like the 1978 Nuclear Non-Proliferation Act) to tighten the conditions of nuclear trade.

The Reagan administration correctly noted that unilateral policies could be self-defeating if they encouraged U.S. nuclear customers to develop their own fuel-cycle facilities or to seek other, more lenient suppliers. But its own approach also contained potential contradictions. In the highly competitive nuclear market of the 1980s, with numerous supplier countries and a shrinking demand for exports, it was not clear how a U.S. commercial revival would bring greater American influence on behalf of nonproliferation interests. Any recovery of U.S. ground lost over the preceding decade would come at the expense of European suppliers. Although they (like Japan) would welcome a more tolerant U.S. policy toward their own domestic nuclear programs, they would hardly applaud an aggressive campaign to increase the U.S. share of the world export market. Instead of encouraging stricter nonproliferation controls, such a campaign could reduce other suppliers' self-restraint, especially since the Reagan administration itself was expounding a more permissive

---

[5] Speech to the Atomic Industrial Forum, December 1, 1981, cited in Joseph Pilat and Warren Donnelly, "The Reagan Administration Policy for Preventing the Further Spread of Nuclear Weapons: A Summary and Analysis of Official Statements," Congressional Research Service Report No. 83–94 S (Washington, DC: Library of Congress, May 6, 1983), p. 13.

[6] Cited in Milton Benjamin, "Administration Becomes Flexible on Gray Area Nuclear Exports," Washington Post, August 8, 1982, p. 11.

philosophy of nuclear trade. The "reliable supplier" motif thus had a two-edged character: ostensibly a strategy for restoring U.S. nonproliferation leadership, it could become simply a self-serving rationale for promoting U.S exports. This tension was apparent in the Reagan administration's handling of the revisionist legacy of the 1970s.

REVISIONISM REVISED: PLUTONIUM AND NUCLEAR EXPORT POLICY

The Reagan administration pursued a selective liberalization of 1970s restrictions on peaceful nuclear relations. Highly critical of the universalism of the Ford-Carter period, Reagan officials espoused a more flexible, discriminatory approach to nuclear trade and cooperation. Restrictive policies would remain in place for high-risk countries (those with manifest weapons ambitions), but elsewhere there would be a presumption in favor of cooperation. General opposition to commercialized plutonium use and transfers of sensitive nuclear facilities (reprocessing and enrichment) gave way to a country-by-country approach. For Europe, Japan, and the domestic U.S. nuclear industry, previous concerns about plutonium were dropped altogether. And while the Reagan administration decided not to ask Congress to repeal the more restrictive NNPA provisions (after early signals that it would do so), it implemented the law creatively to accommodate the interests of the U.S. nuclear customers most affected by it.

On the plutonium issue, the Reagan administration was doubly opposed to the Ford-Carter approach. It considered opposition to plutonium use by U.S. allies to be both unwarranted (since these countries posed little if any proliferation risk) and doomed to failure (since they were committed to reprocessing and breeder-reactor programs). "Past efforts to challenge the carefully considered programs of Japan and EURATOM countries," argued Under Secretary of State Richard Kennedy, "led only to rancorous debates which soured our relations with key allies without enhancing our nonproliferation goals."[7] To impute proliferation risks to allied plutonium use, Arms Control and Disarmament Agency (ACDA) Director Eugene Rostow testified, "is to invite sterile friction based on the illusion of U.S. omnipotence."[8]

Accordingly, the administration announced that it would not "inhibit or set back" allied reprocessing plans. In place of Carter's grudging, case-

---

[7] Statement before the Senate Committee on Governmental Affairs, September 9, 1982, cited in Joseph Pilat and Warren Donnelly, "The Reagan Administration Policy for Preventing the Further Spread of Nuclear Weapons," p. 83. Kennedy later became Reagan's Ambassador-at-Large for nonproliferation policy, a position he retained into the Bush administration.

[8] Statement before the House Foreign Affairs Committee, March 18, 1982, cited in Pilat and Donnelly, "The Reagan Administration Policy," p. 63.

by-case approach to foreign reprocessing of U.S.-origin fuel, Reagan offered to negotiate "programmatic" arrangements under which the United States would give Japan and the EURATOM countries 30-year advance consent for reprocessing and use of the resulting plutonium.[9] The United States would not ask its partners to demonstrate a physical need for spent-fuel transfers or to justify on energy or economic grounds their plans to use plutonium fuels.

The new policy was not a complete reversal, however; during 1980 the Carter administration had been exploring an accommodation with the allies on the plutonium question, including the concept of long-term approvals for reprocessing.[10] Nevertheless, the Reagan solution was markedly less qualified and more open-ended than the Carter proposals. In taking a completely hands-off approach to allied programs (requiring only that IAEA safeguards be in place), the Reagan administration rejected the notion that plutonium per se raised proliferation problems. It associated proliferation risks with countries rather than particular activities and was not self-conscious about creating an explicit double standard for plutonium use, endorsing it for some countries but not for others.

This overt discrimination was a departure from the Ford and Carter policies, and a disavowal of the laborious—but not entirely unsuccessful— U.S. effort in the International Nuclear Fuel Cycle Evaluation (INFCE) to develop consistent and politically sustainable criteria for plutonium activities. Most important, the new policy surrendered the point the United States had won against recycling plutonium in existing nuclear reactors. The Reagan administration also rejected the Ford-Carter premise that U.S. domestic nuclear policy had important implications for the nonproliferation regime. It lifted the ban on domestic reprocessing, promoted the commercialization of plutonium fuel, and briefly sought to use plutonium from civilian power reactors in the U.S. nuclear weapons program. All these initiatives ultimately failed: a market for commercial reprocessing and plutonium use never materialized, and Congress vetoed the military use of civilian plutonium.

The new plutonium policy was strongly backed by the State and Energy Departments—not surprisingly, since it bowed to the preferences of their respective allied and industry constituencies. But it met with opposition in the Defense Department and among nonproliferation leaders in Congress, who questioned how blanket approval of plutonium activities years in advance could be reconciled with the NNPA's "timely

---

[9] See "Reagan Alters Policy on A-Fuel Recycling," *Washington Post*, June 9, 1982, p. 3. For non-EURATOM European countries such as Sweden and Norway, the administration offered 30-year consent for reprocessing only, while plutonium use would still be approved case-by-case. Outside of Europe and Japan, the case-by-case policy would continue to apply to both activities.

[10] See Gerard C. Smith, "A Sound Nuclear Accord With Japan," *Washington Post*, February 19, 1988, p. 19.

warning" standard. Critics also maintained that these activities, potentially placing hundreds of tons of weapons-usable plutonium in domestic and international commerce, posed a high risk of diversion or theft even if the countries involved had no immediate weapons ambitions. But the new policy prevailed; its most important and controversial result was a revised agreement for cooperation with Japan that took effect in 1988. Ironically, the NNPA requirement that such agreements be renegotiated—intended to tighten controls—had instead produced a far more permissive policy on the recovery and use of plutonium from American-origin fuel.[11]

The Reagan administration portrayed this outcome as little more than an acceptance of reality in the face of unshakable allied commitments to reprocessing and plutonium use. But it was already clear in the early 1980s, and more so as the decade progressed, that these plans rested on a precarious base of economic viability and public support. Hence, the real significance of the Reagan policy was to offer moral and material support to beleaguered nuclear establishments in Europe and Japan, in contrast to Carter's unwelcome challenge to those establishments. To have persisted in the challenge would have invited continuing friction with allied governments, but was not necessarily a policy doomed to failure. Moreover, in other areas (for example, the Soviet pipeline controversy and the deployment of intermediate-range U.S. missiles in Europe) the Reagan administration showed that it was prepared to risk serious alliance strains in the pursuit of Cold War policies. Its unwillingness to do so in the case of plutonium policy was due more to substantive dissent from the Ford-Carter policy than to the inherent futility of that policy. In practice, however, the new policy's impact was limited by the steadily receding commercial promise of plutonium fuels, resulting from the slack market for nuclear power itself.

A similar pattern—a loosening of proliferation controls without significant commercial results—also characterized Reagan's nuclear-export policies. Again, a discriminatory approach replaced the previous emphasis on consistency and universality. The administration announced that the United States would "continue to inhibit" exports of sensitive nuclear fuel-cycle technologies "where the danger of proliferation demands," but

---

[11] See Cass Peterson, "U.S. to Allow Unrestricted Transfer of Plutonium," *Washington Post*, April 22, 1988, p. 4; and Warren Donnelly, "U.S.-Japanese Nuclear Cooperation: Revision of the Bilateral Agreement," CRS Issue Brief IB87159 (Washington, DC: Library of Congress, July 22, 1988). A sometimes harsh critic of the Reagan nonproliferation policies was Assistant Secretary of Defense Richard Perle, one of the administration's most conservative officials and probably its most influential arms control policymaker. See Daniel Charles, "DOD Sees Risks in Plutonium Trade," *Science*, November 13, 1987, p. 886; and Frank Gaffney, Jr. (Perle's deputy at Defense), "Plutonium Pact With Japan Guts Proliferation Policy," *Los Angeles Times*, March 7, 1988. See also Perle's testimony in *Nuclear Non-Proliferation and U.S. National Security*, Hearings Before the Senate Committee on Governmental Affairs, 100th Cong., 1st sess., March 5, 1987.

it lifted the general embargo on such exports. This step allowed U.S. firms to bid for a role in Japan's planned commercial-scale reprocessing plant. In an even greater departure from traditional U.S. policy, the administration offered to share highly classified U.S. centrifuge technology with Australia for a joint enrichment venture in that country. Japan and Australia both chose other partners, but the proposed facilities were deferred in response to the declining nuclear fuel market.

Reagan officials indicated that they foresaw sensitive technology cooperation only with advanced industrial countries, but this standard became blurred in the bidding for reactor sales to Mexico in 1981–1982. Mexico had announced plans to import up to 20 reactors over the next two decades, and also expressed interest in acquiring reprocessing and enrichment technology. An intense supplier competition followed, in which the Reagan administration tried to bolster the position of American companies without making explicit commitments to supply sensitive technology. The administration maintained a calculated ambiguity on the issue, hinting that over the long term cooperation in sensitive areas would not be ruled out.[12] Mexico abruptly suspended its nuclear plans amid a severe economic crisis, leaving in doubt what the outcome of the bidding would have been. But the incident suggested the difficulty of drawing firm lines to support a discriminatory nuclear supply strategy and raised questions about the administration's claim that a more aggressive U.S. role in the nuclear market would benefit nonproliferation.

In another delicate area of export policy, the Reagan administration inherited the task of cutting off cooperation with nations refusing to accept full-scope safeguards as required by the NNPA. Congress was not prepared to grant another exemption to India, and South Africa and Brazil—both with unsafeguarded nuclear plants—also faced a termination of U.S. exports. But the Reagan administration had foreign policy interests in better relations with all three nations and wished to avoid applying the law in a punitive way. It therefore arranged or acquiesced in substitute fuel deliveries that allowed these countries to escape any penalty for their failure to meet U.S. export conditions.

The Indian case was the most sensitive, because of New Delhi's threat to declare the Tarapur agreement null and void and to renounce safeguards on the reactors if the United States defaulted on fuel supplies. This outcome was averted by bringing in France to replace the United States as the exclusive supplier of fuel for Tarapur under the 1963 agreement. However, two other long-standing questions—whether India could reprocess Tarapur fuel without U.S. consent, and whether safeguards on the

---

[12] See "Mexican Participation in U.S. Reprocessing, Enrichment Ventures Possible," *Inside Energy*, March 26, p. 1; and Joseph Pilat and Warren Donnelly, "Nuclear Export Policy of the Reagan Administration: A Summary Analysis and Four Cases," Congressional Research Service Report No. 82–70 S (Washington, DC: Library of Congress, April 1982). This report also analyzes the Australian enrichment case.

reactors would terminate with the expiration of the 30-year agreement in 1993—were left in dispute.[13] For both India and the United States, the French solution represented a triumph of broader foreign policy concerns over declaratory nuclear policies, neither side wanting to add the strain of an unfriendly nuclear divorce to the unsettled atmosphere created by the Soviet war in Afghanistan. Although Indian negotiators had initially rejected the arrangement, Indira Gandhi finally decided that the issue would be settled on the basis of "overall bilateral relations with the United States." For its part, the Reagan administration needed a means of placating New Delhi as the United States embarked on a major new program of military assistance to Pakistan.

REAGAN, BUSH, AND PAKISTAN'S BOMB

Pakistan dominated the U.S. nonproliferation agenda through the 1980s, while simultaneously exemplifying that agenda's subordination to the larger Reagan foreign policy design. Bordering on Afghanistan, Pakistan was a front-line state in the renewed Cold War—a bulwark against further Soviet expansion toward the Persian Gulf, the conduit for Western aid to resistance fighters in Afghanistan, and a key link in the anti-Soviet "strategic consensus" that the United States hoped to forge across the Middle East, the Gulf, and South Asia. As it had a decade earlier during the Nixon opening to China, Pakistan again became a beneficiary of U.S. grand strategy. This time, however, the rewards were considerably greater. Raising the stakes well above the spurned proposal of Carter's final year, the Reagan administration offered Islamabad a $3.2 billion, six-year package of economic and military aid, including 40 F-16 fighter-bombers. The planes, more advanced than any previously available to Pakistan, were the heart of the deal, and assured President Zia's acceptance.

The size of the aid offer invited a reprise of the debate on whether the United States could "buy out" Pakistan's nuclear weapons program with conventional arms assistance. But the Reagan administration did not put the question to the test. Persuaded that Zia would refuse to abandon his nuclear plans in return for U.S. aid, the administration was not prepared to jeopardize the package by attaching nonproliferation conditions to it. Lacking this quid pro quo, however, the aid program required congressional action to set aside the Symington amendment (which barred aid to countries acquiring enrichment technology while rejecting full-scope safeguards). The amendment itself contained a waiver provision, but this could be invoked only if the president had received "reliable assurances" that Pakistan was not developing atomic weapons. By not using the

---

[13] See "Tarapur Situation Settled for Present; Major Conflict Still Unresolved," *Nucleonics Week*, December 2, 1982, p. 1.

waiver, the administration in effect admitted that it did not believe Zia's persistent disavowals of nuclear ambitions.[14]

Thus the aid package went forward essentially without strings. The only exception was a separate congressional measure that provided for a cutoff in the event that Pakistan (or other U.S. aid recipients) actually exploded a nuclear device or transferred one to a third party. Critics of the deal maintained that the administration had underestimated U.S. leverage and could have bargained harder. While not disputing the administration's decision to give priority to combating the Soviets in Afghanistan, they argued that this policy was also in Pakistan's interest. Zia was under strong pressure both domestically and from other Islamic countries (especially Saudi Arabia, a major source of economic aid) to support the Afghan rebels, and in fact was already doing so; it was not necessary, then, for the United States to buy Zia's cooperation with U.S. policy on his own terms.[15] But the administration insisted that it had no room to bargain with Zia. In its opinion, U.S. failure to deliver the weaponry desired by Pakistan (above all the F-16s) would lead Zia to walk away from the deal and seek an accommodation with Moscow that would undermine U.S. strategy toward Afghanistan.

Though it refused to seek explicit nuclear concessions, the administration still hoped that the new U.S. aid flow would, over time, help moderate Pakistan's pursuit of the bomb. Pointing out that Pakistan was motivated to obtain nuclear weapons by perceived threats to its security, administration officials argued that conventional military assistance could help alleviate those threats. The argument was not implausible, but it caught the Reagan policy in an awkward contradiction, since the Pakistani nuclear effort was aimed at India.

While sharing U.S. concern about the Soviet presence in Afghanistan, Islamabad continued to regard India as the primary threat to its security. To address Pakistan's underlying nuclear motives, U.S. aid would therefore have to improve the country's military capabilities against India. The United States, however, was at pains to emphasize—and to

---

[14] In presenting the aid program to Congress, Under Secretary of State James Buckley said that Zia had "stated categorically . . . that Pakistan has no intention whatever of developing nuclear weapons," and claimed to accept this statement at face value. But if this were so, the administration could have simply invoked the Symington waiver provision and would not have needed to ask Congress to suspend the amendment itself. See House Committee on Foreign Affairs, *Security and Economic Assistance to Pakistan*, Hearings, 97th Cong., 1st sess., April 27, September 16, 22, and 23, and November 17 and 19, 1981, p. 62.

[15] At the same time, however, Islamic nationalism and Pakistan's newly adopted non-aligned status (it had withdrawn from the U.S.-led CENTO alliance in 1979) made it unlikely that the country would fully support the U.S. "strategic consensus" in the Persian Gulf—for example, by allowing U.S. bases or troop deployments on its territory. See Christopher Von Hollen, "Don't Engulf the Gulf," *Foreign Affairs*, Summer 1981, and his testimony in *Security and Economic Assistance to Pakistan*.

persuade India, which vigorously opposed the deal—that this was not the intent of the aid package. Responding to critics who argued that the F-16's advanced range and capabilities were better suited to striking targets in India than to the purported mission of coping with limited Soviet threats along the Afghan border, the administration noted that India held a commanding three-to-one military advantage over Pakistan, and claimed that the proposed transfers would not appreciably alter the balance of power on the subcontinent. These arguments did little to advance U.S. interests with either side, however. They failed to mollify India, which viewed the deal as catering to Pakistan's pretentions to undeserved regional parity; and they only reminded Pakistan that nuclear weapons remained its only real hope for a military equalizer.[16]

Over the next several years, Pakistan moved steadily to complete its bomb-building capability.[17] Evidence accumulated that work on the Kahuta enrichment plant was continuing, and that Pakistan was also engaged in the full range of activities—warhead design, high-explosives research, assembly of a triggering mechanism, and preparation of a test site—associated with producing a nuclear device. Suggestive, although inconclusive, evidence also pointed to Chinese assistance in these efforts. During the early 1980s, China was reported to be helping Pakistan with uranium enrichment (Chinese technicians having been observed at Kahuta) and had possibly shared nuclear testing and design data as well.[18] Nearly a decade later, more concrete evidence emerged that China may have provided Pakistan with nuclear weapons designs and enough weapons-grade uranium to construct two or more 25-kiloton bombs.[19]

The United States reacted to these developments with a multifaceted but largely ineffective effort to contain Pakistan's program. One thrust (the only even modestly successful one) tried to frustrate the country's technology-acquisition networks through tighter export controls and better coordination among supplier countries. Less productive were a series of warnings, legislative restrictions, and diplomatic initiatives aimed at deterring Pakistan from crossing various nuclear "red lines."

[16] On these issues, see House Committee on Foreign Affairs, *Proposed U.S. Assistance and Arms Transfers to Pakistan: An Assessment*, Staff Report (Washington, DC: GPO, November 20, 1981). For a critical view of the F-16 deal, from a perspective sympathetic to India, see Selig Harrison, "Fanning the Flames in South Asia," *Foreign Policy*, Winter 1981–1982. Harrison notes that the Reagan administration failed to get assurances from Zia that U.S. aid would not be used against India.

[17] For a detailed summary, see Leonard Spector, *The Undeclared Bomb* (Cambridge, MA: Ballinger, 1988), pp. 126ff.

[18] See "U.S. is Holding Up Peking Atom Talks," *New York Times*, September 19, 1982; "China Aids Pakistan on A-Weapons," *Washington Post*, February 28, 1983, p. 1.

[19] Gary Milhollin and Gerard White, "A New China Syndrome: Beijing's Atomic Bazaar," *Washington Post*, May 12, 1991, p. C1; Mark Hibbs, "Despite U.S. Alarm over Algeria, Europeans Won't Blacklist China," *Nucleonics Week*, May 23, 1991, p. 1.

These red lines were communicated directly to President Zia in the early 1980s in several high-level missions headed by Ambassador-at-Large Vernon Walters. Zia was shown sensitive U.S. intelligence information about the Pakistani nuclear program, told that it was a serious "embarrassment" to President Reagan, and warned that if the program persisted the U.S.-Islamabad relationship could be jeopardized. In addition to the red lines contained in U.S. legislation—explosion or transfer of a nuclear device—Zia was asked to suspend work on the enrichment plant, discontinue Pakistan's clandestine "shopping" for nuclear components, and refrain from fabricating a nuclear device. But no explicit threat of sanctions was made, and Zia, understanding America's real priorities, knew that an aid cutoff was unlikely as long as Pakistan did not actually test a weapon.

In 1984, Pakistan completed the Kahuta plant and began to enrich uranium there. The summer of that year saw new reports of Chinese aid to the project and the arrest in Houston of three Pakistanis for attempting to smuggle krytrons (electronic switches used in nuclear weapons) out of the United States. In response, Reagan drew a new line. He wrote Zia asking for assurances that Pakistan would not enrich uranium beyond a 5-percent level of uranium 235 (well below weapons-grade) and warned of "grave consequences" if it did so. Pakistan agreed in writing to this threshold, but then proceeded to ignore it. The unabated pace of Pakistan's nuclear activities, including the reported detonation of a warhead-triggering package, led the following year to two new congressional provisions—one banning aid to countries that violated U.S. export laws to acquire nuclear components (the Solarz amendment), and the other linking Pakistani aid to an annual certification by the president on Islamabad's nuclear program (the Pressler amendment). Under the latter, the president was required to certify at the start of each fiscal year that Pakistan did not "possess" a nuclear device, and that continued U.S. aid would significantly reduce the risk that it would do so.

By 1987, when the six-year U.S. aid package expired, the administration was forced to admit that it had failed as a nonproliferation inducement. Pakistan had, in effect, called the U.S. bluff. According to intelligence estimates, Pakistan was now producing 93.5-percent weapons-grade uranium and had virtually attained a weapons capability, even if the components of the devices had not actually been assembled. That is, the country was approaching the "bomb-in-the-basement" capability earlier acquired by Israel.[20] Statements by Zia and A. Q. Kahn—the head of the

---

[20] Bob Woodward, "Pakistan Reported Near Atom Arms Production," *Washington Post*, November 11, 1986, p. 1. By early 1988, according to an apparently well-informed press report, Pakistan had accumulated enough bomb-grade uranium for several weapons and had warhead components ready for assembly on short notice. Hendrick Smith, "A Bomb Ticks in Pakistan," *New York Times Magazine*, March 6, 1988.

Kahuta project—boasted that Pakistan had indeed acquired a nuclear weapons option, while continuing to insist that there was no intention to exercise it. And another Pakistani national—later found to be an agent of the government—was apprehended in the United States for nuclear-relevant smuggling activities.

These events inspired congressional moves to tie any renewal of military assistance to a verified halt in Pakistan's production of fissile material.[21] The administration acknowledged that Pakistan had violated U.S. laws and Zia's assurances to Reagan, but still argued for the no-strings policy. (The Arms Control and Disarmament Agency dissented, recommending that aid be withheld at least temporarily as a message to Zia.) State Department officials pleaded the continuing priority of countering the Soviets in Afghanistan. In addition, they argued that a U.S. cutoff would not only free Pakistan of any external constraints on its nuclear program (and feed a growing nationalist backlash there against U.S. interference), but would signal to India that Pakistan had crossed the nuclear threshold. The result could be to precipitate an overt South Asian nuclear arms race.[22]

Following a brief halt in aid to Pakistan in the fall of 1987, the administration ultimately prevailed. Congress approved a new $4.02 billion program of military and economic assistance and suspended the Symington amendment for an additional 30 months. Reagan satisfied the Pressler amendment by certifying that Pakistan still did not "possess" a nuclear device—an increasingly strained semantic exercise. Completing the rout of U.S. nonproliferation policy, he then waived the Solarz amendment (prohibiting aid to countries in violation of U.S. nuclear export laws) to remove the final obstacle to the aid package.[23]

The Reagan administration may well have been correct in its initial premise that U.S. aid provided inadequate leverage to halt the Pakistani nuclear program. But the question was moot in light of the administration's dominant interest in buying Zia's support for its anti-Soviet

---

[21] See Charles Van Doren, "Pakistan, Congress, and the Nonproliferation Challenge," *Arms Control Today*, November 1987, and the interview with Sen. John Glenn in the same issue.

[22] See Don Oberdorfer, "Panel Rejects Cut in Aid to Pakistan," *Washington Post*, April 4, 1987; Michael Gordon, "U.S. Official Urges New Aid to Pakistan," *New York Times*, October 23, 1987; and testimony of Richard Kennedy in House Committee on Foreign Affairs, *Pakistan and U.S. Non-Proliferation Policy*, Hearings, 100th Cong., 1st sess., October 22, 1987. A blunt speech against the nuclear program by U.S. Amb. Deane Hinton in February had fed the already growing anti-American feelings in Pakistan. See Steven Weisman, "Pakistan's Nuclear Aims Worrying U.S.," *New York Times*, February 20, 1987, p. 3; and "Pakistan Stiffens on Atom Program," *New York Times*, March 22, 1987, p. 15.

[23] David Ottaway, "Reagan Likely to Clear Aid to Pakistan," *Washington Post*, January 15, 1988, p. 1.

agenda.[24] This fact allowed Pakistan to escape a choice between U.S. aid and the development of nuclear weapons, and deprived later U.S. warnings and appeals of credibility. Given the decision not to play the strongest U.S. card, these efforts amounted to little more than an attempt to talk Pakistan out of its nuclear program—advice that Zia correctly calculated he could ignore. Seeing the opportunity to have his nuclear program without sacrificing U.S. support, he took it.

This unwillingness to place the Pakistani aid program on the line also weakened the U.S. hand in dealing with the Indian side of the South Asian nuclear equation. Like its predecessor, the Reagan administration understood the need to address the problem of Pakistan in a regional context, but was frustrated by its inability to sway India. Although relations with New Delhi improved somewhat following the Tarapur fuel compromise (there were modest increases in trade, transfers of computer technology, and talks on limited military assistance), U.S. influence over Indian policy remained slight.

India repeatedly protested U.S. F-16 sales to Pakistan, and persisted in rejecting bilateral nonproliferation formulas—such as Islamabad's proposals for a nuclear-free zone or test ban—that equated the two countries. Pakistan, in turn, flatly refused U.S. requests for inspections of the Kahuta plant in the absence of Indian reciprocity.[25] (During these years, India began to produce unsafeguarded plutonium on a large scale, but held back from developing nuclear weapons.) India's own mixed motives regarding the Pakistani program were a further complicating factor in the U.S. search for a coherent regional strategy. Although troubled by Pakistan's nuclear progress, New Delhi also appreciated that at some point that progress might threaten U.S. aid to Pakistan. Hoping for a cutoff, India had little incentive to make conciliatory moves that might only facilitate the continued flow of U.S. weapons to its adversary. A final obstacle was the fact that China remained a basic reference point for Indian nuclear policy. Without China's involvement (which American diplomacy was unable to bring about), no regional plan for nuclear controls was acceptable to New Delhi.

---

[24] The administration's Cold War perspective was dramatized in mid-1986 when the Soviet Union (apparently reflecting Indian concerns) warned Pakistan to curb its nuclear program. In response, the United States sent a strong message to Moscow reiterating American support for Pakistan and warning against Soviet interference in its affairs. See Bob Woodward and Don Oberdorfer, "Superpowers Spar on Pakistan Bomb," *Washington Post*, July 15, 1986, p. 1.

[25] Michael Gordon, "Pakistan Rejects Atomic Inspection," *New York Times*, August 6, 1987, p. A1; "Pakistan Proposes Nuclear Test Ban in South Asia," *New York Times*, September 25, 1987; Steven Weisman, "India Rejects Idea for Nuclear Ban," *New York Times*, October 11, 1987, p. 15. See also Richard Haass, "South Asia: Too Late to Remove the Bomb?" *Orbis*, Winter 1988, and Senate Committee on Foreign Relations, *Nuclear Proliferation in South Asia: Containing the Threat*, Staff Report (Washington, DC: GPO, 1988).

The 1987 aid-renewal process turned out to be the high-water mark of U.S. indulgence toward the Pakistani nuclear program. Over the remainder of the decade, Islamabad's successful balancing act was threatened from several directions. In early 1989, the Soviet Union withdrew from Afghanistan, removing the key premise of U.S. policy in the region since the end of the Carter administration. No longer an essential U.S. partner, Pakistan was now far more vulnerable to American pressure on the nuclear issue. A new rationale for continued U.S. support appeared, however, when Pakistan turned toward democracy after Zia's death and elected Benazir Bhutto as president in 1988. Encouraged by this trend, and hopeful that Bhutto would curb the nuclear program and move toward a rapprochement with India, the incoming Bush administration gave her the benefit of the doubt and offered to supply Pakistan with an additional 60 F-16s.[26]

But 1990 brought new evidence of South Asia's precarious regional and domestic stability. India and Pakistan came to the brink of a new war over Kashmir, prompting a high-level U.S. mission to try to defuse tensions and avoid a nuclear crisis.[27] Months later, Bhutto was removed from office under charges of corruption. Meanwhile, new intelligence reports indicated that Pakistan's bomb program had reached a point that would no longer allow the president to certify that Islamabad did not "possess" a nuclear device. As a result, U.S. aid was suspended—despite efforts by the Bush administration to find a way around the legal requirement—at the end of fiscal year 1990.[28]

Pakistan's nuclear relations with India improved somewhat, and negotiations on a "nuclear nonattack" agreement—initially proposed in 1988 by Bhutto—continued even after she was removed from office and India's Rajiv Gandhi was assassinated. Nonetheless, early in 1991, Japan, the United Kingdom, Germany, and the Netherlands felt compelled to impose an embargo on the export of defense-related equipment to Pakistan

---

[26] David Ottaway, "U.S. Relieves Pakistan of Pledge Against Enriching Uranium," *Washington Post*, June 15, 1989, p. A38; House Committee on Foreign Affairs, *Proposed Sale of F-16s to Pakistan*, Hearings, 101st Cong., 1st sess., August 2, 1989. Bhutto and Indian Prime Minister Rajiv Gandhi (who led India from his mother's death in 1984 until late 1989) briefly improved relations between the two countries, and signed an agreement to ban attacks against each other's nuclear facilities.

[27] Michael Gordon, "War Over Kashmir is Feared by U.S.," *New York Times*, June 17, 1990, section 1, p. 15; Leonard Spector, "India-Pakistan War: It Could Be Nuclear," *New York Times*, June 7, 1990, p. 23.

[28] R. Jeffrey Smith, "Administration Unable to Win Hill Support for Continued Aid to Pakistan," *Washington Post*, October 10, 1990, p. 14. In support of continuing aid, Bush cited Pakistan's role in the U.S.-led military force opposing Iraq in the Persian Gulf. In the previous two years, Reagan and Bush had certified Pakistan's nonpossession of nuclear weapons with growing caveats and qualifications. See Michael Gordon, "Nuclear Course Set by Pakistan Worrying U.S.," *New York Times*, October 12, 1989, p. A1.

because of the growing conviction that Pakistan possessed nuclear weapons.[29]

AN ILLUSORY "CHINA CARD"

Beginning with its first nuclear test in 1964, China played a recurrent, if often indirect, role in shaping U.S. interests and perspectives on proliferation. But not until the Reagan administration did the United States engage Beijing directly on the issue, and make a serious bid for its participation in the nonproliferation regime. Ironically, in light of Reagan's history of vocal hostility to communist China, this effort became the leading initiative on nonproliferation by a president who otherwise largely neglected the subject. The vehicle for U.S. overtures to China was an agreement for peaceful nuclear cooperation that embodied the classic mix of political and commercial motives—and wishful thinking—of the Atoms for Peace era, and in the end produced equivocal and disappointing results.

Reagan laid the foundation for the nuclear initiative early in his administration when, following the logic of his larger anti-Soviet strategy, he embraced the 1970s U.S. rapprochement with China. Secretary of State Alexander Haig moved quickly to establish closer ties with China ("the most important country in the world," he asserted) as a means of applying pressure on Moscow. China was reclassified as a "friendly but nonaligned" nation, allowing sales of defensive weapons and dual-use technologies, and the United States agreed to limit future arms sales to Taiwan. Haig's successor, George Shultz, emphasized U.S. support for Chinese modernization through bilateral economic links and transfers of American civil technology.[30] The nuclear agreement was the centerpiece of this strategy.

The commercial stakes in nuclear cooperation with China were potentially vast. Beijing planned an extensive nuclear power program; with a government-to-government umbrella agreement in place, the moribund U.S. nuclear industry would be eligible to compete for up to $7 billion in anticipated sales of reactors and associated equipment. As with the Tarapur agreement 20 years before, the expected economic dividends reinforced broader political and strategic interests in nuclear collaboration.

---

[29] "Pakistan and India to Implement Accord on Nuclear Plant Attacks," *Nucleonics Week*, January 3, 1991, pp. 3–4; Rauf Siddiqi and Shahid-ur-Rheman Khan, "Nonproliferation Proposal Rejected," *Nucleonics Week*, June 13, 1991, pp. 15–16; Gus Constantine, "Pakistan Wants Regional Talks on Nuclear Arms," *Washington Times*, June 14, 1991, p. A8.

[30] Haig, *Caveat*, pp. 194ff.; Banning Garrett and Bonnie Glaser, "From Nixon to Reagan: China's Changing Role in American Strategy," in Kenneth Oye et al., eds., *Eagle Resurgent*, pp. 171ff.

But as in the Indian case, divergent nonproliferation policies plagued the negotiations.[31]

There were two main difficulties. First, China adamantly refused to accept IAEA safeguards on technology imported from the United States, considering such inspections an infringement of its sovereignty. This stance was awkward but not unmanageable, in the Reagan administration's view. Since China was already a nuclear weapon state, it argued, the danger that material might be diverted from peaceful to military uses was moot. (Critics disputed this claim, and argued that U.S. atomic energy laws required safeguards on all exports regardless of the nuclear status of the recipient.) More damaging was China's long tradition of opposition to nonproliferation policies and its more recent record of assistance to suspect nuclear programs. In addition to helping Pakistan's program, China had provided unsafeguarded nuclear exports (heavy water and enriched uranium, respectively) to Argentina and South Africa, both NPT holdouts and assumed to be pursuing the nuclear weapons option.

The Reagan administration again regarded nuclear cooperation as a lever to change China's behavior and obtain its support of the nonproliferation regime, and for once this strategy was at least partially rewarded. Beijing joined the IAEA in 1983 and announced that in the future it would require safeguards on its nuclear exports. It refused, however, to given written assurances of its conversion to the cause of nonproliferation. Instead, U.S. negotiators settled for a verbal affirmation, in a January 1984 White House toast by Premier Zhao Ziyang, that "We do not engage in nuclear proliferation ourselves, nor do we help other countries develop nuclear weapons." On this basis, the two sides completed the negotiations and produced a text that was initialed by Zhao and Reagan during the president's state visit to China in June.

Almost immediately the agreement began to unravel amid allegations that China was continuing to assist the Pakistani enrichment program. Attempts by Shultz and other American officials to obtain more explicit disavowals were summarily rebuffed by China's defense minister.[32] Fearing that the controversy would doom the agreement, the administration delayed submitting it to Congress for a year. During that time, the United States became satisfied—and was able to persuade congressional leaders—that Chinese personnel had been withdrawn from Kahuta and that other assistance to Pakistan's weapons effort had ceased. In July 1985,

---

[31] For a detailed account of the negotiations and their aftermath, see Patrick E. Tyler, "A Few Spoken Words Sealed China Atom Pact," *Washington Post*, January 12, 1986, p. 1.

[32] Leslie Gelb, "Pakistan Link Perils U.S.-China Nuclear Pact," *New York Times*, June 22, 1984; Leslie Gelb, "Peking Said to Balk at Nuclear Pledges," *New York Times*, June 23, 1984. For a cautious assessment of Chinese-Pakistani nuclear collaboration, see Charles Van Doren and Rodney Jones, *China and Nuclear Non-Proliferation: Two Perspectives*, Occasional Paper no. 3, Programme for Promoting Nuclear Non-Proliferation (Southampton, U.K.: Center for International Policy Studies, University of Southampton, 1989), esp. pp. 22–24.

Reagan signed the agreement and sent it to Congress. There it met severe criticism for its failure to require IAEA safeguards (the text provided vaguely for "exchanges of information and visits" to be arranged in the future) and for its loose wording on U.S. approval rights over the re-processing of American fuel. But China's high political stock in the mid-1980s, and the lure of multi-billion-dollar nuclear sales, overrode these doubts.[33] The agreement was approved on the condition that no exports could be licensed under it until the president issued certifications on China's commitment to nonproliferation and two other points.[34] Within a few years, however, China's reactor program was dramatically scaled back, and U.S. relations with Beijing cooled over the latter's missile sales to the Middle East and continuing indications of aid to Pakistan. The presidential certifications needed to authorize U.S. nuclear sales were never issued.

The Bush administration's nonproliferation policy towards China was complicated by the president's personal commitment to good relations with that country, stemming from Bush's experience as the American envoy in the 1970s. Following China's violent repression of prodemocracy forces in June 1989, however, Congress voted economic sanctions, including a ban on nuclear exports, in effect suspending the 1985 nuclear cooperation agreement.[35] Thus, one of the cornerstones of the Reagan nonproliferation policy crumbled in the hands of his successor.

Nuclear issues continued to be major irritants in U.S. relations with China. For example, China was revealed to have supplied Algeria with a research reactor that some feared could contribute to Algerian nuclear

---

[33] The U.S. nuclear industry lobbied heavily for the agreement, arguing that without it the United States would concede the China market to German and French firms. See J. Ernest Beazley, "Opposition to China-U.S. Nuclear Treaty Could Derail American Reactor Contracts," *Wall Street Journal*, September 26, 1984. On the agreement's textual lapses and the congressional debate, see Daniel Horner and Paul Leventhal, "The U.S.-China Nuclear Agreement: A Failure," *The Fletcher Forum*, Winter 1977, and Peter A. Clausen, "A Porous Nuclear Pact," *New York Times*, October 5, 1985, p. 23.

[34] The other points were verification of the peaceful use of U.S.-supplied materials and U.S. veto rights over reprocessing of American fuel. See Warren Donnelly, *Implementation of the U.S.-Chinese Agreement for Nuclear Cooperation*, CRS Issue Brief IB86050 (Washington, DC: Library of Congress, September 8, 1988).

[35] "Authorization Bill Contains Sanctions Against China," *Congressional Quarterly*, November 11, 1989, pp. 3083–84. See also George Lardner, Jr., "White House Defers Deal for Nuclear Equipment," *Washington Post*, June 12, 1989, p. A26. In the late 1980s, China sold Silkworm missiles to Iran and intermediate-range East Wind ballistic missiles to Saudi Arabia, and promoted a new family of short-range ballistic missiles to Syria and other countries. See Martin Navias, "Ballistic Missile Proliferation in the Third World," *Adelphi Papers* 252, Summer 1990, p. 22. Press reports allege that the Saudi ambassador to the United States, Prince Bandar, requested nuclear weapons from China for the East Wind missiles the day after the Iraqi invasion of Kuwait. Jack Anderson and Dale Van Atta, *Washington Post*, December 12, 1990, p. G15; *The Sunday Times* (London), December 16, 1990, p. 1.

weapons potential; the Chinese government first denied that it had supplied the reactor, then later acknowledged the transaction. Only after the reactor's existence was publicly divulged by the U.S. government did Algeria agree to place the reactor under IAEA safeguards.[36]

Ending a two-year boycott of high-level diplomatic exchanges with China following the Tiananmen Square massacre, Secretary of State Baker visited Beijing in November 1991. While the Chinese leadership reiterated China's previously announced willingness to consider signing the NPT, it nonetheless refused to bow to Baker's entreaties to curb its nuclear technology export activities to worrisome countries such as Iran, or to use its influence to dampen North Korea's nuclear weapons aspirations.[37] Since President Bush had made it clear in advance that he would veto congressional attempts to pressure China by depriving it of its most-favored-nation trade status, it is not surprising that Baker was able to exercise so little leverage over the Chinese government.[38]

SOUTH AFRICA, LATIN AMERICA, AND THE MIDDLE EAST

Regional proliferation trends were sharply mixed during the 1980s. In the Middle East, as in South Asia, the decade saw a steady worsening of the situation. In Africa and South America, however, "problem countries" edged closer to the nuclear weapons option, but then pulled back under the influence of domestic moves toward democracy. In comparison with the high-level attention devoted to Pakistan, the United States was only marginally involved with proliferation developments in these other regions. Each case, however, revealed the U.S. predilection for treating the nuclear question as subordinate to other, Cold War–related U.S. interests in the countries concerned.

South Africa

South Africa developed its own enrichment technology during the 1970s, and was beginning to produce weapons-grade uranium in an unsafeguarded pilot plant as the 1980s began. Pretoria's nuclear weapons motives seemed clear, and presumably reflected both military and politi-

---

[36] Bill Gertz, "China Helps Algeria Develop Nuclear Weapons," *Washington Times*, April 11, 1991, p. A3; Mark Hibbs, "Cooling Towers are Key to Claim Algeria is Building Bomb Reactor," *Nucleonics Week*, April 18, 1991, pp. 7–8; Ann MacLachlan and Mark Hibbs, "Algeria Confirms Secret Reactor; Questions about Purpose Remain," *Nucleonics Week*, May 2, 1991, p. 3.

[37] Thomas L. Freidman, "Baker's China Trip Fails to Produce Pledge on Rights," *New York Times*, November 18, 1991, p. A1.

[38] *The Economist*, November 9, 1991, p. 36.

cal interests of the country's beleaguered apartheid regime. A nuclear option might serve as a last-resort deterrent against invasion from neighboring states aimed at overturning South Africa's white minority government, or as a bargaining card in negotiations on the country's future.[39] When Carter left office, U.S. relations with Pretoria were deteriorating over the latter's racial policies and were at an impasse on the nuclear issue.

The Reagan administration announced a new policy of "constructive engagement" toward South Africa. Pressure for racial reform would be eased to reduce the regime's sense of isolation and insecurity, and the United States would stress Pretoria's role as a counterweight to Soviet inroads in southern Africa—largely the result of Cuba's intervention in the civil war in neighboring Angola.[40] The policy had a nuclear corollary. Although the 1978 Nuclear Non-Proliferation Act prevented the United States from supplying fuel for South Africa's Koeberg reactors—as had been planned earlier—the Reagan administration softened this sanction by allowing U.S. uranium brokers to arrange for Pretoria to obtain the fuel it needed in Europe. In addition, the administration approved exports to South Africa of nuclear components and dual-use items not covered by the NNPA, arguing that such sales would maintain a channel of influence over South African nuclear policy.[41] But in the mid-1980s, even limited nuclear cooperation was swamped by the growing controversy over apartheid. Constructive engagement collapsed in the face of growing public and congressional opposition and increasingly violent repression of anti-apartheid forces in South Africa. Under sanctions imposed by Reagan and Congress, all nuclear exports to South Africa were prohibited, as were U.S. imports of uranium from that country.

At the end of the decade, however, under President F. W. deKlerk, South Africa began a series of unprecedented racial reforms that appeared

---

[39] See Michele Flournoy and Kurt Campbell, "South Africa's Bomb: A Military Option?" *Orbis*, Summer 1988; and Richard Betts, "A Diplomatic Bomb for South Africa?" *International Security*, Fall 1979. Concern over South Africa's nuclear intentions became acute in 1977 when an apparent underground nuclear test site was discovered in the Kalahari Desert. Under pressure, Pretoria agreed to dismantle the site, but continued to pursue a weapons option. In 1979, a U.S. satellite detected a flash over the South Atlantic that closely resembled a nuclear explosion, prompting speculation that South Africa, perhaps in cooperation with Israel, had tested a nuclear device. U.S. government experts were divided in their assessment of the event, which remains mysterious.

[40] See Chester Crocker, "South Africa: A Strategy for Change," *Foreign Affairs*, Winter 1980–1981; David Gordon, "Southern Africa," in Robert Litwak and Samuel Wells, Jr., eds., *Superpower Competition and Security in the Third World* (Cambridge, MA: Ballinger, 1988).

[41] According to a report by the General Accounting Office, South Africa became the second-largest recipient of U.S. dual-use equipment in the nuclear sector in Reagan's first two years. Cited in Gunther Hellman, "The Collapse of 'Constructive Engagement': U.S. Foreign Policy in Southern Africa," in Helga Haftendorn and Jakob Schissler, eds., *The Reagan Administration: A Reconstruction of American Strength?* (New York: Walter de Gruyter, 1988), p. 277.

to signal the demise of the apartheid system. In parallel, the South African government modified its nuclear policy, closing the unsafeguarded enrichment plant and indicating that it was prepared to sign the NPT if other southern African states did so as well.[42] Although difficult questions remained unsettled (such as the status of any weapons material already produced), and a right-wing backlash against reform could not be excluded, the proliferation threat in South Africa was declining in urgency as the 1990s began.

South America

South America saw a similar mellowing of the nuclear threat during the Reagan-Bush period. Brazil and Argentina, with a long history of national rivalry and military interest in nuclear weapons, had both been stigmatized by the Carter nonproliferation and human-rights policies. In the 1980s, both made progress toward nuclear capabilities by mastering uranium-enrichment technologies, while continuing to reject the NPT and its safeguards requirements.[43]

As with South Africa, the Reagan administration sought better U.S. relations with the two authoritarian regimes to further its anticommunist priorities. Carter-era confrontation on human-rights abuses was halted and U.S. arms sales to Latin America increased as Reagan tried to build a common front in support of the Nicaraguan "contra" rebels and other efforts to combat Soviet influence in the Western Hemisphere.[44] Again, there was a nuclear component to the strategy. The administration gave Brazil a free escape route from the NNPA-mandated cutoff of fuel supplies, suspending the country's U.S. enrichment contract so that it could purchase fuel elsewhere without financial penalty. For Argentina, Reagan approved transfers of U.S. heavy water and dual-use computer technology.[45]

United States rapprochement with Argentina was cut short by the latter's 1982 invasion of the Falkland Islands and its ensuing war with Britain over the disputed territory. In the aftermath of Argentina's defeat,

---

[42] Anne MacLachlan and Mark Hibbs, "South Africa Ready to Sign NPT If Other States in the Region Do Likewise," *Nucleonics Week*, October 27, 1990, p. 20–23.

[43] See David Albright, "Bomb Potential for South America," *Bulletin of the Atomic Scientists*, May 1989. Brazil's weapons effort, a secret program run by the military, was separate from the safeguarded civil nuclear program based on the 1975 deal with Germany. The civil program, the object of the Carter administration's protests, virtually collapsed during the 1980s because of economic and technical setbacks.

[44] See Robert Pastor, "The Reagan Administration and Latin America: Eagle Insurgent," in Oye et al., eds., *Eagle Resurgent*.

[45] *Washington Post*, July 19, 1982, p. 1. On the Brazilian fuel case, see Joseph Pilat and Warren Donnelly, "Nuclear Export Policy of the Reagan Administration," (footnote 13), pp. II–7 to II–12.

however, a civilian government replaced the discredited military regime and took steps to contain the country's nuclear program. When Brazil also returned to civilian rule, the two countries deescalated their nuclear rivalry and adopted confidence-building measures including mutual visits to sensitive nuclear facilities. In 1990, the Brazilian president publicly exposed his country's secret nuclear weapons program and announced that it would be shut down. Soon after, both countries renounced the pursuit of nuclear weapons and declared their willingness to negotiate full-scope safeguards agreements with the IAEA, perhaps establishing a bilateral agency similar to EURATOM for the purpose of conducting safeguards inspections.[46]

Israel and the Middle East

Throughout the 1980s, the Israeli nuclear program remained the "dog that didn't bark" in U.S. policy. Following the precedent set under Nixon and honored by Carter, the United States took no official note of the Israeli program and did not raise it in relations between the two countries.[47] If anything, the Reagan administration was even less inclined than its predecessors to jeopardize U.S.-Israeli ties over the nuclear issue, because in the wake of the Iranian revolution it viewed Israel as the chief anti-Soviet bastion in the Middle East. Israel's heightened importance as a U.S. "strategic asset" survived early strains over its attack on Iraq's Osirak nuclear reactor and its invasion of Lebanon, and led to unprecedented levels of aid by mid-decade.[48]

The June 1981 air strike against Iraq presented the Reagan administration with its first proliferation-related crisis and tested its ability to calibrate an appropriate response.[49] On the one hand, Israel was not only a close ally but was legitimately threatened—although not in the near term—by Iraq's highly suspect nuclear program; and the strike, which destroyed the French-built reactor and set back Iraq's program by several

---

[46] Shirley Christian, "Argentina and Brazil Renounce Nuclear Weapons," *New York Times*, November 11, 1990, p. 1; *Gazeta Mercantil* (São Paulo), May 24, 1991, as reported in *Proliferation Issues*, July 10, 1991, p. 8.

[47] On the Carter administration's tolerance of the Israeli program, see Gerard Smith and Helena Cobban, "A Blind Eye to Nuclear Proliferation," *Foreign Affairs*, Summer 1989, pp. 62–63. Proliferation was a nonissue in the Carter-sponsored Camp David negotiations that led to a peace treaty between Israel and Egypt; a Senate proposal to link subsequent U.S. aid to the two countries' signing of the NPT was decisively defeated. See also Smith's testimony in Senate Committee on Governmental Affairs, *Nuclear Nonproliferation Policy*, Hearings, 97th Cong., 1st sess., June 24, 1981.

[48] See Philip S. Khoury, "The Reagan Administration and the Middle East," in Kyvig, ed., *Reagan and the World*, pp. 72ff.; and Sanford Lakoff, "The 'Reagan Doctrine' and U.S. Policy in the Middle East," in Steven L. Spiegel et al., eds., *The Soviet-American Competition in the Middle East* (Lexington, MA: Lexington Books, 1988), pp. 130ff.

[49] See Haig, *Caveat*, pp. 182ff.

years, was undeniably an effective nonproliferation measure. On the other hand, the incident awkwardly underlined Washington's proliferation double standard, undercut the credibility of the NPT system (Iraq being a treaty member and the reactor subject to IAEA safeguards), and violated U.S.-Israeli agreements barring the offensive use of American-supplied aircraft. Balancing these considerations in Israel's favor, the Reagan administration briefly delayed delivery of four new F-16s, but blocked punitive action by the UN and the IAEA. When the latter threatened to eject Israel over the issue in 1982, the United States withdrew from the agency for several months and successfully diverted the attempt.[50]

The mild reaction to the Osirak raid set the pattern for subsequent U.S. indulgence of the Israeli nuclear weapons program. In late 1981, a congressional measure aimed at Pakistan—requiring a cutoff of U.S. aid to countries manufacturing nuclear bombs—was withdrawn when the State Department warned its sponsors that it might inadvertently punish Israel.[51] In 1986, the Reagan administration made no response to the most detailed revelations yet about Israeli nuclear activities. Mordechai Vanunu, a former technician at the Dimona complex, reported that Israel possessed an arsenal of up to 200 warheads, some employing nuclear fusion (the technique of the H-bomb), and that these weapons had been integrated into the nation's military forces and strategy.[52] This information, considered credible by expert analysts who debriefed Vanunu (later abducted by Israeli agents, convicted of espionage and treason, and sentenced to prison), indicated a far more advanced program than earlier assumed. Three years later, there were new disclosures about Israeli collaboration with South Africa on the development of ballistic missiles and (less conclusively) nuclear weapons. This time, U.S. officials protested to Tel Aviv (whose cooperation with South Africa would have violated

---

[50] See Lawrence Scheinman, *The International Atomic Energy Agency and World Nuclear Order* (Washington, DC: Resources for the Future, 1987), pp. 211–18. Scheinman concludes that "U.S. behavior showed that the importance it attached to nonproliferation policy was distinctly in second place when it came to supporting Israel." In extensive congressional hearings on the Osirak attack, the Israeli program was scarcely mentioned, much less acknowledged as a spur to Arab nuclear efforts. See Senate Committee on Foreign Relations, *The Israeli Air Strike*, Hearings, 97th Cong., 1st sess., June 18, 19, and 25, 1981. Adding further to the U.S. reluctance to punish Israel was a major controversy during 1981 over U.S. plans to sell advanced Airborne Warning and Control System (AWACS) planes to Saudi Arabia.

[51] Judith Miller, "2 in House Withdraw Atom Curb," *New York Times*, December 9, 1981, p. 8.

[52] "Revealed: The Secrets of Israel's Nuclear Arsenal," London *Sunday Times*, October 5, 1986. Some analysts, while crediting the bulk of Vanunu's claims, estimate a smaller arsenal of fewer than 100 weapons. See Leonard Spector and Jacqueline Smith, *Nuclear Ambitions: The Spread of Nuclear Weapons, 1989–1990* (Boulder, CO: Westview Press, 1990), p. 159.

sanctions against defense aid to that country), but dropped the issue when Israel bluntly refused to discuss it.[53]

The Reagan administration's indulgence of Israel was apparently strained to the limit when it was discovered in 1985 that an American civilian employee of U.S. Naval Intelligence, Jonathan Pollard, had passed top-secret defense information to Israel. One of Israel's purposes in the spying was to gain U.S. intelligence data on the Soviet Union that would improve Israel's ability to target the USSR with its growing nuclear force. At the direction of Prime Minister Shamir, however, the information obtained from Pollard was immediately turned over to the Soviet Union as a "good will gesture" that would improve Israeli-Soviet relations. Although there was a strong reaction inside the U.S. government, publicly the ramifications of the Pollard case were downplayed so as not to damage U.S. relations with an Israel that became, during the Reagan administration, increasingly described as the U.S.'s "strategic partner" in the Middle East.[54]

As George Bush took office in 1989, two related but conflicting trends were emerging. First, the United States was increasingly (if still only implicitly) treating the Israeli nuclear capability as legitimate and unalterable, and defining the Middle East proliferation problem in terms of the threat to Israel from the Arab countries. This skewed perspective largely precluded a regional policy—such as the one the U.S. tried to pursue in South Asia—that accounted for the role of Israeli nuclear weapons in motivating Arab programs. Second, however, the U.S. double standard on behalf of Israel was becoming increasingly strained in light of the Vanunu and South Africa disclosures, the obvious contrast between U.S. pressure on Pakistan and benign neglect toward Israel, and rising concern about Arab nuclear, missile, and chemical weapons programs. In the late 1980s, public references to Israel's nuclear capability became more frequent and explicit. Arab leaders openly justified chemical weapons as a counter to Israel's bomb; Israeli officials became less artful in their nuclear disclaimers and hinted at a policy of nuclear retaliation in response to Arab chemical attacks.[55]

The 1990 Persian Gulf crisis brought these trends into sudden and sharp relief. The Iraqi takeover of Kuwait belatedly drew attention not only to Baghdad's own advanced weapons programs but to the whole phenomenon of Middle East proliferation, the interaction between chem-

---

[53] Michael Gordon, "U.S. Says Data Suggest Israel Aids South Africa on Missile," *New York Times*, October 27, 1989; David Ottaway and Jeffrey Smith, "U.S. Knew of 2 Nations' Missile Work," *Washington Post*, October 27, 1989.

[54] Seymour Hersh, *The Samson Option: Israel, America, and the Bomb* (New York: Random House, 1991), chap. 21.

[55] See Edward Cody, "Talks Show Growing Arab Consensus that Chemical Arms Balance Nuclear," *Washington Post*, January 13, 1989, p. 24; and Spector and Smith, *Nuclear Ambitions*, p. 158.

ical and nuclear threats, and the resulting risk that any conflict might quickly escalate into a regional conflagration. The crisis also served to underscore President Saddam Hussein's bid to make Iraq the dominant military power in the region, and the West's shortsighted complicity in this bid.

Just as Israel had profited from the U.S. fixation on the Soviet threat in the Middle East, Iraq was the beneficiary of Western hostility to Iran following the Shah's overthrow. Convinced that Iran posed the greater threat, the United States tilted strongly toward Baghdad in the Iran-Iraq war (started by Iraq) that lasted through most of the 1980s—restoring diplomatic relations, offering commodity credits, organizing an arms embargo against Iran, and turning a blind eye to Hussein's repeated use of chemical weapons in the conflict.[56] The war ended in Iran's defeat in 1988, but the United States continued to view Iraq as a potential moderating force in the region despite new evidence of Baghdad's nuclear and chemical threats.

In the late 1980s, Saddam Hussein energetically revived the Iraqi nuclear weapons program that had been dormant since the Osirak raid.[57] Using the clandestine techniques successfully pioneered by Pakistan, Baghdad began building a centrifuge enrichment plant and acquiring components for nuclear warheads. In March 1990, Iraqi agents were caught smuggling warhead detonators out of Great Britain.[58] Subsequently, Hussein threatened to destroy "half of Israel" with chemical weapons in response to any new Israeli attack, and in an interview with an American newspaper "spoke with almost clinical detachment of a war in which Israeli nuclear weapons would be offset by Iraq's chemical capability."[59] Congressional attempts to impose economic sanctions in response to these threats were opposed by the Bush administration until the August 1990 Iraqi invasion of Kuwait finally reversed its calculation of U.S. interests toward Iraq. The White House then declared the Iraqi nuclear program to be a severe threat to regional security and to American troops deployed in the Gulf following the invasion. Responding to opinion polls indicating that the destruction of Hussein's nuclear potential was the only rationale for war supported by a majority of the public, administra-

---

[56] See Mark Heller, "Soviet and American Attitudes Toward the Iran-Iraq War," in Spiegel et al., eds., *The Soviet-American Competition in the Middle East*, p. 177.

[57] Glenn Frankel, "Iraq Said Developing A-Weapons," *Washington Post*, March 31, 1989, p. 1; Patrick Tyler, "Iraq Nuclear Program Stirs Debate," *Washington Post*, June 4, 1989, p. 35. See also Spector and Smith, *Nuclear Ambitions*, pp. 190ff.

[58] Michael Isikoff and George Lardner, Jr., "Bomb Parts Seized on Way to Iraq," *Washington Post*, March 29, 1990, p. 1. Despite these activities, most experts judged Iraq to be several years away from an actual weapons capability as of 1990.

[59] Karen E. House, "Iraqi President Hussein Sees New Mideast War Unless America Acts," *Wall Street Journal*, June 28, 1990, p. 1.

tion officials began to invoke this theme as a justification for sending in U.S. troops.[60]

Iraqi nuclear installations were purposely targeted during the initial air phase of the war.[61] Some of these, such as the Tuwaitha nuclear research facility near Baghdad, were under the IAEA inspection regime, but there was surprisingly little protest from the international community.[62]

But the major surprises were to come in the wake of the U.S. victory in the war: UN inspectors discovered an Iraqi nuclear weapons program of much greater scope and sophistication than had previously been suspected, along with a panoply of missile programs and gas- and germ-warfare facilities. This discovery led to a dramatic confrontation between IAEA inspectors and Iraqi authorities, which, for a time, looked as if it might trigger a renewal of hostilities.[63] That a country such as Iraq could build a clandestine nuclear weapons program, employing thousands of people in dozens of separate components, called into question the adequacy of U.S. intelligence, challenged the effectiveness of Western nations' export controls, and raised doubts about the adequacy of the existing international safeguards regime. That many of these nuclear facilities had escaped destruction during the war raised further questions about the effectiveness of the American bombing.

Having waged war in part to disarm Iraq's nuclear potential, the Bush administration was faced with the irony of a military victory that revealed a significant failure of the United States's nonproliferation policies.

CONCLUSION

The Gulf war thus served to redirect attention to the threat of nuclear proliferation. Throughout the 1980s, the issue had been eclipsed by the preoccupation with Cold War conflicts and superpower diplomacy. Preoccupied with reversing the perceived weakness of its predecessor, the

---

[60] Michael Gordon, "U.S. Aides Press Iraqi Nuclear Threat," New York Times, November 26, 1990, p. 13. Most experts placed a usable Iraqi nuclear capability several years in the future, however. See Malcolm Growne, "Unless Stopped, Iraq Could Have A-Arms in 10 Years, Experts Say," New York Times, November 11, 1990, p. 1; and Michael Wines, "Hard Data Lacking on Iraqi Nuclear Threat," New York Times, November 30, 1990, p. 12.

[61] Mark Hibbs, "U.S. Says Iraqi Reactors Hit: No Confirmation from Baghdad," Nucleonics Week, January 24, 1991, p. 1.

[62] Ann MacLachlan and Margaret Ryan, "Allied Bombing of Iraqi Reactors Provokes No Safeguards Debate," Nucleonics Week, January 31, 1991, p. 1.

[63] David Albright and Mark Hibbs, "Iraq's Nuclear Hide-and-Seek," Bulletin of the Atomic Scientists, September 1991, pp. 14–23; Maureen Dowd, "Bush Accuses Iraq of Lying About Arms," New York Times, June 30, 1991, p. A6.

Reagan administration had largely disregarded the importance of non-proliferation in U.S. national security policy. Repeating the pattern of the Nixon-Kissinger era, its nonproliferation policy was marked by complacency and neglect and relegated to the periphery of U.S. foreign policy concerns. Like the previous cycle of indifference, which ended with the Indian nuclear explosion, the pattern of the 1980s was broken by a proliferation-related crisis in 1991. Moreover, the events of 1989–1991 also resembled those of 15 years earlier in that they marked an important watershed in world politics and U.S. foreign policy as well as for non-proliferation.

Coming in the wake of the liberation of Eastern Europe and the virtual end of East-West antagonism, the Persian Gulf war was widely seen as ushering in the post–Cold War era of world politics. The crisis was remarkable for the close superpower cooperation and the absence of what had previously been the overriding risk in such situations—that a regional conflict would ignite a central nuclear confrontation. At the same time, Iraq's aggression exemplified the risks of a world no longer defined by familiar postwar patterns of bipolar competition and restraint.

Indeed, the breakup of the Soviet Union itself was an example of the novel proliferation threats that the U.S. was forced to confront in the early 1990s. As the Russian empire unraveled, and the constituent republics increasingly asserted their independence from the central government in Moscow, American worries grew about the ultimate disposition of the Soviet Union's enormous nuclear arsenal. Theoretical proliferation scenarios in which nuclear weapons might play a role in a civil war or military coup d'état became more realistic following the Moscow coup of August 1991.[64] Part of the Bush administration's preference for the maintenance of a strong central government in Moscow was apparently based on its fear of possible nuclear proliferation resulting from the breakup of the Soviet Union.[65]

The Bush administration accelerated the pace of bilateral nuclear arms negotiations with Gorbachev's central government, and took unilateral acts such as the announced phaseout of tactical nuclear weapons from Western Europe,[66] making it easier for the Soviet central government to pull its own far-flung nuclear arsenal back into the Russian republic. The United States also recognized that assertive nationalism in, for example, the Ukraine could result in the emergence of a new nuclear weapons state with one of the largest nuclear arsenals in the world. The United States was faced with the prospect of negotiating separate accords

---

[64] Michael Dobbs, "General Withdrew Missiles into Shelter During Coup: KGB Officers Tell of Key Unit Disobeying Orders," *Washington Post*, August 28, 1991, p. A1.

[65] Andrew Rosenthal, "Nuclear Arms Issue Is Driving U.S.-Soviet Policy," *New York Times*, December 10, 1991, p. A10.

[66] John E. Yong, "Bush Plan Emerged After Failed Coup," *Washington Post*, September 28, 1991, p. 23.

with the constituent republics.[67] The emergence of a Commonwealth of former Soviet republics exercising control over Soviet nuclear weapons did not resolve all concerns about the dangers inherent in the evolving Soviet situation.[68]

The Bush administration also had to confront the possibility that the economic collapse of the Soviet Union might lead Soviet nuclear scientists who were thrown out of work at home to become nuclear weapons mercenaries working abroad in clandestine weapons programs.[69] Alternatively, enterprising Soviet nuclear scientists and bureaucrats might seek to capitalize on one of the Soviet Union's few marketable advanced technologies and try to sell nuclear weapons technologies to the highest bidders.[70] These unprecedented possibilities invited the question of whether the post–Cold War world would on balance be more or less hospitable to U.S. and global nonproliferation efforts.

[67] Michael Wines, "Baker Will Visit Ukraine to Discuss Nuclear Question," *New York Times*, December 3, 1991, p. A1; William C. Potter, "Ukraine as a Nuclear Power," *Wall Street Journal*, December 4, 1991, p. A14.

[68] Thomas L. Friedman, "U.S. Says 4 Republics Vow to Carry-out Nuclear Arms Cuts," *New York Times*, December 19, 1991, p. A1; Serge Schmenann, "Declaring Death of the Soviet Union, Russia and 2 Republics Form New Commonwealth," *New York Times*, December 10, 1991, p. A1.

[69] Andrew Rosenthal, "U.S. Fears Spread of Soviet A-Arms," *New York Times*, December 16, 1991, p. 9.

[70] William C. Potter, "Russia's Nuclear Entrepreneurs," *New York Times*, November 7, 1991, p. A15.

Chapter
8

Nonproliferation After the Cold War

*F*or 45 years, America's nonproliferation policy was made and implemented in the shadow of the Cold War rivalry. The specter of a nuclear-armed Soviet Union inspired the first U.S. attempts to prevent the spread of the bomb; subsequent U.S. policies on proliferation were often conceived and shaped according to Washington's preoccupation with the Soviet problem. Just as the Cold War largely defined U.S. foreign policy throughout the decades following World War II, it also largely determined American perspectives on the nature of the proliferation threat, the range of choice for dealing with it, and the costs and benefits of alternative policies. This impact, as the evolution of U.S. policy over the decades repeatedly shows, was two-sided: the contest with Moscow provided both a powerful motive to oppose the spread of nuclear weapons and a frequent constraint on such opposition. This fact suggests that the why and how of U.S. nonproliferation in the post–Cold War world may not be straightforward.

Although the future is uncharted territory, the patterns and lessons of the past still have relevance. In particular, the problem of meshing nonproliferation with the pursuit of other U.S. interests and goals will remain. This book has examined the foreign policy logic of America's response to the spread of nuclear weapons in the belief that this is the most realistic focus for assessing past performance and making recommendations for the future. Simply put, the foreign policy dog typically wags the nonproliferation tail. Policymakers will continue to address nonproliferation, not in a vacuum or as an end in itself but in relation to their wider concerns, as one U.S. national interest among others. They will pursue it because—and to the extent that—they believe proliferation threatens vital U.S. interests and that measures to prevent it are tolerably consistent with the key premises of American foreign policy. From the start, American policymakers recognized and espoused nonproliferation as an important U.S. national interest. Consistently, the United States took the lead in creating and upgrading the institutions of the global nonproliferation regime.[1] At times, these efforts were well integrated with the broader goals of U.S. foreign and national security policy. Frequently, however, gaps and discontinuities appeared, and nonproliferation was pursued at cross-purposes with (and, more often than not, sacrificed to) other interests. The coherence, effectiveness, and credibility of U.S. nonproliferation efforts have suffered as a result. The task for the future is not to make nonproliferation always the top priority—an unrealistic and probably undesirable goal—but to weave it more successfully into the fabric of U.S. foreign policy.

PATTERNS

Since 1945, U.S. policymakers have believed that nonproliferation serves a number of American interests. The spread of nuclear weapons to additional countries has been thought to increase the chances of nuclear war generally and of a catalytic superpower conflict in particular; raise the risks of extending deterrence to overseas allies; impede efforts to stabilize the U.S.-Soviet balance through arms control and crisis management; abridge U.S. influence and access in the Third World; and threaten overseas allies and military forces of the United States. In addition to these intrinsic reasons to oppose the spread of the bomb, nonproliferation policies have also served important instrumental purposes for the United States. Peaceful nuclear cooperation was pursued for its economic and political benefits (to counter Soviet influence and promote European unity, for example) as well as to discourage proliferation; the Non-Proliferation Treaty served as a major vehicle for U.S.-Soviet rapprochement in addition to its explicit objectives.

But these U.S. interests in nonproliferation have not been consistent. Interacting with other U.S. objectives and with the overarching foreign policy agendas of successive administrations, their relative priority has varied over time and from one country to another. Much of this variation is due to four related factors: the changing aims of U.S. policy toward the Soviet Union; the level of East-West tensions; the alternation of expanding and contracting impulses in U.S. foreign policy; and different U.S. interests toward nations seeking nuclear weapons.

---

[1] For an interesting historical balance sheet, see Lewis A. Dunn, "Four Decades of Nuclear Non-proliferation Policy: Some Lessons from Wins, Losses, and Draws," *The Washington Quarterly*, Summer 1990.

The Cold War Prism

Typically, relations with the Soviet Union have stood at the top of the U.S. foreign policy agenda and have heavily influenced or, indeed, dominated the assessment of nuclear proliferation. The rise and fall of nonproliferation has thus been closely correlated with the requirements of American policy toward Moscow (see Table 8.1). When nonproliferation has directly served those requirements, it has risen in priority. Such was the case during the period of U.S. nuclear monopoly (when depriving Moscow of the bomb was a self-evident vital interest), and again during the mid-1960s when Johnson saw the Non-Proliferation Treaty as a way to improve superpower relations. The only other period in which non-proliferation gained a comparable status, the mid- to late 1970s, was a time when the dominance of U.S.-Soviet relations in Washington's world-view was temporarily challenged by the "global issues" agenda. By the

Table 8.1   FOREIGN POLICY AND NONPROLIFERATION

Period	Foreign policy focus	Nonproliferation
1945–50	Beginning of Cold War; containment policy.	U.S. monopoly period; Baruch Plan; 1946 Atomic Energy Act (denial).
1950s	Height of Cold War; New Look and massive retaliation; NATO nuclearization.	1954 and 1958 Atomic Energy Act; Atoms for Peace, IAEA; U.K. cooperation.
Early 1960s	Flexible response; globalism; Cuban crisis and U.S.-Soviet thaw (partial test ban).	MLF; opposition to French bomb; Dimona inspections.
Mid-1964–68	U.S.-Soviet détente; Vietnam; globalism peaks.	NPT; MLF dropped; acquiescence to Israeli bomb.
1969–74	Vietnam; Nixon doctrine; opening to China; SALT; Middle East conflict.	Low priority and attention.
1975–79	Post-Vietnam retrenchment; energy crisis; human rights.	Post-India revival; Glenn-Symington, NNPA, Suppliers Group; antiplutonium initiative; Pakistani aid cutoff.
1980–88	Cold War revival; arms buildup; Reagan doctrine (Afghanistan).	Downgraded; acquiescence to allied plutonium use, Pakistani bomb.
1989–	End of Cold War; Persian Gulf war; growing emphasis on economic competition.	Pakistani aid suspension, concern about Iraq, North Korea; anti-bomb trends in South America and South Africa; growing threat of commerce in nuclear technology.

same token, nonproliferation lost priority when it clashed with the perceived imperatives of U.S. policy toward Moscow—in the 1950s, when the political and military demands of NATO nuclear strategy required some delegation and sharing of nuclear responsibilities with the allies; and in the 1980s, when policies toward the Soviet Union prompted the United States to downplay the proliferation threat posed by American partners in the Third World.

The Level of East-West Tension

A related pattern follows from the Cold War prism. Since the Soviets obtained the bomb, there has been an inverse relationship between the level of East-West tension and the priority of U.S. nonproliferation efforts. Periods of détente have been more favorable to these efforts than periods of intense U.S.-Soviet rivalry. In part this simply reflects the fact that the Soviet threat has controlled the attention of Washington at times of sharp confrontation; when that threat has receded from the foreground, other security issues have assumed greater importance. Another reason is that acute Cold War periods have generally heightened the tension between America's nonproliferation and Soviet policies. East-West polarization has encouraged the United States to be more tolerant of the nuclear programs of anti-Soviet allies and clients, while détente has weakened security ties with these nations and encouraged the expression of the shared superpower interest in nonproliferation.

Expansion versus Retrenchment

The early 1970s were an exception to the above rule: in the Nixon administration a lessening of superpower tension was accompanied by diminished attention to the proliferation threat. The Nixon-Kissinger foreign policy illustrates another historical pattern, however. Periods of concern about the burdens of containment and the perils of overextension—that is, the post-Korean period and the last years of the Vietnam war—saw a relaxation of U.S. nonproliferation policy. In these periods, policymakers were sensitive to the potential costs of a strict nonproliferation policy in terms of U.S. overseas obligations. While not endorsing the spread of nuclear weapons to U.S. allies, Presidents Eisenhower and Nixon were comparatively tolerant of it. In their view, a greater European (or Israeli) nuclear role was not entirely inimical to U.S. interests and could serve as a form of Cold War burden-sharing, enabling the United States to limit its own direct involvement in countering Soviet power. In contrast, when the United States defined its global role and interests in more expansive, open-ended terms—especially in the Kennedy and Johnson administrations—nonproliferation rose in importance. The risks of proliferation then loomed larger than the political costs of more vigorous efforts to prevent it.

In the mid-1970s, this pattern was broken. The Ford and Carter administrations uneasily combined post-Vietnam U.S. retrenchment with a strong emphasis on nonproliferation. The result was a disparity between ends and means that hampered the effectiveness of U.S. policy. The Reagan years, on the other hand, saw a revival of U.S. global activism but relative complacency about the threat of proliferation.

Country Variations

These broad aggregate trends, though suggestive, necessarily gloss over a major source of the fluctuations and discontinuities that have marked U.S. nonproliferation policy—differences between specific cases facing American policymakers. Differences in the U.S. interests at stake in particular countries, and in their susceptibility to U.S. influence, have precluded a uniform and consistent American policy against the spread of nuclear weapons.

Two countries, Great Britain and Israel, received especially favored treatment. United States nonproliferation legislation was deliberately crafted in the 1950s to permit aid to the British nuclear weapons effort, and in later decades to avoid penalizing Israel for its own weapons program. In both cases, a determined U.S. bid to deny nuclear weapons would have exacted high political costs with no guarantee of success. Tolerance of nuclear weapons in these two countries was also encouraged by the close U.S. political relations with each, the relative compatibility of their security perspectives with those of the United States, their domestic stability, and the low risk that their weapons would be used in ways that would directly threaten U.S. interests. Where these conditions were lacking, American concern about the spread of nuclear weapons was greater. France was considered a less reliable ally than Britain. India was nonaligned and frequently out of line with American Cold War policies. Pakistan, though a U.S. ally against the Soviet Union, wanted nuclear weapons against India—an interest that the United States did not share. South Africa's motives for obtaining nuclear weapons bore little relation to U.S. interests, despite the congruence of the two countries' Cold War security perspectives.

In many cases the intensity and results of U.S. nonproliferation efforts have varied directly with the leverage available to the United States. The greatest U.S. success (though achieved at the cost of considerable strain) was in formalizing the nonnuclear status of Germany and Japan through the NPT. Taiwan and South Korea, friendly nations heavily dependent on Washington, were not as easily persuaded by security ties with the United States to abandon the nuclear option, but were vulnerable to direct pressures to desist from weapons activities. Brazil and Argentina, though nominally in the American sphere of influence, were less amenable to pressure because of their relatively slight dependence on U.S. aid, their indigenous capabilities, and their strong nationalistic resistance to U.S.

political and economic domination. Domestic political evolution, rather than outside nonproliferation policies, brought about a shift toward nuclear restraint in these countries. A similar pattern prevailed in South Africa, where the regime's international isolation because of the apartheid issue left few levers for influencing its nuclear policy incentives. With the demise of apartheid, it would become possible for the United States and others to offer inducements (such as a resumption of peaceful nuclear cooperation) in return for Pretoria's renunciation of nuclear weapons and acceptance of international controls.

Another group of would-be nuclear powers—North Korea, Iraq, Iran, and Libya—lies outside the traditional Western collective security system. These states present the United States with a different mix of interests and potential for influence. Like the Soviet Union during the Cold War and China before 1970, they are essentially adversaries of the United States (although, if they should be in conflict, as in the Iran-Iraq war, the United States may favor one over the other—in that particular case, Iraq). As such they inspire no U.S. ambivalence: their acquisition of nuclear weapons would clearly threaten American interests—posing a menace to U.S. allies and military forces and increasing the risk of nuclear terrorism. But if there are no mitigating factors to constrain U.S. nonproliferation efforts toward such countries, there are few levers (short of coercive force) by which the United States could shape their nuclear incentives. United States economic, political, and military relations with these countries are weak or nonexistent, so the usual bilateral carrots and sticks for pursuing nonproliferation are not at hand.

DILEMMAS

The interplay between nonproliferation and other U.S. interests has confronted American policy with recurring dilemmas, cross-pressures, and sources of ambivalence. Throughout the nuclear age, these have inhibited vigorous efforts to prevent the bomb's spread, setting limits on the price the United States was willing to pay for nonproliferation. United States policymakers, confronted with the true implications of a maximum nonproliferation effort, have seldom seriously entertained such a course. At the same time, they have considered an unrestrained proliferation of nuclear weapons to be equally unacceptable. In practice, then, policy outcomes have been a rough balancing between two sets of costs. The historical record reflects the shifting nature of these calculations (see Table 8.2).

The Dove's Dilemma

A perennial constraint on U.S. nonproliferation efforts is the tension between Washington's desire to limit overseas commitments and military

Table 8.2 FOREIGN POLICY COSTS OF PROLIFERATION AND NONPROLIFERATION

Period	Perceived foreign policy costs of proliferation	Costs of maximum NP policy	Costs of actual NP policy
Late 1940s	Soviet acquisition of nuclear weapons threatens West.	U.S. gives up bomb to international control.	Denial policy alienates U.K.
1950s	Allied nuclear forces violate optimum NATO division of labor (wasteful).	Military: continued denial policy weakens NATO and alienates U.K. Civil: forfeits political and economic benefits of peaceful cooperation (or: maximum IAEA threatens U.S. weapons program).	Double standard for allied sharing alienates France; Atoms for Peace with weak controls accelerates spread of nuclear technology.
Early 1960s	New national nuclear forces undermine NATO flexible response, endanger U.S.-Soviet and global stability, threaten catalytic war.	Strict U.S. nuclear monopoly in NATO alienates allies, especially FRG (turns to Gaullist France or Soviets).	Nassau agreement and MLF provoke NATO crisis over nuclear sharing.
Mid-1960s	Chinese bomb leads to widespread Third World proliferation, endangers stability and U.S. global access.	Maximum NPT (with security guarantees and disarmament pledges) threatens U.S. autonomy; hard-line policy against Israel threatens U.S. interests in Middle East.	NPT strains U.S.-allied relations, alienates India; acquiescence in Israeli bomb undercuts U.S. credibility.

1969–74	Proliferation inevitable; does not threaten vital U.S. interests, and may selectively serve U.S. interests.	NP pressure on allies and Third World clients futile and potentially harmful to U.S. ties.	Middle East, South Asia, and China diplomacy insensitive to proliferation issue; mild reaction to India test weakens U.S. credibility.
1975–79	Global instability; threat to world order.	Expanded U.S. overseas commitments and military role to reduce proliferation motives; breach with allies and Third World states over rigid export and plutonium restrictions.	Revisionist policies, though moderated, strain relations with allies and Third World states.
1980–88	Global instability; regional nuclear arms races.	Jeopardizes security ties with key anti-Soviet partners.	Acquiescence in Pakistani bomb undercuts U.S. credibility; growing nuclear threat in Middle East not addressed.
1989–	Global instability; threat to U.S. allies and overseas military forces; nuclear terrorism.	Active diplomacy to promote regional nonproliferation regimes; probable strain on relations with Israel and others; meaningful constraints on vertical proliferation (e.g., test ban, deep reductions).	Continued risk of emergence of additional nuclear weapons countries.

assistance and the desire of potential nuclear weapons states for security guarantees. This is the "dove's dilemma"—how to stop proliferation without becoming the world's policeman. Except in the cases of Western Europe and Japan, the United States has generally been unable to fully alleviate the insecurities that prompt other countries to pursue a nuclear weapons option. Even in the full flush of U.S. global interventionism in the 1960s, the Kennedy and Johnson administrations were not willing to give binding guarantees to India or Israel, or to assume new U.S. security obligations under the NPT. Subsequently, the Nixon Doctrine and the Carter administration's anti-interventionism and moral qualms about conventional arms sales weakened the U.S. hand in combating proliferation. In the Pakistani case, there was a fatal gap between Islamabad's fear of India and Washington's view that the U.S.-Pakistan alliance applied only to the Soviet threat.

The Hawk's Dilemma

The "hawk," less reticent about projecting American power abroad, has faced a different dilemma: how to deny nuclear weapons to others without forfeiting U.S. nuclear prerogatives and freedom of action. Consistently, the United States pulled back from an integrated, nondiscriminatory approach to nuclear arms control that would have imposed restraints on its own weapons development program. In the 1940s, U.S. faith in the "winning weapon" as a necessary counter to Soviet power made relinquishing the U.S. bomb too high a price to pay for nonproliferation. In the 1950s, nonproliferation might have been aided by a more potent IAEA or a nuclear test ban, but these would have interfered with U.S. and NATO nuclear policies. In the 1960s and beyond, the United States rejected a firm linkage between superpower arms control and the NPT obligations of nonnuclear states. And throughout, the American strategists fashioned increasingly elaborate doctrines premised on the military utility and efficacy of nuclear weapons, while insisting on the irrationality of other nations seeking them. This double standard, divorcing the "horizontal" and "vertical" dimensions of nuclear policy, was a persistent handicap to the legitimacy and persuasiveness of U.S. nonproliferation efforts.

The dove's dilemma and hawk's dilemma both underscore the costs of nonproliferation policy and the difficult trade-offs facing policymakers on the issue. Moreover, the two dilemmas are linked in an ironic fashion: America's Cold War alliances, arguably the most effective nonproliferation measures of the postwar period, played a key role in the vertical growth of nuclear forces. In particular, it was the extension of deterrence to Western Europe, and the effort to make credible the U.S. threat to resort to nuclear war in its defense, that drove the development of warfighting strategies and their ever-escalating weapons "requirements."

Clients, Carrots, and Sticks

A third recurring dilemma concerns the application of leverage against the nuclear programs of American allies and client states. Here a kind of Catch-22 has prevailed, epitomized by the cases of Israel and Pakistan. Both countries (though in different degrees) were valued strategic partners in the East-West conflict. While American leverage was substantial in theory, it could not be fully exploited without harm to U.S. regional and Cold War interests. In neither case did Washington want to risk a break by exerting maximum pressure for nonproliferation, preferring instead to maintain security ties and supply conventional arms in hopes of reducing incentives for nuclear weapons in these countries. This strategy failed to satisfy either country that it could safely forgo a nuclear option, and as a result the U.S. embrace—offered without meaningful strings—signaled a tacit acquiescence in proliferation. But policymakers were never persuaded that the opposite policy—credibly linking U.S. aid to nonproliferation—would have worked any better. At critical junctures in relations with Israel and Pakistan, U.S. policymakers believed that a cutoff would be counterproductive not only in terms of broader U.S. Cold War interests but in proliferation terms as well, and would serve only to increase the target's nuclear incentives and forfeit U.S. influence.

A parallel dilemma appeared in the field of peaceful nuclear cooperation, in the tension between "reliable supply" policies and the use of American supplier leverage to exert pressures on U.S. nuclear partners. In establishing safeguards under the Atoms for Peace policy, and again in implementing the Carter antiplutonium policy, the United States concluded that maximizing the power of America's dominant market position would risk hastening the demise of that position—driving customers to other suppliers—in addition to straining U.S. relations with the countries concerned.

The Indeterminacy of Risks

Finally, the nature of foreign policy risk assessments has often worked to the detriment of strong nonproliferation efforts. Policymakers operate with imperfect information about the present and cannot see into the future to weigh the true risks of alternative courses of action. The consequences of proliferation, however serious, are generally perceived as long-term and hypothetical. The political and economic costs of hard-line nonproliferation policies, in contrast, are often immediate and concrete. This disparity, and the short time-horizons that normally dominate policy decisions, make it difficult to maintain a high priority for nonproliferation against seemingly more pressing, though perhaps ephemeral, interests. This dilemma is reinforced by the bureaucratic organization of foreign policy. In the State Department, the regional bureaus have frequently counseled against tough nonproliferation measures that would endanger U.S. diplomacy in their areas of responsibility. Combined with the more

Soviet-centered orientation of the most senior policymakers, this tendency has put nonproliferation officials at a double disadvantage in the competition for priority on the foreign policy agenda.

It was easier to acquiesce in favored treatment for Great Britain, self-inspection for EURATOM, a flawed nuclear agreement with India, or nuclear deception by Israel, than to apply a firm, consistent nonproliferation policy. Yet these decisions sowed the seeds of later frictions and crises that carried their own high costs. To take another example, the decision to place the arming of Pakistan ahead of nonproliferation in that country was premised on a view of the Soviet threat—in Afghanistan and globally—that in hindsight was greatly exaggerated. By 1987, when the U.S. aid package was renewed without strings, the Soviet empire was on the brink of collapse. The threat to U.S. interests posed by Moscow's misadventure in Afghanistan is now seen as transitory, while the dangers of a nuclear confrontation in South Asia continue to grow. (This is not to deny that U.S. arming of the resistance forces in Afghanistan undoubtedly hastened Moscow's decision to cut its losses there.)

BEYOND THE COLD WAR

The ending of the Cold War transforms the setting for U.S. nonproliferation policy, altering the dynamics of the proliferation threat, the constraints and opportunities for halting it, and its interaction with American national interests. It is too early to discern these effects in detail, but a number of plausible trends can be sketched out. Just as the superpower rivalry itself had mixed implications for proliferation, post–Cold War trends are likely to be similarly mixed. On the one hand, the decline of U.S.-Soviet conflict should ease some of the dilemmas and cross-pressures that have hampered nonproliferation policy in the past. At the same time, however, this decline may also erode some historic checks on the spread of nuclear weapons (see Table 8.3).

Good News?

As in earlier periods of détente, when preoccupation with the superpower nuclear confrontation receded, the proliferation issue should now command relatively more attention as a security threat. Developments such as the growth of nuclear tensions in the Middle East and South Asia and the expiration of the NPT's 25-year term in 1995 reinforce this probability. But the end of the Cold War could create favorable conditions for action on the problem that did not exist previously. The removal of East-West rivalry as a chronic factor in regional security conflicts is especially important, because it alters the calculus of superpower interests toward several of the leading nuclear aspirants. With local rivals no longer serving as U.S. and Soviet surrogates, and their conflicts no longer tests of superpower

Table 8.3   PROLIFERATION AFTER THE COLD WAR

Good News?	Bad News?
Improved prospects for U.S.-Soviet cooperation and enhanced UN role to resolve regional conflicts (esp. Middle East and South Asia) that inspire proliferation.	Weakening of Cold War security relations increases proliferation motives, exacerbates regional conflicts.
Superpowers devote more attention and resources to Third World proliferation threat.	Domestic preoccupations and reduced interest in Third World produces U.S.-Soviet disengagement and complacency about proliferation.
Reduced superpower tendency to tolerate nuclear programs of regional allies and clients (e.g., Pakistan, Israel, North Korea, Iraq).	Reduced superpower leverage over former Cold War allies and clients.
U.S.-Soviet arms control eases regime double standard, helps NPT renewal; demise of warfighting strategies sends signal of disutility of nuclear weapons.	U.S.-Soviet arms cuts lower threshold for entry into nuclear club, encourage proliferation.
United Europe takes more active non-proliferation role; French and British nuclear forces are merged into a "European deterrent."	Postbipolar Europe fragments, proliferates.
Improved cooperation in export controls.	Export controls decline because of relaxed East-West technology-transfer restrictions, vulnerability of new Third World suppliers to oil and financial leverage, disintegration of Soviet Union.
Reconciliation reduces proliferation threat in North and South Korea.	North Korean isolation exacerbates proliferation motives, feeds renewed bomb interest in South Korea and Japan.
South Africa joins NPT as apartheid is peacefully ended.	Violent breakdown in South Africa revives nuclear threat.

influence and credibility, Washington and Moscow should feel less pressure to subordinate nonproliferation to client-state relations. For example, Pakistan's ability to obtain U.S. aid on its own terms, a function of its value in the anti-Soviet encounter, has declined sharply. Although Israel will undoubtedly still have special claims on American policy, its role as a U.S. "strategic asset" is devalued by the demise of the Soviet threat in the Middle East, removing at least one factor in Washington's indulgence of the Israeli nuclear program. In the same way, Moscow's incentives to tolerate suspect nuclear activities on the part of former Third World partners have diminished.

A related change is the potential for stronger cooperative efforts on behalf of nonproliferation. While superpower cooperation has been better and more sustained on this issue than in other areas, the Cold War set limits on solutions to the problem. There is now a greater opportunity for the superpowers to act jointly to address regional conflicts, and to reinvigorate the United Nations as an effective instrument of peace keeping and conflict resolution. The multilateral response to the Iraq-Kuwait crisis may be a harbinger of future possibilities. The Cold War's end made possible not only a UN mandate for economic sanctions against Iraq but also the large-scale projection of U.S. military force into the region without danger of sparking a superpower confrontation. The Gulf war stimulated broader diplomatic initiatives on Middle East peace and security, and may lead to regional arms control. More determined efforts to achieve a settlement between India and Pakistan, and to defuse their nuclear competition, may also become feasible in the new setting. Multilateral diplomacy, and regional settlements to reduce nuclear motivations at the source, offer the best hope for resolving the U.S. "dove's dilemma"—curtailing proliferation while keeping America's security burdens within politically and economically acceptable bounds.

The "hawk's dilemma" could be eased as well in the post–Cold War world. With the end of the East-West confrontation, the nuclear arms race has lost its original engine. The withdrawal of Soviet armies from Central Europe has eliminated the historic rationale for American reliance on nuclear forces and on warfighting strategies designed to make their use credible. As a result, a wholesale contraction in the role of nuclear weapons in superpower security policies has become possible, and with it a chance to soften the nonproliferation regime's nuclear double standard.

For the first time, the superpowers are on an arms control trajectory that displays more than token observance of their commitments under NPT Article VI. Under the 1991 Strategic Arms Reduction Treaty (START), they will begin to reduce their nuclear arsenals, albeit only modestly. Subsequent agreements are likely to make deeper cuts, and to constrain the modernization of nuclear forces. In September 1991, President Bush announced the unilateral phaseout of tactical weapons based in Europe and at sea, and soon after President Gorbachev pledged further unilateral Soviet reductions. Tighter restrictions on nuclear testing, flatly rejected by the United States during the 1980s, are also likely, although a comprehensive test ban—the symbolic litmus test of Article VI compliance—still faces strong official resistance.

Bad News?

These optimistic scenarios have a flip side, however. The bipolar world of the Cold War, despite its risks and inequalities, did provide a measure of structure, predictability, and hierarchy that helped keep proliferation in check. United States and Soviet alliances relieved insecurities that might otherwise have prompted a much more wide-spread pursuit of nuclear options. Fears of catalytic war provided a strong rationale for superpower nonproliferation efforts; escalation risks tended to inhibit regional conflicts. The emergence of a more fragmented and fluid world order could, in contrast, unleash new forces for proliferation. The weakening of Cold War collective security arrangements may create uncertainty and insecurity among states that formerly enjoyed the patronage of the superpower antagonists, and proliferation is possible even among the constituent republics of the former Soviet superpower. At the same time, leverage over potential proliferants may decline. The result could be the worst of worlds: increased incentives for proliferation combined with reduced outside influence over aspiring nuclear weapons states.

Hints of these trends were apparent in the early 1990s. Again, the case of Pakistan is instructive. The suspension of U.S. aid in October 1990 signaled that the United States had become more willing to punish Islamabad's pursuit of the bomb in the aftermath of the Cold War. This very willingness, however, was in part a measure of Washington's reduced interest in Pakistan, which in turn could make it difficult for the United States to reestablish and preserve a bilateral relationship that offers Pakistan meaningful incentives for nuclear restraint. The immediate response to the aid suspension was an upsurge of nationalistic, anti-American feeling in Pakistan (to which Prime Minister Benazir Bhutto fell victim) and a heightened determination to resist U.S. nonproliferation pressures.[2]

Among Moscow's Third World allies, the evidence of fragmentation is more dramatic. North Korea, perceiving itself isolated and betrayed by the Soviet reconciliation with South Korea, has emerged as a significant proliferation concern.[3] Arab countries such as Iraq, Syria, and Libya experienced a sudden and unsettling loss of Soviet backing—economic, political, and military—under the Gorbachev policies of retrenchment and rapprochement with the West.[4] Though the demise of the super-powers' Middle East rivalry has opened up new possibilities for coopera-

---

[2] Steve Coll, "U.S. Seeking Deal on Pakistani Aid," *Washington Post*, December 1, 1990, p. A12; Steve Le Vine, "Pakistan's Nuclear Stand Firm," *Washington Times*, December 5, 1990, p. A9.

[3] Though it signed the NPT in 1985, North Korea has yet to complete an IAEA safeguards agreement covering its large research reactor and a plutonium-extraction plant that is under construction. See Leonard Spector and Jacqueline Smith, *Nuclear Ambitions* (Boulder, CO: Westview Press, 1990) pp. 123ff. Persistent U.S. attempts to win Chinese help in pressuring North Korea to forswear nuclear weapons were apparently unsuccessful (press reports).

[4] See Mary Curtius, "Soviets' Mideast Retreat Alters Power Equation," *Boston Globe*, April 3, 1990, p. 1.

tive action, it may also have increased pressures for proliferation by former Soviet clients and reduced Soviet influence over them. It is doubtful, for example, that Iraq would have felt free to invade Kuwait while Cold War restraints still prevailed in the region.

There is also a danger that export-control discipline, already significantly undermined in Iraq, will be harder to maintain in the post–Cold War world. The easing of Western restrictions on technology transfers to the East, and the dispersion of Soviet nuclear scientists, could inadvertently facilitate leaks of dual-use technologies to nuclear programs in the Third World. The unification of the West European market in 1992 could create a "lowest common denominator" situation in which clandestine nuclear transactions can more easily evade a limited European export control system. Former Soviet satellite countries in Eastern Europe, such as Romania, could become new sources of illicit aid to Third World programs, while increased, commercially motivated exports by "second tier" nuclear suppliers such as India and Argentina may further increase proliferation risks in the Third World.

WHY PROLIFERATION MATTERS

In sum, the end of the Cold War presents new proliferation risks as well as opportunities. The challenge to nonproliferation policy is to contain the former while exploiting the latter. For the United States, the task will be to establish a strong priority for nonproliferation in planning for the post–Cold War world order. This requires, in turn, that the United States articulate and sustain a clear national interest in the issue, avoiding the peaks and valleys of attention, and the gaps between nonproliferation and foreign policy that have marked the past. A better integrated approach would overcome the opposite errors of the last two cycles of U.S. policy: the Ford-Carter syndrome, in which nonproliferation received a high priority but was inadequately anchored in, or supported by, the traditional agenda of national security policy; and the Reagan-Bush pattern, in which the traditional agenda was revived at the expense of nonproliferation, and the latter's role in American security neglected. New temptations to downplay the issue may arise in the future. The two most likely causes of neglect are complacency and fatalism. Complacency would result from a perception that the Third World is no longer an area of vital U.S. interest now that the Cold War has abated. As regional rivalries cease to be proxy conflicts that hold the potential for triggering a superpower confrontation, the problem of local proliferation may be judged less urgent. Fatalism would reflect a belief that proliferation is inevitable and irreversible, and that policies should be aimed more at managing than preventing the problem. The objective would be to assimilate de facto weapons states into the nuclear club, formally acknowledging their status and seeking to establish stable regional deterrent balances.[5]

Neither response, however, is consistent with long-term U.S. security interests and the creation of a stable post–Cold War order. Although proliferation no longer threatens to catalyze a U.S.-Soviet nuclear conflict, the Third World nuclear threat is not self-contained. It is linked by strategic, economic, and geographic factors to Western interests, and thus poses risks from which the United States cannot realistically hope to insulate itself:

- Proliferation in the Middle East, still a region of vital interest to the West despite the end of the Cold War, could endanger access to oil, threaten American allies and military forces, and increase the risks that terrorist groups would obtain nuclear weapons. Moreover, the spread of medium- and long-range missiles in the area increases the danger that Middle East conflicts and instabilities could embroil Russia and Western Europe.
- South Asia is a region of less immediate strategic importance, but the implications of proliferation there reverberate beyond the subcontinent. The South Asian and Middle East conflicts are linked through Pakistan's ties to the Arab states; both India and Pakistan are potential suppliers of nuclear assistance and technology to proliferators elsewhere; and the open deployment or use of nuclear weapons in a South Asian conflict would be a damaging blow to global nonproliferation norms.
- On the Korean peninsula, an outbreak of proliferation would endanger U.S. strategic interests in the Pacific and erode Japan's non-nuclear policy.
- In Brazil and Argentina, the direct proliferation threat has subsided, but both countries have economic and energy vulnerabilities that could be exploited by third parties to obtain access to nuclear weapons technology and expertise.
- Should South Africa descend into violent disorder, the country's nuclear capability could become a stake or a hostage in domestic conflicts, with unpredictable but potentially serious consequences.

---

[5] An extreme view—of academic interest but never persuasive to policymakers—holds that proliferation is by nature a stabilizing development and therefore to be welcomed. See Kenneth Waltz, "The Spread of Nuclear Weapons: More May be Better," *Adelphi Papers*, no. 171 (London: International Institute for Strategic Studies, 1981). A recent variation argues for a nuclear Germany as the key to stability in post–Cold War Europe. See John J. Mearscheimer, "Back to the Future: Instability in Europe After the Cold War," *International Security*, Summer 1990. For the argument that U.S. interests in the Third World have declined, see Steven Van Evera, "Why Europe Matters, Why the Third World Doesn't," *Journal of Strategic Studies*, vol. 13:2, June 1990. On the "proliferation-management" strategy, see Shai Feldman, "Managing Nuclear Proliferation," in Jed Snyder and Samuel Wells, eds., *Limiting Nuclear Proliferation* (Cambridge, MA: Ballinger, 1985).

- The breakup of the Soviet Union, if it results in an unraveling of export controls or an exodus of nuclear experts willing to market their talents, will aggravate any or all of these situations.

If complacency about proliferation is unwarranted, fatalism is equally so. The "proliferation management" strategy may become unavoidable as a last resort in some cases, but as a general approach to the spread of nuclear weapons it is premature and unrealistic. The turnaround of nuclear policies in South Africa, Argentina, and Brazil suggests that even entrenched weapons programs may be reversed as political conditions evolve, and warns against defeatism. A management approach would legitimize and in effect reward such programs, undercutting their domestic critics and sending a counterproductive signal to other countries contemplating a nuclear option.

Furthermore, hopes for stable deterrence among new nuclear states are overly sanguine. The postwar U.S.-Soviet balance, often invoked to justify such hopes, is not an apt model. Unlike the superpowers, putative nuclear rivals in the Middle East and South Asia share common—and often disputed—borders and have histories of recurrent armed conflict over deeply rooted territorial, religious, and ethnic quarrels. As shown by the Kashmir and Persian Gulf crises of 1990, these disputes can erupt at any time. The instability and powerful military influence characteristic of many Third World regimes compound the danger, as does the pervasive threat of terrorist activity in the Middle East. In short, the prospect that deployed nuclear forces in the Third World would actually be used, or would trigger preventive strikes to avert their use, is more likely than the optimistic proliferation-management scenario concedes.

As the 1990s began, U.S. policymakers showed some awareness of these realities. The Bush administration's attempts to defuse the Kashmir confrontation were largely motivated by concern over the nuclear side of the crisis. Similarly, the need to eliminate Saddam Hussein's nuclear threat was offered as a leading rationale for military action against Iraq. Nonproliferation was once again being taken seriously as a hard-headed U.S. national security interest. It remained unclear, however, whether this was yet another short-lived peak of concern or the prelude to a more thoughtful and persistent strategy to contain proliferation.

A STRATEGY FOR THE 1990s

There are two broad tasks for a revitalized strategy—to preserve and strengthen the global regime, and to deal with the handful of proliferation problem countries. Both tasks call for a closer meshing of nonproliferation with other dimensions of U.S. foreign and national security policy. At the regime level, the 1995 NPT renewal—when the parties must decide to extend the treaty for a specified period or indefinitely—is a key watershed. A collapse of the treaty is improbable; for the most part, its non-nuclear members believe it serves their interests despite shortcomings in the performance of the nuclear weapon states. But a long-term renewal is not likely—and wide support for tighter export controls, sanctions, and other steps to upgrade the regime is even less so—in the absence of further progress toward superpower nuclear disarmament. This was the message of the 1990 NPT review conference, which ended in disarray over U.S. refusal to endorse a nuclear test ban.[6]

The NPT renewal and post–Cold War superpower arms control may thus converge to invite a revival, under more auspicious circumstances, of the comprehensive approach to nuclear control that marked the early disarmament plans of the 1940s and 1950s. With the collapse of the Soviet threat, the United States should reconsider the road not taken at that time, when self-restraint was thought an unacceptable price for restraint by others. A new, integrated arms control framework would encompass both the vertical and horizontal dimensions of the arms race. In addition to sharp numerical reductions in superpower forces, it would halt the qualitative arms race through limits on weapons testing and the production of fissile materials. The extension of these limits to potential nuclear states would effectively relink nonproliferation to U.S. and Russian disarmament.

Superpower arms control, of course, would not directly mitigate the nuclear incentives of the leading problem countries. It would, however, strengthen the political pressure against states that reject nonproliferation commitments, particularly those like India that have invoked the discriminatory aspect of the NPT as a justification for their rejection. In addition, the possible demonstration effect of a very visible U.S. and Russian "loss of faith" in Cold War nuclear theologies should not be discounted. Over time, such a change could affect foreign perceptions of the military utility and prestige value of nuclear arms and influence domestic policy debates in countries considering nuclear weapons. Furthermore, very deep cuts in U.S. and Russian nuclear forces would have ripple effects with relevance to nonproliferation. At some point they would require that the smaller nuclear powers—Britain, France, and China—be drawn into the process. China's involvement could in turn create new options for breaking the India-Pakistan impasse. In this way, the historical chain of proliferation might begin to be reversed.

Another neglected regime issue that merits revisiting is the accumulation of plutonium in peaceful nuclear programs. Just as the Cold War's end makes possible a fresh approach to nuclear arms control, the evolving economics of nuclear power, resulting in the virtual abandonment of plans for a transition to breeder reactors, could facilitate tighter controls on civilian plutonium. The Carter campaign on this question was

---

[6] Leonard Spector and Jacqueline Smith, "Treaty Review: Deadlock Damages Nonproliferation," *Bulletin of the Atomic Scientists*, December 1990.

beset by foreign resistance and domestic indecision. The Reagan retreat, however, was imprudently hasty and sweeping. The reprocessing of European and Japanese spent fuel—essentially as a temporary, politically expedient waste-management procedure, divorced from energy or economic logic—is producing a steadily growing "overhang" of surplus plutonium.[7] The handling, transport, and storage of this material defy the capacity of IAEA safeguards and national security systems to assure against diversions to states or terrorist groups with nuclear ambitions. A new initiative to restrict civil reprocessing would predictably create diplomatic friction, but the alternative is an increasingly severe proliferation threat.

The above steps would upgrade and tighten the global nonproliferation regime, but still leave the nuclear problem countries to be dealt with on their own terms. As in the past, a uniform American policy toward these cases is not realistic. Variations in U.S. interests and influence, and in the motivations and capabilities of each country, will compel a flexible approach. Nevertheless, the record suggests some guidelines for improving the coherence and effectiveness of U.S. policy.

First, the United States should engage specific cases on a more steady, consistent basis. Especially in South Asia, nonproliferation efforts have been impaired by the intermittent and erratic nature of U.S. involvement, fluctuating in response to the changing requirements of Cold War diplomacy. Toward Pakistan, the United States shifted back and forth between a punitive nonproliferation policy that failed to address Islamabad's security needs and a strategic embrace that ignored the nuclear problem—an all-or-nothing pattern neither pole of which gave Pakistan credible incentives to rein in its nuclear program. A more calibrated middle road would link U.S. aid levels to specified measures of nuclear restraint. A similar formula could be applied to Israel, indicating a second guideline for future policy: Israel's historic exemption from U.S. nonproliferation policy should be reassessed. The double standard in Israel's favor—however compelling to policymakers in the past—has become increasingly dubious in the wake of the Vanunu revelations, the suspension of aid to Pakistan, and the harsh U.S. response to Iraq's nuclear program. Continued refusal to acknowledge the Israeli program and its role in the proliferation dynamics of the region will present a serious obstacle to arms control and wider peace efforts in the region.[8]

---

[7] See Frans Berkhout, Tatsujiro Suzuki, and William Walker, "The Approaching Plutonium Surplus: A Japanese-European Predicament," *International Affairs*, 66, 3 (1990). Japan is going forward with its controversial plan to use plutonium fuels in its nuclear energy program (newspaper reports).

[8] On the possibilities for addressing the Israeli nuclear capability in Middle East arms control arrangements, see Avner Cohen and Marvin Miller, *Nuclear Shadows in the Middle East: Prospects for Arms Control in the Wake of the Gulf Crisis* (Cambridge, MA: MIT Center for International Studies, December 1990).

A third guideline, related to the first two, is that the United States should broaden the multilateral dimension of its nonproliferation policy. Historically, U.S. dominance in this field has been two-edged. American initiative provided the stimulus for regime building—from the IAEA to the NPT and the Nuclear Suppliers Group—during most of the postwar period. Yet this unique role also had a negative side: it tended to hold nonproliferation hostage to the vagaries of U.S. foreign policy, and sometimes prejudiced foreign support by fostering a perception that nonproliferation was a self-serving and distinctly American interest. In the post–Cold War world, interest and responsibility will have to be spread more widely. The United States does not command the levers to reverse proliferation trends in the problem countries. Broad multilateral coalitions, bridging the former East-West divide as well as the North-South one, are required if export controls and sanctions are to be effective. Similarly diverse support is needed for diplomatic initiatives to settle the regional disputes that drive proliferation, especially in the Middle East and South Asia.

If the United States cannot dictate these efforts or determine their outcome, enlightened and persistent American involvement—unhampered by the hesitations and ambivalence of the past—would dramatically improve their chances of success. In that case, the final decade of the century could see the nuclear menace in all its dimensions brought under control. Horizontal and vertical proliferation, intertwined at the Cold War's beginning, could abate together in the wake of its demise.

Appendix
1
Nuclear Technology and Proliferation

There are five acknowledged nuclear weapon states: the United States, which built the world's first atomic bombs in 1945, the Soviet Union (1949), Great Britain (1953), France (1961), and China (1964). After China's entry into the nuclear club, the process of proliferation became more ambiguous and covert. A number of countries have effectively crossed the nuclear threshold while officially disavowing nuclear status. Others have sought to obtain a weapons capability—or keep the option open—under the guise of civilian nuclear-energy programs. Increasingly, proliferation occurs through clandestine markets in nuclear components and dual-use technologies, which have both military and civilian applications. Except for India, which conducted an alleged "peaceful nuclear explosion" in 1974, none of the proliferation candidates of recent years has openly tested a nuclear device—once the hallmark of entry into the club.

The motives of aspiring nuclear weapon states are generally straightforward. Most of these countries are involved in chronic regional conflicts and rivalries. They want nuclear weapons to enhance their national security, deter or threaten adversaries, and gain added international status and influence—the same reasons that motivated the original nuclear powers.

On the technical side, there are few nuclear secrets left, and the barriers to nuclear weapons development by a determined country have steadily eroded. The key hurdle remains the acquisition of fissile material, whose atoms can be split in an explosive chain reaction releasing huge amounts of energy. The two principal fissile materials, plutonium and uranium-235, are obtained in quite different ways. Plutonium, which does not exist in nature, is a by-product of uranium-fueled nuclear reactors; it can be separated from the other waste products of these reactors through reprocessing and then fashioned into weapons. Uranium-235 is a rare isotope accounting for only about 0.7 percent of naturally

Peter A. Clausen, "Nuclear Proliferation," Union of Concerned Scientists briefing paper, May 1991.

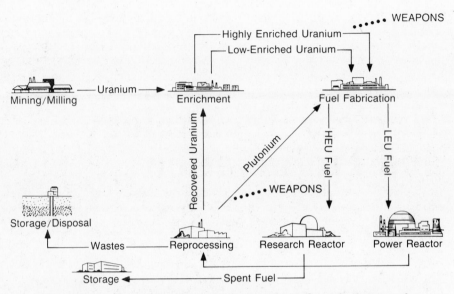

The civilian nuclear-fuel cycle entails opportunities to divert fissile materials to weapons use: either highly enriched uranium or plutonium recovered by reprocessing spent reactor fuel.

occurring uranium (most of the remainder being nonfissile U-238). Weapons-grade uranium—normally 90 percent or more U-235—is produced through enrichment, a laborious and technically demanding process of separating uranium atoms by mass to obtain a progressively higher concentration of U-235.

A single nuclear weapon requires about 5–10 kilograms (11–22 lb.) of plutonium or 15–25 kilograms (33–55 lb.) of highly enriched uranium (HEU). The lower amounts demand more sophisticated design techniques. In a plutonium bomb, the nuclear material is surrounded by chemical high-explosive "lenses," which trigger the weapon by compressing the core into a critical mass—the minimum mass of material needed to sustain a chain reaction. A uranium bomb may employ either this technique (called implosion) or the "gun" technique, in which two subcritical masses of material are suddenly brought together.

PROLIFERATION AND THE PEACEFUL ATOM

There is an inherent overlap between the technologies and materials used to produce nuclear weapons and those used in peaceful nuclear research and electric-power programs. About 250 kilograms (550 lb.) of plutonium are produced each year by a typical nuclear power reactor. Early plans assumed that this material would be recycled as the expansion of nuclear power depleted world uranium resources. Under this scenario, reactor fuel would be reprocessed to recover the plutonium, which would then be fabricated into new fuel elements. Eventually, the nuclear industry was to shift to fast-breeder reactors, which produce more plutonium than they consume. These plans have foundered as the stagnation of nuclear power growth has left uranium resources abundant and cheap.

Uranium enrichment also plays a role in peaceful nuclear programs. Most power-reactor fuel contains uranium enriched to about 3 percent U-235. The United States, two European consortia, and the Soviet Union provide commercial enrichment services for most of the world's power reactors, but several other countries have also mastered the technology.

The overlaps between peaceful and military uses of nuclear technology pose a basic challenge to nonproliferation policy. A "safeguards" system of inspections and other accounting procedures, administered by the International Atomic Energy Agency (IAEA), has been created to detect and thus deter diversions of material from civilian programs to military uses. Parties to the Non-Proliferation Treaty (NPT)—who pledge not to obtain nuclear weapons—must submit their entire civilian nuclear programs to IAEA inspection (called full-scope safeguards); others are obliged to accept safeguards only on materials imported from abroad as required by the particular supplier.

Appendix
2

Treaty on the Non-Proliferation of Nuclear Weapons*

Done at Washington, London, and Moscow July 1, 1968; Ratification advised by the Senate of the United States of America March 13, 1969; Ratified by the President of the United States of America November 24, 1969; Ratification of the United States of America deposited at Washington, London, and Moscow March 5, 1970; Proclaimed by the President of the United States of America March 5, 1970; Entered into force March 5, 1970

The States concluding this Treaty, hereinafter referred to as the "Parties to the Treaty,"

Considering the devastation that would be visited upon all mankind by a nuclear war and the consequent need to make every effort to avert the danger of such a war and to take measures to safeguard the security of peoples,

Believing that the proliferation of nuclear weapons would seriously enhance the danger of nuclear war,

The conformity with resolutions of the United Nations General Assembly calling for the conclusion of an agreement on the prevention of wider dissemination of nuclear weapons,

Undertaking to cooperate in facilitating the application of International Atomic Energy Agency safeguards on peaceful nuclear activities,

Expressing their support for research, development and other efforts to further the application, within the framework of the International Atomic Energy Agency safeguards system, of the principle of safeguarding effectively the flow of

---

* 21 UST 483: TIAS 6839. For a list of states which are parties to the Treaty, see Dept. of State publication, *Treaties in Force*.

source and special fissionable materials by use of instruments and other techniques at certain strategic points,

Affirming the principle that the benefits of peaceful applications of nuclear technology, including any technological by-products which may be derived by nuclear-weapon States from the development of nuclear explosive devices, should be available for peaceful purposes to all Parties to the Treaty, whether nuclear-weapon or non-nuclear-weapon States,

Convinced that, in furtherance of this principle, all Parties to the Treaty are entitled to participate in the fullest possible exchange of scientific information for, and to contribute alone or in cooperation with other States to, the further development of the applications of atomic energy for peaceful purposes,

Declaring their intention to achieve at the earliest possible date the cessation of the nuclear arms race and to undertake effective measures in the direction of nuclear disarmament,

Urging the cooperation of all States in the attainment of this objective,

Recalling the determination expressed by the Parties to the 1963 Treaty Banning Nuclear Weapon Tests in the Atmosphere, in Outer Space and Under Water in its Preamble to seek to achieve the discontinuance of all test explosions of nuclear weapons for all time and to continue negotiations to this end,

Desiring to further the easing of international tension and the strengthening of trust between States in order to facilitate the cessation of the manufacture of nuclear weapons, the liquidation of all their existing stockpiles, and the elimination from national arsenals of nuclear weapons and the means of their delivery pursuant to a treaty on general and complete disarmament under strict and effective international control,

Recalling that, in accordance with the Charter of the United Nations, States must refrain in their international relations from the threat or use of force against the territorial integrity or political independence of any State, or in any other manner inconsistent with the Purposes of the United Nations, and that the establishment and maintenance of international peace and security are to be promoted with the least diversion for armaments of the world's human and economic resources,

Have agreed as follows:

ARTICLE I

Each nuclear-weapon State Party to the Treaty undertakes not to transfer to any recipient whatsoever nuclear weapons or other nuclear explosive devices or control over such weapons or explosive devices directly, or indirectly; and not in any way to assist, encourage, or induce any non-nuclear-weapon State to manufacture or otherwise acquire nuclear weapons or other nuclear explosive devices, or control over such weapons or explosive devices.

ARTICLE II

Each non-nuclear-weapon State Party to the Treaty undertakes not to receive the transfer from any transferor whatsoever of nuclear weapons or other nuclear explosive devices or of control over such weapons or explosive devices directly, or indirectly; not to manufacture or otherwise acquire nuclear weapons or other nuclear explosive devices; and not to seek or receive any assistance in the manufacture of nuclear weapons or other nuclear explosive devices.

ARTICLE III

1. Each non-nuclear-weapon State Party to the Treaty undertakes to accept safeguards, as set forth in an agreement to be negotiated and concluded with the International Atomic Energy Agency in the cordance with the Statute of the International Atomic Energy Agency and the Agency's safeguards system, for the exclusive purpose of verification of the fulfillment of its obligations assumed under this Treaty with a view to preventing diversion of nuclear energy from peaceful uses to nuclear weapons or other nuclear explosive devices. Procedures for the safeguards required by this article shall be followed with respect to source or special fissionable material whether it is being produced, processed or used in any principal nuclear facility or is outside any such facility. The safeguards required by this article shall be applied on all source or special fissionable material in all peaceful nuclear activities within the territory of such State, under its jurisdiction, or carried out under its control anywhere.

2. Each State Party to the Treaty undertakes not to provide: (a) source or special fissionable material, or (b) equipment or material especially designed or prepared for the processing, use or production of special fissionable material, to any non-nuclear-weapon State for peaceful purposes, unless the source or special fissionable material shall be subject to the safeguards required by this article.

3. The safeguards required by this article shall be implemented in a manner designed to comply with article IV of this Treaty, and to avoid hampering the economic or technological development of the Parties or international coopera- tion in the field of peaceful nuclear activities, including the international ex- change of nuclear material and equipment for the processing, use or production of nuclear material for peaceful purposes in accordance with the provisions of this article and the principle of safeguarding set forth in the Preamble of the Treaty.

4. Non-nuclear-weapon States Party to the Treaty shall conclude agreements with the International Atomic Energy Agency to meet the requirements of this article either individually or together with other States in accordance with the Statute of the International Atomic Energy Agency. Negotiation of such agree- ments shall commence within 180 days from the original entry into force of this Treaty. For States depositing their instruments of ratification or accession after the 180-day period, negotiation of such agreements shall commence not later than the date of such deposit. Such agreements shall enter into force not later than eighteen months after the date of initiation of negotiations.

ARTICLE IV

1. Nothing in this Treaty shall be interpreted as affecting the inalienable right of all the Parties to the Treaty to develop research, production and use of nuclear energy for peaceful purposes without discrimination and in conformity with articles I and II of this Treaty.

2. All the Parties to the Treaty undertake to facilitate, and have the right to participate in, the fullest possible exchange of equipment, materials and scientific and technological information for the peaceful uses of nuclear energy. Parties to the Treaty in a position to do so shall also cooperate in contributing alone or together with other States or international organizations to the further development of the applications of nuclear energy for peaceful purposes, especially in the territories of non-nuclear-weapon States Party to the Treaty, with due consideration for the needs of the developing areas of the world.

ARTICLE V

Each Party to the Treaty undertakes to take appropriate measures to ensure that, in accordance with this Treaty, under appropriate international observation and through appropriate international procedures, potential benefits from any peaceful applications of nuclear explosions will be made available to non-nuclear-weapon States Party to the Treaty on a non-discriminatory basis and that the charge to such Parties for the explosive devices used will be as low as possible and exclude any charge for research and development. Non-nuclear-weapon States Party to the Treaty shall be able to obtain such benefits, pursuant to a special international agreement or agreements, through an appropriate international body with adequate representation of non-nuclear-weapon States. Negotiations of this subject shall commence as soon as possible after the Treaty enters into force. Non-nuclear-weapon States Party to the Treaty so desiring may also obtain such benefits pursuant to bilateral agreements.

ARTICLE VI

Each of the Parties to the Treaty undertakes to pursue negotiations in good faith on effective measures relating to cessation of the nuclear arms race at an early date and to nuclear disarmament, and on a treaty on general and complete disarmament under strict and effective international control.

ARTICLE VII

Nothing in this Treaty affects the right of any group of States to conclude regional treaties in order to assure the total absence of nuclear weapons in their respective territories.

ARTICLE VIII

1. Any Party to the Treaty may propose amendments to this Treaty. The text of any proposed amendment shall be submitted to the Depositary Governments which shall circulate it to all Parties to the Treaty. Thereupon, if requested to do so by one-third or more of the Parties to the Treaty, the Depositary Governments shall

convene a conference, to which they shall invite all the Parties to the Treaty, to consider such an amendment.

2. Any amendment to this Treaty must be approved by a majority of the votes of all the Parties to the Treaty, including the votes of all nuclear-weapon States Party to the Treaty and all other Parties which, on the date the amendment is circulated, are members of the Board of Governors of the International Atomic Energy Agency. The amendment shall enter into force for each Party that deposits its instrument of ratification of the amendment upon the deposit of such instruments of ratification by a majority of all the Parties, including the instruments of ratification of all nuclear-weapon States Party to the Treaty and all other Parties which, on the date the amendment is circulated, are members of the Board of Governors of the International Atomic Energy Agency. Thereafter, it shall enter into force for any other Party upon the deposit of its instrument of ratification of the amendment.

3. Five years after the entry into force of this Treaty, a conference of Parties to the Treaty shall be held in Geneva, Switzerland, in order to review the operation of this Treaty with a view to assuring that the purposes of the Preamble and the provisions of the Treaty are being realized. At intervals of five years thereafter, a majority of the Parties to the Treaty may obtain, by submitting a proposal to this effect to the Depositary Governments, the convening of further conferences with the same objective of reviewing the operation of the Treaty.

ARTICLE IX

1. This Treaty shall be open to all States for signature. Any State which does not sign the Treaty before its entry into force in accordance with paragraph 3 of this article may accede to it at any time.

2. This Treaty shall be subject to ratification by signatory States. Instruments of ratification and instruments of accession shall be deposited with the Governments of the United States of America, the United Kingdom of Great Britain and Northern Ireland and the Union of Soviet Socialist Republics, which are hereby designated the Depositary Governments.

3. This Treaty shall enter into force after its ratification by the States, the Governments of which are designated Depositaries of the Treaty, and forty other States signatory to this Treaty and the deposit of their instruments of ratification. For the purposes of this Treaty, a nuclear-weapon State is one which has manufactured and exploded a nuclear weapon or other nuclear explosive device prior to January 1, 1967.

4. For States whose instruments of ratification or accession are deposited subsequent to the entry into force of this Treaty, it shall enter into force on the date of the deposit of their instruments of ratification or accession.

5. The Depositary Governments shall promptly inform all signatory and acceding States of the date of each signature, the date of deposit of each instrument of ratification or of accession, the date of the entry into force of this Treaty, and the date of receipt of any requests for convening a conference or other notices.

6. This Treaty shall be registered by the Depositary Governments pursuant to article 102 of the Charter of the United Nations.

ARTICLE X

1. Each Party shall in exercising its national sovereignty have the right to withdraw from the Treaty if it decides that extraordinary events, related to the subject matter of this Treaty, have jeopardized the supreme interests of its country. It shall give notice of such withdrawal to all other Parties to the Treaty and to the United Nations Security Council three months in advance. Such notice shall include a statement of the extraordinary events it regards as having jeopardized its supreme interests.

2. Twenty-five years after the entry into force of the Treaty, a conference shall be convened to decide whether the Treaty shall continue in force indefinitely, or shall be extended for an additional fixed period or periods. This decision shall be taken by a majority of the Parties of the Treaty.

ARTICLE XI

This Treaty, the English, Russian, French, Spanish and Chinese texts of which are equally authentic, shall be deposited in the archives of the Depositary Governments. Duly certified copies of this Treaty shall be transmitted by the Depositary Governments to the Governments of the signatory and acceding States.

IN WITNESS WHEREOF the undersigned, duly authorized, have signed this Treaty.

DONE in triplicate, at the cities of Washington, London and Moscow, the first day of July one thousand nine hundred sixty-eight.

Index